Catalysis at Surfaces

Catalysis at Surfaces

Ian M. Campbell

School of Chemistry
University of Leeds

London New York
CHAPMAN AND HALL

First published in 1988 by Chapman and Hall Ltd
11 New Fetter Lane, London EC4P 4EE
Published in the USA by Chapman and Hall
29 West 35th Street, New York NY 10001

© 1988   Ian M. Campbell

Printed in Great Britain at the
University Press, Cambridge

ISBN 0 412 31880 6 (hardback)
ISBN 0 412 28970 9 (paperback)

British Library Cataloguing in Publication Data

Campbell, Ian M. (Ian McIntyre), *1941–*
    Catalysis at surfaces.
    1. Heterogenous catalysis
    I. Title
    541.3'95

    ISBN 0-412-31880-6
    ISBN 0-412-28970-9 Pbk

Library of Congress Cataloging in Publication Data

Campbell, Ian M. (Ian McIntyre), *1941–*
    Catalysis at surfaces/Ian M. Campbell
        p.   cm.
    Bibliography: p.
    Includes index.
    ISBN 0-412-31880-6.   ISBN 0-412-28970-9 (pbk.)
    1. Catalysis.   2. Surface chemistry.   I. Title.
QD505.C36   1988
660.2'995—dc19   88-4383

Contents

Preface   vii

Glossary   ix

1   Introduction to catalysis   **1**
1.1   Historical   1
1.2   The basis of catalytic action   1
1.3   Catalysts in action   6
1.4   Concluding remarks   10

2   General aspects of catalysis at surfaces   **11**
2.1   General classification of bulk-solid materials as catalysts   11
2.2   Nature and classification of enzymes   14
2.3   Basic thermodynamics of heterogeneous catalysis   17
2.4   Aspects of the kinetics of surface catalysed reactions   36
2.5   Concluding remarks   51

3   The constitution of catalytic surfaces   **52**
3.1   Basic physical forms of catalytic surfaces   52
3.2   The creation of catalytic surfaces   67
3.3   Concluding remarks   83

4   The detection of adsorbates on solid surfaces   **85**
4.1   Crystal faces and cleaved surfaces of metals   86
4.2   The effects of pressure on surface phenomena   90
4.3   Destructive techniques for surface investigation   91
4.4   Non-destructive techniques for surface investigation   100
4.5   Concluding remarks   130

5   Chemisorption processes at solid surfaces   **132**
5.1   Transition metal surfaces   132
5.2   Redox oxide surfaces   142
5.3   Solid acid surfaces   145
5.4   Concluding remarks   159

6   Catalytic actions on solid surfaces   **161**
6.1   Reactions catalysed by transition metals   161
6.2   Oxidation reactions on redox catalysts   168
6.3   Hydrocarbon conversions on solid acid surfaces   174
6.4   Reforming catalysts   178
6.5   Concluding remarks   182

7   Catalytic action by enzymes   **183**
7.1   Origin of reactivity at the active site   183
7.2   The pH-sensitivity of enzyme catalysis   186
7.3   Roles of metal centres in enzymes   190
7.4   Examples of enzymes in industrial use   193
7.5   Concluding remarks   198

8   Industrial processes based on solid catalysts   **200**
8.1   Hydrogenation of vegetable oils   200
8.2   Ammonia and nitric acid productions   203
8.3   Methanol synthesis   205
8.4   Synthesis gas conversion processes   209
8.5   Ethylene oxide production   215
8.6   Sulphuric acid production   217
8.7   Linear polyethylene production   220
8.8   Catalytic cracking   223
8.9   Synthetic gasoline production   224
8.10 Some processes using zeolite catalysts   233
8.11 Concluding remarks   238

      Further reading   239

      Index   245

Preface

'Many bodies...have the property of exerting on other bodies an action which is very different from chemical affinity. By means of this action they produce decomposition in bodies, and form new compounds into the composition of which they do not enter. This new power, hitherto unknown, is common both in organic and inorganic nature...I shall ...call it catalytic power. I shall also call catalysis the decomposition of bodies by this force.
J. J. Berzelius (1836) Edinburgh New Philosophical Journal, XXI, 223.

This quotation marks the origin of the term catalysis in a scientific context. The earlier literary meaning was 'the breakdown in law and order'. Perhaps Berzelius' train of thought was that catalytic action appeared to defy the scientific laws and principles as formulated in 1836.

It is remarkable that this quotation, with some substitution of modern wording, can represent a fair summary of our present view of catalysis. There is now recognized a broad division of catalytic systems under the headings homogeneous and heterogeneous. In the former the catalyst is generally a dissolved species whilst in the latter it is usually an insoluble solid, with the action restricted to the surface. This book concerns heterogeneous catalysis, which is the more important for industrial applications.

The major tasks in the book are to describe and explain the significant features of a wide variety of solids which offer active surfaces for catalysis, together with the microscopic actions which lead ultimately to the evolution of the reaction products. The outstanding general point is that only a few particular kinds of solid materials are able to effect most individual catalytic reactions. The reasoned choice of a catalyst suitable for a specific conversion process can only be made, other than from experience, with an understanding of the nature of the interactions at the molecular level which take place within the zone of contact of the solid and fluid phases concerned. Considerable emphasis will be put accordingly on investigational techniques which permit identification of intermediate species existing on the surface and hence elucidation of the chemical mechanisms of significance. It is important to realize at the outset that the usual surface effecting heterogeneous catalytic conversion is not uniform at the microscopic level. Many aspects of the theory which will be developed as the book progresses are based upon the existence of localized active sites, which offer special interactive and reactivity-inducing properties for reactant and intermediate species. Major attention will extend to processes of industrial significance.

Heterogeneous catalysis extends far wider than the actions at the external surfaces of bulk solids, even if these provide the main catalysts used presently in industrial-scale processes. Research effort is now directed strongly at catalysts which are to be regarded as molecular entities or localized microstructures attached to solid surfaces which are often in themselves inert. Many of these systems could be described as 'heterogenized' homogeneous catalysts. Also, in a similar vein, a particular feature of this book is the recognition that enzymes and living cells are to be viewed as heterogeneous catalysts, especially as they are used in industrial-scale processes. A further important aspect is catalytic action occurring on the internal surfaces of microporous solids. These materials may be synthesized with the application of principles which may be described as 'molecular engineering' so that they restrict the access of potential reactants or products through the pores. As a consequence of the resultant size- and shape-selectivity, these catalysts can induce 'unusual' pathways of reaction yielding valuable products.

This book has developed from courses given to undergraduate students over a number of years. Although it is pitched mainly at this level, it brings in many of the recent exciting discoveries of novel types of solid catalysts. Furthermore it demonstrates the rapidity of the pace of development of the subject over the last decade or so, which reflects the widespread application of sophisticated procedures for examining the details of surfaces since about 1970. These techniques can be regarded as having removed catalysis from the status of 'advanced witchcraft' to make it a well-founded, but nevertheless still amazing, branch of main science.

Ultimately it must be recognized that in a book designed to provide a broad introduction there are severe limitations on the depth to which individual topics can be pursued. A carefully-selected list of further reading suggestions appears at the end of the text with a view to allowing readers to extend their interests in particular aspects. Also, following, there is a glossary of common and systematic names of organic compounds referred to in the text: most of the literature of catalysis uses the common names and thus the book has acceded to this custom and usage.

I. M. C.
Leeds, 1987

Glossary

Common and systematic nomenclature for organic compounds referred to in the text by common names.

Common name	Systematic name	Formula
Acetaldehyde	Ethanal	CH_3CHO
Acetic acid	Ethanoic acid	CH_3COOH
Acetylene	Ethyne	C_2H_2
Acrolein	Propenal	$CH_2{=}CHCHO$
Benzene-*cis*-glycol	1,2-Dihydroxybenzene	$o\text{-}C_6H_4(OH)_2$
Cumene	Isopropylbenzene	$(CH_3)_2CH{-}C_6H_5$
Ethylene	Ethene	C_2H_4
Ethylene glycol	1,2-Ethanediol	$CH_2OH.CH_2OH$
Ethylene oxide	1,2-Epoxyethane	C_2H_4O
Formaldehyde	Methanal	$HCHO$
Formic acid	Methanoic acid	$HCOOH$
Glutaraldehyde	1,5-Pentanedial	$OHC(CH_2)_3CHO$
Maleic anhydride	*cis*-Butenedioic (acid) anhydride	$OC{-}CH{=}CH{-}CO$ with bridging O
Propylene	Propene	$CH_3CH{=}CH_2$
Styrene	Ethenylbenzene	$C_6H_5{-}CH{=}CH_2$
Vinyl chloride	Chloroethene	$CH_2{=}CHCl$
o-Xylene	1,2-Dimethylbenzene	$o\text{-}C_6H_4(CH_3)_2$
p-Xylene	1,4-Dimethylbenzene	$p\text{-}C_6H_4(CH_3)_2$

1

Introduction to catalysis

1.1 Historical

A modern statement of the original concept proposed by Berzelius (see Preface) is that a catalyst is a substance which accelerates the rate of a chemical reaction whilst it may be recovered chemically unchanged at the end of the reaction. On many occasions, the effect of the catalyst appears to be absolute rather than relative: under the conditions concerned the presence of the catalyst is essential for the achievement of a significant rate of reaction. On other occasions, a particular catalyst may act to induce 'unusual' reaction pathways, leading to products which would not otherwise be obtained from the reactants concerned.

Action now recognized as heterogeneous catalysis induced by the presence of surfaces was reported first almost two hundred years ago. Table 1.1 sets out a series of significant dates in the relevant historical records.

1.2 The basis of catalytic action

The apparently absolute effect of catalysis by surfaces can be demonstrated in many systems. For instance at ambient temperature, a stoichiometric mixture (2 : 1 v/v) of hydrogen and oxygen will not react significantly in the gas phase, even if it is left for years. The potential reaction to form water is nevertheless highly feasible on the thermodynamic basis of having a large negative value of the standard Gibbs (free energy) function change :

$$2H_2(g) + O_2(g) \rightarrow 2H_2O(g), \Delta G^{\ominus}_{298} = -457 \text{ kJ mol}^{-1}$$

However there are no elementary reactions of significant rate under these conditions, so that the process is precluded kinetically. This is not too

Table 1.1 Important early dates of advances in catalysis at surfaces

Year	Investigator(s)	Phenomenon
1796	van Marum	Dehydrogenation of alcohols contacted with metal surfaces
1817	Davy, Döbereiner	Glowing of metals in contact with mixtures of air and combustible gases
1825	Faraday	Surface-induced combustion of hydrogen
1831	Phillips	Patent for sulphur dioxide oxidation on platinum
1836	Berzelius	Definition of catalysis
1869	von Hoffmann	Partial oxidation of methanol to formaldehyde on silver
1875	Squire, Messel	Industrial scale oxidation of sulphur dioxide on platinum
1894	Takamine	First patent for an extracted enzyme catalyst
1905	Sabatier, Sanderens	Hydrogenation of unsaturated hydrocarbons on nickel
1913	—	First ammonia synthesis plant operated at Oppau, Germany (1.3×10^8 kg fixed nitrogen per annum)
1915	Langmuir	First quantitative theory of adsorption
1925	H. S. Taylor	First detailed theory of contact catalysis

surprising since hydrogen and oxygen are molecules with fairly strong bonds, which are required to be broken in the course of the reaction. Dissociation of the isolated molecules to generate atoms only occurs at temperatures of the order of thousands of degrees Kelvin.

It is then an apparently absolute effect that contact of hydrogen/oxygen mixtures with a platinum surface at ambient temperatures results in quite rapid reaction. The immediate point of interest is how the introduction of the metal surface overcomes the kinetic preclusion which exists in the homogeneous system. The explanation, of general importance for heterogeneous catalytic systems, is that the presence of the surface allows the exploitation of chemical reaction pathways other than those available in the gas phase alone. To anticipate matters which will be discussed at length later, the metal surface induces the breaking of the bonds in hydrogen and oxygen, even at low temperatures. The resultant atoms are

Table 1.2 'Full' conversions induced by solid catalysts

Reaction	Catalyst	T/K	$\Delta G^{\ominus}_{298}/kJ\,mol^{-1}$
$H_2O_2 \rightarrow H_2O + \frac{1}{2}O_2$	Mn_2O_3	310	-125
$CO + \frac{1}{2}O_2 \rightarrow CO_2$	Pt	500	-257
$C_2H_6 + H_2 \rightarrow 2CH_4$	Ni	500	-69
$CH_4 + 2O_2 \rightarrow CO_2 + 2H_2O$	Co_3O_4	600	-801
$N_2 + 3H_2 \rightarrow 2NH_3$	Fe	700	-33
$SO_2 + \frac{1}{2}O_2 \rightarrow SO_3$	V_2O_5	800	-70

not free but are bound chemically to the surface. Nevertheless they can link together subsequently to form the eventual product. Evidently this does not alter the platinum permanently; the metallic surface exists at the completion of reaction. One key feature of catalytic action is exemplified here. The catalyst participates chemically in the conversion process by being involved in the formation of chemical bonds, but these bonds are only of a transient nature.

The above action may be regarded as catalysis of the most straightforward variety, the product (water) being the most stable on a thermodynamic basis. There are many other instances of such 'full' conversions induced by solid catalysts, some of which are given in Table 1.2, with typical catalysts and suitable temperatures (T) used to effect each process indicated. The values of $\Delta G^{\ominus}_{298}$ (for gas phase reactants and products) are negative in each case, so that the processes may be regarded as thermodynamically feasible at ambient temperature. Yet each process has in fact an insignificant rate at the temperature listed in the absence of a catalyst. The products shown would be generated in the gas phase systems themselves at much higher temperatures.

Catalysis might be a useful but rather uninteresting phenomenon if its accomplishments were restricted to allowing systems to achieve their most thermodynamically stable states only. But in the majority of catalytic processes used industrially, the products are not those expected for full conversions. This feature of catalysis, whereby reactions can be turned onto unusual pathways, greatly enhances its value and makes it a thoroughly fascinating branch of science.

Selectivity is the term used to describe the ability of a catalyst to induce the formation of particular products. The differing, highly selective actions of various catalysts on one reactant at approximately the same temperature are illustrated in Table 1.3. All of these processes proceed to close to maximum theoretical yields of the products specified. None corresponds to the full conversion which would proceed to methane, water and solid

Table 1.3 Catalytic conversions of ethanol vapour at approximately 600 K

Catalyst	Principal products
Copper metal	Acetaldehyde, hydrogen
Alumina	Ethylene, water
MgO–SiO$_2$ (Na$_2$O) (1 : 1 (0.1%) w/w)	Buta-1,3-diene, water
ZSM-5 zeolite	Synthetic gasoline, water

carbon. It is common for bulk solid catalysts to induce more than one conversion route concurrently. For instance, when a hydrocarbon and oxygen react over oxide catalysts to yield partial oxidation products (e.g. carbonyl species) oxidation to carbon oxides proceeds usually to some extent in parallel. Consider a simple general scheme in which a reactant A undergoes a variety of parallel reactions, one of which yields a particular product B. The percentage selectivity (S_B) to B would be defined as

$$S_B = \frac{\text{Number of moles of A converted to B}}{\text{Total number of moles of A consumed}} \times 100\%$$

Table 1.4 indicates the importance of selective (partial) oxidation in the chemical industry, when maximization of selectivities towards desired products is a major concern. At the same time, the elucidation of the microscopic action on the catalyst surface, wherein the selectivity originates, is a primary interest from the scientific viewpoint.

There are three main requirements of an industrial catalyst. It must induce a rate of conversion which allows the process to be conducted with a realistic contact time. It must achieve an acceptable selectivity for the desired product(s). Also it must be sufficiently robust and stable under the operating conditions to minimize the need for its regeneration or replacement. The major differences between homogeneous (in the same phase as the reactants) and heterogeneous (bulk solid) catalysts are highlighted under these requirements. Homogeneously-catalysed processes, typically in a liquid phase, are often characterized by high selectivities but low activities relatively; they work generally under mild temperature (≤ 350 K) conditions, which preserve the catalytic entity. The usual homogeneous catalysts, organometallic species or enzymes for examples, are molecules with particular structures. The active site (the specific part of the entity associated with the catalytic action) of one homogeneous catalyst is exactly the same on each of its molecules. Identical active sites interact with reactant molecules in the same manner to achieve

Table 1.4 Major products of the usage of heterogeneous catalysis

Reactant(s)	Product	Typical catalyst(s)	Global production/ kg year^{-1}
Crude oil	Hydrocarbon fuels	Platinum/silica–alumina Platinum/acidic alumina Metal-exchanged zeolites	1×10^{12}
SO_2, O_2	Sulphuric acid	V_2O_5	1.4×10^{11}
N_2, H_2	Ammonia	Fe	9×10^{10}
NH_3, O_2	Nitric acid	Pt/Rh	2.5×10^{10}
CO, H_2	Methanol	Cu/ZnO	1.5×10^{10}
C_2H_4, O_2	Ethylene oxide	Ag	1×10^{10}
Unsaturated vegetable oils, H_2	Hydrogenated vegetable oils	Ni	8×10^9
C_2H_4	Polyethylene	Cr(II), Ti(III)	6×10^9
CH_3OH, O_2	Formaldehyde	Mixed Fe,Mo oxides	5×10^9
C_3H_6, NH_3, O_2	Acrylonitrile	Mixed Bi,Mo oxides	3×10^9
o-Xylene, O_2	Phthalic anhydride	V_2O_5	2×10^9
n-Butane, O_2	Maleic anhydride	V_2O_5	4×10^8

high selectivity overall. But with a dissolved catalyst, the number of active sites within a volume of the reactor is relatively small under normal conditions, so that the activity per unit volume of the reaction medium is correspondingly restricted. In contrast, it will become clear as the text develops that solid catalysts usually present active sites of various structures at the microscopic level on the same surface: these can be expected to have differing interactions with reactant molecules which may promote differing reaction pathways to result in lower individual selectivities. But now the number of active sites which can be offered to reactants within a given volume does not depend upon factors such as solubility in a fluid phase of the catalyst. Furthermore the operating temperature is not limited by the characteristics of a solvent; reaction rates are promoted in general by higher temperature. Most solid catalysts are quite stable at temperatures of say 500 K, well above the usual temperature range employed with homogeneous catalysts. Thus relatively high activities, with perhaps lower selectivities, may be expected of solid catalysts as compared with dissolved catalysts in general.

Despite the higher energy demands imposed by operation at high temperatures, processes based upon solid catalysts are used widely in the chemical industry. This reflects not only the high activities achievable but also the ease of separation of the products which are in a different phase from the catalyst. The usage of homogeneous catalysts on the other hand necessitates the appendage to the process of an efficient operation for recovery of both products and often expensive and sometimes poisonous catalysts.

Not every part of the surface of a solid catalyst on a microscopic scale may be active catalytically and the effective sites may have widely different activities. For quantitative purposes, it is necessary to specify the surface density of individual sites where catalytic action takes place and their average activity. The *turnover frequency* during a heterogeneous catalytic reaction is then expressed by the number of reactant molecules converted (turned over) by the average active site in unit time. The highest values known for solid surfaces are between 10^5 and $10^6\,\mathrm{s}^{-1}$.

The attachment of a molecule derived from a fluid phase on to a surface is termed *adsorption*. When this involves weak interactions, such as van der Waals forces, physical adsorption or *physisorption* has occurred. For example, the physisorption of oxygen (O_2) on titania (TiO_2) involves a binding energy equivalent to about $5\,\mathrm{kJ\,mol}^{-1}$, not unexpectedly similar to the latent heat of condensation of oxygen ($6.8\,\mathrm{kJ\,mol}^{-1}$). When chemical bonds create the attachment to the surface, chemical adsorption or *chemisorption* has occurred. The binding energy in chemisorption usually exceeds $50\,\mathrm{kJ\,mol}^{-1}$. *Desorption* is the reverse process to adsorption, when the attachment to the surface is broken. In any catalytic reaction on a surface, essential components of the mechanism are chemisorption of reactants and desorption of products. Chemisorption, rather than physisorption, must be involved to explain the ability of different catalysts to divert conversion of reactants along routes to different products (Table 1.3).

This section focuses attention upon microscopic action at surfaces, which will be a major theme of this book. The aim is to allow fundamental understanding of the basis for the use of particular catalysts in specific conversion processes.

1.3 Catalysts in action

This section will set the context of the book, in illustrating the importance of catalytic actions throughout the world.

The most prevalent chemical process on Earth is photosynthesis, the mechanism through which growing plants fix solar energy. The details of how carbon dioxide, derived from the air, is ultimately converted to carbohydrates, principally cellulose, are not important here. But the significant point is that natural catalysts of a protein nature, known as enzymes, are vital for inducing many of the stages of the overall process.

It is relevant to point out that these enzyme molecules are not free entities, but are attached to surfaces in the plant cell structures. The global achievement of photosynthesis is the formation of about 2×10^{14} kg of dry biomass each year. This is then the largest scale of any catalytic process on our planet.

Catalysis is of central importance in the chemical industry, with heterogeneous systems dominant. In exemplification, the overall statistics for main chemical products in the United States of America may be considered. These reveal that some 43% of the total production depends on the application of catalysts, divided 36% and 7% between heterogeneous and homogeneous actions respectively, when oil refining is excluded. In fact, just one product of heterogeneous catalysis, sulphuric acid, accounts for over 10% of the total on the same basis. It is interesting to note in passing that one of the yardsticks proposed for judging the state of development of a nation is its production of sulphuric acid on a *per capita* basis. This amplifies the viewpoint that heterogeneous catalysis is a mainstay of the world economy. Table 1.4 lists major industrial products which are dependent upon the usage of solid catalysts, together with recent global production amounts. The main point to be drawn from the Table is that a wide variety of solid materials is used for catalytic synthesis in industry. But for a specified process, only particular materials prove to be effective. The objective in the following chapters is to gain some understanding of these specific catalytic activities offered by different solid surfaces.

Heterogeneous catalysis is also employed for a variety of other purposes, including control of air pollution. Major problems in this connection are the emissions of pollutants such as nitric oxide (NO) from combustion systems. This pollutant species originates in the equilibrium represented as

$$N_2 + O_2 \rightleftharpoons 2NO$$

which is established at the high temperatures within combustion chambers. The corresponding equilibrium constant has values which increase sharply with rising temperature: at 300 K, 1200 K and 2500 K, the values of $K^\ominus$ are 6×10^{-31}, 3×10^{-7} and 4×10^{-3} respectively. It is then evident that if the backward reaction process represented as

$$2NO \rightarrow N_2 + O_2$$

could proceed rapidly enough to adjust nitric oxide levels to equilibrium values as the temperature falls along the exhaust system, there would be no pollution problem. But, in the gas phase, the actual rates of reactions are too slow to achieve significant adjustment from the high-temperature levels. This kinetic limitation suggests a potential for catalytic reduction of nitric oxide levels, together with those of carbon monoxide and hydrocarbon species which also emerge at exhaust as the result of insufficiently fast rates of homogeneous reaction in the exhaust system. In fact, these pollutant emissions from vehicles are controlled, particularly in the USA and Japan, by the incorporation of catalytic converters into the exhaust systems. The usual converter units have an internal honeycomb structure created by a ceramic material and catalytic surfaces within produced by deposition of platinum (90%) and rhodium (10%) (not alloyed) to a mass loading of 0.25%. At operating temperatures of around 1000 K, the metallic surfaces catalyse a series of reactions which result in the conversion of all three types of pollutants to the corresponding inert products, carbon dioxide, water and nitrogen. Thus the levels of the pollutant species are lowered towards those corresponding to equilibrium at 1000 K. Accordingly known as 'three-way' catalytic converters, these units in typical operation reduce the emissions of each of the pollutants by over an order of magnitude. Here it is the activity of the catalyst, together with its ability to tolerate the presence of sulphur compounds in the hot exhaust gases, which governs the choice of the material used.

Electricity generating plants have a basic anomaly for which catalysis offers a solution. The central operation is the raising of high-pressure steam at temperatures of the order of 900 K using, in conventional plants, combustion chambers which achieve flame temperatures of above 2000 K. The latter feature results in rather high emissions of nitric oxide, certainly in comparison with those which would be expected if the combustion could be conducted with peak temperatures nearer to 1000 K. Pertinently, an outstanding feature of a heterogeneous catalytic process in comparison with its homogeneous equivalent in general is the significantly lower temperature coefficient (or apparent Arrhenius activation energy) associated with its rate. The consequence in the case of combustion systems is that only heterogeneous processes can be fast enough at temperatures below 1500 K to sustain continuous action. Heterogeneous combustion turns out to be quite easy to induce: almost any ceramic material will produce it at temperatures of the order of 1000 K. The surface-catalysed rates of reaction are large enough to meet the self-sustaining condition, which is that heat generation rates must balance heat-loss rates. The presence of the solid leads to radiative heat losses far in excess of those which would arise in a purely gaseous system: on this account alone the temperature achieved in the heterogeneous system will be expected to be considerably lower than that in the conventional flame. Further losses to embedded steam pipes can also be tolerated.

Two modes of heterogeneous combustion are finding increasing usage. 'Within-wall' gas-firing of kilns lined with porous ceramic blocks can result in nitric oxide generation rates about an order of magnitude less than in a conventional kiln. Also fluidized-bed combustion systems are likely to achieve general application in future power stations. Here combustion occurs within a bed of small solid particles, such as sand or coal ash. The rapid movement of gases upwards through the bed causes grains to rise in the wake of the bubbles, with grains elsewhere falling under the influence of gravity in compensation. Fluidization describes the resultant apparent 'boiling' motions of the particles. The combustion occurs heterogeneously on the surfaces of the grains typically at temperatures of the order of 1200 K, yielding much reduced nitric oxide emissions compared to conventional flames as a consequence. This order of temperature then matches more closely the peak temperature of the steam required to be obtained.

In another area of general interest, heterogeneous catalytic action is an essential component of many of the processes used in the steam gasification of coal or other carbonaceous solids. The objective in these systems is the production of a mixture of carbon monoxide and hydrogen, which may then pass as the feedstock ultimately for the synthesis of methanol or hydrocarbon fuels, topics for discussion in Chapter 8. It has been found that addition of alkali carbonates (M_2CO_3) greatly enhances both rates and yields in gasification. The catalytic effect concerned can be described in terms of three steps

$$M_2CO_3(s) + C(s) \rightarrow M_2O(s) + 2CO(g)$$
$$M_2O(s) + H_2O(g) \rightarrow 2MOH(s)$$
$$2MOH(s) + CO(g) \rightarrow M_2CO_3(s) + H_2(g)$$

In combination these steps yield the overall conversion represented as

$$C(s) + H_2O(g) \rightarrow CO(g) + H_2(g)$$

The solid catalyst particles have mobility on the solid structure of the carbon. The role of the alkali carbonate is then to abstract carbon from the solid, releasing it in the form of carbon monoxide to the gas phase. In the subsequent steps the alkali element is restored to the carbonate form, as required in true catalytic action. It is worth mentioning a secondary catalytic action which occurs in these systems. Alkali-element solids also have the ability to catalyse the so-called water-gas shift reaction, which is represented by the equation

$$CO + H_2O \rightarrow CO_2 + H_2$$

This has the result, proceeding in the direction indicated, of enriching the product gas mixture in hydrogen at the expense of some of the carbon monoxide generated in the primary gasification process.

On other occasions, catalysis has the ability to create hazards, in particular by triggering explosions. It is evident that a mixture of, for example, a hydrocarbon vapour with air may be induced to explode by contact with a catalytically active metal. A possible mode is ignition propagating homogeneously into the gas phase from hot spots created by rapid catalytic oxidation proceeding on the metallic surface. Various bulk chemicals are hazardous because of their susceptibility to catalytic decomposition. For example, concentrated solutions of hydrogen peroxide can represent serious hazards due to the readiness with which decomposition can occur in contact with solids at relatively low temperatures (see Table 1.2), with consequent liberation of potentially large amounts of heat and oxygen. Metals in general, particularly if the surface is rough, can constitute a potential danger in this respect if they are allowed to make contact with either liquid or vapour phase hydrogen peroxide. In fact in this connection, any surface should be regarded as likely to create a hazardous situation if it is hotter than 390 K.

1.4 Concluding remarks

This introductory chapter should have convinced the reader of the general importance of catalytic action at surfaces. The last section especially has taken a broad sweep through systems in which the presence of solid materials acting as catalysts is essential for the basis of many large-scale processes. It is legitimate to regard heterogeneous catalysis as the major aspect of catalysis as it occurs in the world today. This will become even more apparent when discussion in Chapter 3 extends to the means of attachment of homogeneous catalytic entities to surfaces and the advantages which are thereby gained.

2

General aspects of
catalysis at surfaces

Three main aims are pursued in this chapter. The first is to classify broadly the catalysts which are discussed in the book. The other two concern the characterization of catalytic actions, through thermodynamic and kinetic parameters respectively which may be investigated without resort to sophisticated techniques which allow surfaces to be examined and analysed at the microscopic level. The resultant aims here are to achieve basic levels of understanding of adsorption/desorption processes and the dependences of the rates of catalytic reactions upon partial pressures or concentrations of individual species in the contacting fluid phase.

2.1 General classification of bulk-solid materials as catalysts

At this stage the objective is simply to produce a summary of main experience of the catalytic abilities of broad classes of solid materials. The origins of the various *functionalities* (i.e. the abilities to induce particular routes of conversion) will be discussed in subsequent chapters. Nevertheless it is important to gain an early impression of the general types of solids which may serve to catalyse a particular mode of reaction. Table 2.1 summarizes the major functionalities of bulk solid materials with respect to their catalytic actions, with illustrative examples of the reactions induced by certain materials. This Table is not intended to be an all-embracing list of the functionalities of the various classes of solids. For instance there is a far wider spectrum of processes catalysed by solid oxides mixed at the molecular level than can be set down in a reasonably concise tabulation. Exposition on these actions will appear in Chapter 6.

Table 2.1 General classification of bulk solids as catalysts

Type of solid	Main catalytic functionalities	Examples of reaction (catalyst)
Transition metals	Hydrogenation	$\begin{cases} N_2 + 3H_2 \longrightarrow 2NH_3 \ (Fe) \\ C_2H_4 + H_2 \longrightarrow C_2H_6 \ (Ni) \end{cases}$
	Dehydrogenation	$H_3C\!-\!\bigcirc \longrightarrow H_3C\!-\!\bigcirc + 3H_2 \ (Pt)$
	Hydrogenolysis	$C_2H_6 + H_2 \longrightarrow 2CH_4 \ (Os)$
	Oxidation	$CO + \tfrac{1}{2}O_2 \longrightarrow CO_2 \ (Ir)$
	Oxidation (deep)	$\begin{cases} C_2H_4 + 3O_2 \longrightarrow 2CO_2 + 2H_2O \ (Co_3O_4) \\ CO + \tfrac{1}{2}O_2 \longrightarrow CO_2 \ (Cr_2O_3) \end{cases}$
	Oxidation (selective)	$n\text{-}C_4H_{10} + 3\tfrac{1}{2}O_2 \longrightarrow \text{(maleic anhydride)} + 4H_2O \ (V_2O_5)$
Transition metal oxides	Oxidation (steam)	$C_3H_6 + \tfrac{1}{2}O_2 \xrightarrow{H_2O} CH_3COCH_3 \ (SnO_2\text{–}MoO_3)$
	Oxidative dehydrogenation	$\bigcirc\!-\!CH_2CH_3 \longrightarrow \bigcirc\!-\!CH{=}CH_2 + H_2O \ (Fe_2O_3)$
	Ammoxidation	$C_3H_6 + \tfrac{3}{2}O_2 + NH_3 \longrightarrow CH_2{=}CHCN + 3H_2O \ (Bi_2O_3\text{–}MoO_3)$
	Hydrogenation	$C_4H_6 + 2H_2 \longrightarrow C_4H_{10} \ (ZnO)$
	Oxidation–reduction	$CO + H_2O \longrightarrow CO_2 + H_2 \ (Fe_3O_4)$
	Decomposition	$N_2O \longrightarrow N_2 + \tfrac{1}{2}O_2 \ (NiO)$

Main group oxides (insulator oxides)

Dehydration $C_2H_5OH \longrightarrow C_2H_4 + H_2O$ (Al_2O_3)

Dehydration $i\text{-}C_3H_7OH \longrightarrow C_3H_6 + H_2O$ $(V_2O_5\text{–}Al_2O_3)$
               1-Butene $\longrightarrow$ Butene isomers $(SiO_2\text{–}TiO_2)$

Acidic mixed oxides

Isomerization

Cracking

Polymerization e.g. oligomerization   Propylene $(C_3) \longrightarrow$ Dimer (C_6), Trimer (C_9), etc. $(TiO_2\text{–}ZrO_2)$

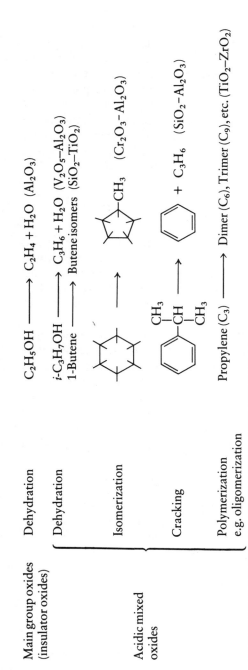

$(Cr_2O_3\text{–}Al_2O_3)$

$+\ C_3H_6$ $(SiO_2\text{–}Al_2O_3)$

Even the limited nature of Table 2.1 indicates an essential point: it is crucial that a reasoned choice of the catalyst for inducing a particular type of reaction is made. Thus a major objective for following chapters is to achieve an understanding of the factors which allow a particular surface to be effective in catalysing one type of reaction but not another. In this connection, the *mechanism* induced at the surface will be of paramount importance. The mechanism of a complex reaction process is the set of distinguishable, elementary reaction steps which occur in sequence to generate the observed products. The elucidation of mechanism, involving the identification of the intermediate species of a transient nature existing on the surfaces, will be the basis of a major part of this book.

2.2 Nature and classification of enzymes

Enzymes are protein molecules and are thus totally unlike the solid catalysts of Table 2.1 in general nature. As catalysts, enzymes exert much more selective actions than do solid surfaces generally. However, an important tenet of this book is that enzyme action is to be regarded as an aspect of catalysis at surfaces, for which explanation is necessary in the first place.

Enzymes are very large molecules indeed, with cross-sectional dimensions extending up to 100 nm or so. On a size scale, these dimensions place enzymes between the usual inorganic species which act as homogeneous catalysts and the solid surfaces which induce heterogeneous catalysis. Table 2.2 shows a selection of relative molecular mass ranges of some common enzymes: these extend over an order of magnitude. The main bulk of the enzyme molecule is composed of amino acid units (residues) joined together through peptide linkages. The long chain, with of

Table 2.2 Relative molecular mass (ranges) of some common enzymes

Enzyme (type)	Relative molecular mass/10^3
Lysozyme	13.9
Dehydrofolate reductase	18
Chymotrypsin	22.6
Amylases	50–60
Glucose isomerases	167–191
Invertases Catalases	240–280

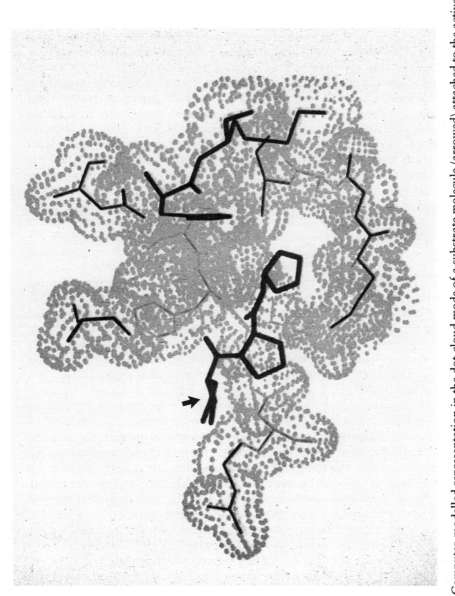

Fig. 2.1 Computer-modelled representation in the dot-cloud mode of a substrate molecule (arrowed) attached to the active site of the enzyme elastase. Reproduced with permission of the Royal Society of Chemistry from *Computer graphics as an aid to drug design*, C. H. Hassall (1985) *Chemistry in Britain*, January, **21**, 43.

the order of hundreds of such residues, is coiled in on itself so that the enzyme molecule as a whole has a globular shape at the microscopic level. In this normal configuration, the interior tends to be hydrophobic in nature. The essentially hydrocarbon parts of the amino acid residues, including sections of the main chain composed of —CH_2— units together with alkyl and aromatic side chains, tend to be directed inwards, whereas hydrophilic side groups, such as —CH_2OH, —NH_2 and —$COOH$ are located at the external surface preferentially. Thus there is some immediate justification for a view that an enzyme molecule creates a true surface, separating hydrophilic from hydrophobic natures. The interior of the giant molecule might be considered to be in some ways akin to an organic phase.

A key feature of the catalytic activity of enzymes at the microscopic level is that only a small part of the external surface of the molecule provides the active site: this often takes the general form of a cleft. The critical factor for the high specificity of associated catalytic action is the necessity that the reactant molecule (or substrate in the conventional terminology of this topic) must fit snugly into this cleft in such a way as to make intimate contacts with some of the amino acid residues in this vicinity. Figure 2.1 shows a computer-modelled graphic representation of a particular substrate molecule bound to the enzyme elastase (a serine protease), evidently within a cleft-like depression in the surface of an irregular globular entity.

The binding forces within an enzyme molecule, responsible for maintaining the overall molecular shape and more critically the configuration at the active site, are relatively weak. Accordingly the activities of enzymes in general are very susceptible to destruction by heating: relatively few enzymes can function as catalysts at temperatures much above 330 K. This can be discussed using a macroscopic analogy of a loosely fastened assembly of scaffolding (corresponding to the molecule) and a walkway (corresponding to the active site) on top of the structure. The existence of the latter would be threatened by a high wind, which through the analogy would correspond in effect to increased thermal energy applied to the enzyme active site. Pursuing this analogy further, the scaffolding and the enzyme structure would be expected to be stabilized to some extent if attachments were made to firm solid surfaces. In the case of the enzyme molecule this process involves its attachment to the surface of an insoluble solid material, a process termed *immobilization* (see Section 3.2.4). Immobilized enzymes would thus be expected to show higher thermal stabilities than the corresponding free forms, which is observed in many instances. Almost invariably the enzymes used in catalytic processes are immobilized, so that the resultant catalytic action is then truly heterogeneous in nature.

A further point of association with some of the solid materials which are used as heterogeneous catalysts is that many enzyme molecules incorporate

Table 2.3 Examples of enzymes incorporating metallic elements

Enzymes	Metallic elements
Glucose isomerases	Mg or Co or Mn (or combinations)
Alcohol dehydrogenase ⎫ Carboxypeptidase ⎬	Zn
Superoxide dismutase	Zn, Cu
Nitrogenases	Fe and Mo or V
Peroxidases ⎫ Catalases ⎬	Fe

metal atoms (in various oxidation states) within their structures and these are essential for the catalytic action at the active sites. Table 2.3 lists a few examples of such enzymes, indicating the metallic element(s) concerned. Most of the metallic elements appearing in this Table can be seen to be common components of many of the solid catalysts, particularly of the oxides which catalyse oxidation reactions, in Table 2.1 and later in Sections 5.2 and 6.2.

The main discussion of the details of the catalytic actions of enzymes will be reserved to Chapter 7. At this stage the remaining task is the classification of enzymes. It is very rare for a particular enzyme to induce more than one reaction pathway with a given substrate: this is in evident contrast with the situation with solid catalysts when it is quite common for parallel reactions to different products to occur. The systematic classification of enzymes is based therefore upon the general type of reaction which they catalyse. In the scheme of classification adopted by international convention, six primary divisions are recognized and allocated identifying numbers as shown in Table 2.4. In so far as industrial and general usages of enzymes are concerned, the most important classes are hydrolases (3) and isomerases (5). The former predominate, accounting for around 90% of the total amounts of all enzymes produced in industry. Table 2.5 indicates some applications of enzymes in large scale processes.

2.3 Basic thermodynamics of heterogeneous catalysis

2.3.1 *Adsorption isotherms*

A dynamic equilibrium will be achieved eventually when a species from a fluid phase interacts with a solid surface in the absence of net chemical conversion. Then the rate of adsorption will be equal to the rate of

Table 2.4 The system of classification of enzymes

Primary division number	Class name	Typical catalytic action	Representative members
1	Oxidoreductases	Oxidation, reduction	Dehydrogenases, oxidases
2	Transferases	Transfer of a functional group from donor to acceptor	Aminotransferases, kinases
3	Hydrolases	Hydrolytic cleavage of bonds	Esterases, proteases, amylases, lipases
4	Lyases	Eliminative cleavage of bonds, addition across double bonds	Decarboxylases, hydratases
5	Isomerases	Configurational changes	Glucose isomerase
6	Synthetases	Linkage of molecules	Peptide synthetase

Table 2.5 Major enzyme usages on an industrial scale

Enzyme	Primary division	Principal usage
Malic acid dehydrogenase	1	Improvement of fruit juices and wines
Amylglucosidases ⎱ Amylases ⎰	3	Glucose production from starch
Cellulases	3	Glucose production from cellulose
Alkaline proteases	3	Biological washing powders
Rennin	3	Cheese production
Pectinases	3	Clarification of fruit juices
Penicillinases	3	Production of penicillin derivatives
Aspartases	4	Production of L-aspartic acid
Glucose isomerases	5	Corn syrup production

desorption. An adsorption isotherm (equation) is an expression relating parameters involved in this type of dynamic equilibrium at a defined temperature.

Only the simplest forms of adsorption isotherms are required for the purposes of this book. The reader is referred to more specialist books on surface phenomena as such for the more complex forms of equations which represent adsorptive behaviour with high precision. Here the only forms needed are those which allow straightforward application to measure the surface area offered by a given amount of a particular solid or to interpret in general terms the dependences of the rates of catalytic reactions on the experimental variables.

The original approach developed by Langmuir (Table 1.1) is still of considerable value today. In this the surface is regarded as presenting an array of identical sites for adsorption, each capable of adsorbing just one molecule or atom. This postulate leads to the limiting concept of a *monolayer* of adsorbed species, which is created when every surface site is occupied. When a monolayer has formed, no further adsorption can occur in this theory. The procedure for developing the isotherm equation is then to equate expressions for the rates of adsorption and desorption within the dynamic equilibrium at a particular temperature: the result is known as the Langmuir adsorption isotherm when the conditions defined above are imposed.

Consider a homogeneous fluid phase containing a concentration c of a species A above a surface upon which A is the only significant adsorbate (adsorbed species). At equilibrium there will be a certain amount of A adsorbed on the surface: in principle this creates effectively a surface concentration of A, but this has been regarded as an inaccessible parameter. The more realistic working parameter is the fraction of the total number of sites on the surface which is occupied by adsorbed A (either at a particular instant or averaged over a period of time), designated as θ. This parameter is proportional to the effective surface concentration of A evidently. Then $1 - \theta$ corresponds to the fraction of sites vacant (i.e. not occupied by adsorbed A).

Following the principles of mass action, the rate of desorption of A from the surface, regarded as a first order kinetic process, will be proportional to the surface concentration of A and hence to θ. This process may be represented as

$$A \text{ (ads)} \rightarrow A \text{ (fluid phase)}$$

using (ads) to indicate the adsorbed species. On the other hand, the rate of adsorption of A will depend upon c, which controls the rate of bombardment of the surface by A. When a molecule impinges on to the surface, there are two possibilities. It may arrive at a vacant site, when it has a finite statistical probability of being adsorbed there. But alternatively, when the molecule arrives at a site at which another molecule is already adsorbed, it has zero probability of being adsorbed. It is then clear that the rate of adsorption of A will be only a fraction of its rate of bombardment of the surface. Other than by constants at a defined temperature, the rate of adsorption of A is reduced compared to its rate of bombardment by the probability of its arrival at a site which is vacant: this probability is measured by the fraction of surface sites vacant, $1 - \theta$. Thus the rate of adsorption of A is proportional to the product $c \times (1 - \theta)$. Equating the rates of adsorption and desorption gives

$$k_a c (1-\theta) = k_d \theta \tag{2.1}$$

in which k_a and k_d are the effective rate constants for adsorption and desorption respectively. Equation (2.1) may be rearranged straightforwardly to yield an expression for θ

$$\theta = \frac{k_a c}{(k_a c + k_d)} = \frac{c}{(c + (k_d/k_a))} \tag{2.2}$$

This is one form of the Langmuir adsorption equation.

Most often in the systems relevant to heterogeneous catalysis the fluid phase will be gaseous, when the partial pressure of A, p_A, will be proportional to c in equation (2.2). An alternative form of the Langmuir adsorption equation appropriate to these circumstances is

$$\theta = \frac{b p_A}{(b p_A + 1)} = \frac{p_A}{(p_A + B)} \tag{2.3}$$

The constants, k_d/k_a in equation (2.2) and $B = b^{-1}$ in equation (2.3), will be proportional to the standard equilibrium constant, $K^{\ominus}$, for the dynamic equilibrium represented as

$$A(ads) \rightleftharpoons A(fluid\ phase)$$

In turn therefore, these constants are related to the other thermodynamic parameters associated with this equilibrium through the familiar equations

$$\Delta G^{\ominus} = \Delta H^{\ominus} - T\,\Delta S^{\ominus} = -RT\ln K^{\ominus} \qquad (2.4)$$

where $\Delta G^{\ominus}$, $\Delta H^{\ominus}$ and $\Delta S^{\ominus}$ are the standard changes in Gibbs (free energy) function, enthalpy and entropy respectively associated with the desorption of 1 mole of A(ads).

Equation (2.3) generates a plot of θ *versus* p_A of the general form shown in quantitative illustration in Fig. 2.2. Three distinct sections may be distinguished in this plot: (i) below point P; $p_A \ll B$ and θ is a linear function of p_A effectively; (ii) above point Q; $p_A \gg B$ and $\theta = 1$ effectively; (iii) between points P and Q, a curved plot of decreasing gradient as p_A increases.

Figure 2.3 shows particular examples of plots for the adsorption of nitrogen and hydrogen on a zeolitic solid. The amount of gas (expressed in terms of the volume V which it would occupy in the gas phase under

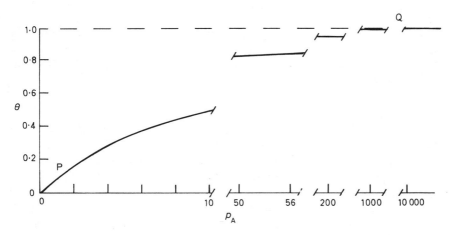

Fig. 2.2 Plot of the form of the Langmuir adsorption isotherm for a single gaseous adsorbate (A), corresponding to equation (2.3). θ is the fraction of the equivalent surface sites covered by adsorbed A molecules and p_A is the partial pressure of A (expressed in arbitrary units) in the gas phase. The value of the constant B used here is 10 in the same units as p_A. The significance of the points identified as P and Q is discussed in the text.

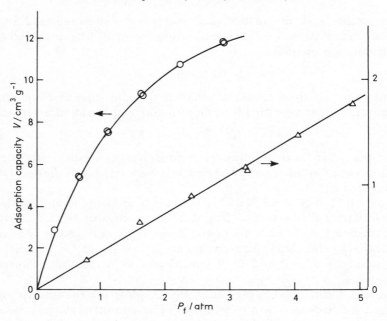

Fig. 2.3 Plots of the adsorption capacities (*V*) of an ion-exchanged (using potassium chloride) form of the natural zeolite clinoptilolite *versus* the final equilibrium pressure, p_f, for nitrogen gas (○) (left-hand vertical scale) and for hydrogen gas (△) (right-hand vertical scale) at ambient temperature. (1 atm = 1.013 bars = 1.013×10^5 Pa). Reproduced with permission of Butterworth & Co. (Publishers) Ltd. from *Hydrogen recovery from hydrogen–nitrogen mixture by selective adsorption on natural clinoptilolite*, M. Abrudean, A. Bâldea and D. Axente (1985) *Zeolites*, 5, 211.

standard conditions) adsorbed on unit mass of the solid (termed the specific adsorption capacity) will be proportional to θ for each final equilibrium pressure, p_f. Nitrogen is more strongly adsorbed than is hydrogen; the plot for nitrogen shows progression into the section between P and Q in Fig. 2.2, whereas the plot for hydrogen corresponds to the section below point P only. Let the specific adsorption capacity corresponding to a monolayer be represented by V_m. Then the ratio V/V_m corresponds to θ and equation (2.3) can be re-expressed in the form (equating p_f in the diagram to p_A)

$$V/V_m = p_A/(p_A + B)$$

With straightforward rearrangement this leads to the equation

$$1/V = 1/V_m + B/V_m p_A \qquad (2.5)$$

This predicts that a plot of the reciprocal of V *versus* the reciprocal of p_A should be linear: it can be extrapolated to obtain the value of the reciprocal of V_m. For example, in the case of the data for nitrogen in Fig. 2.3, this procedure led to a value of $19.5 \, \text{cm}^3 \, \text{g}^{-1}$ for V_m.

To digress, it is interesting to see that the data of Fig. 2.3 suggest a method for using this solid adsorbent to effect separation of hydrogen from a mixture of nitrogen and hydrogen. When such a gas mixture flows through a column packed with this solid, the stronger adsorption of nitrogen means that it will progress more slowly than hydrogen. Thus reasonably pure ($\geqslant 98\%$) hydrogen emerges for a period of time before ultimately the nitrogen 'breaks through': at this stage the entire column will have achieved adsorptive equilibrium with the nitrogen. This process, operating at ambient temperature, is evidently more attractive than a cryoscopic separation procedure on the grounds of energy economy. Similar procedures can be applied to achieve separation of oxygen from air and have been used as a crucial preliminary stage in the production of liquid nitrogen.

Further examples of plots displaying the characteristics expected on the basis of the Langmuir adsorption equation appear later (see Figs 2.9, 2.10 and 4.16).

The BET (Brunauer, Emmett, Teller) gas adsorption technique is accepted as the standard procedure for obtaining a good estimate of the surface areas of finely divided and porous solids (*IUPAC Commission on Colloid and Surface Chemistry including Catalysis, Pure and Applied Chemistry* (1985), **57**, 603–619). Nitrogen is generally used as the adsorptive (i.e. the gas which is adsorbed) at temperatures close to the normal condensation point (77 K). Under these conditions the monolayer of physisorbed molecules is close packed, resembling a one molecule thick layer of liquid nitrogen covering the entire accessible surface. On this basis the volume occupied by a molecule in the monolayer and in the actual liquid (e.g. liquid nitrogen) phase are presumed to be identical. Thus using the density of this liquid phase in conjunction with the determined amount of gas incorporated into the monolayer, the underlying surface area of the solid may be evaluated. Multiplication of the number of molecules in the monolayer of nitrogen by the cross-sectional area of the assumed cubic volume occupied by the molecule in liquid nitrogen ($1.62 \times 10^{-19} \, \text{m}^2$) yields the surface area of the solid. An additional feature of adsorption under these conditions is that less strongly adsorbed layers tend to develop on top of the initially-adsorbed monolayer with approach to atmospheric pressure of nitrogen (p^0) in a phenomenon known as multilayer adsorption.

The simplest forms of BET isotherm (conventionally termed Type II) are illustrated in Fig. 2.4. The 'knees' in these plots are sharply developed near

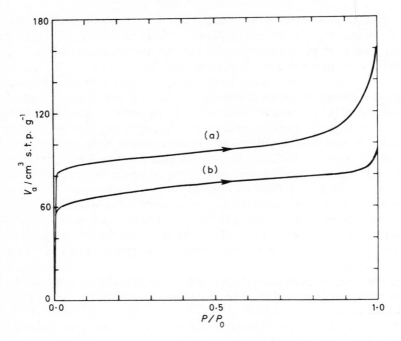

Fig. 2.4 Specific adsorption capacities, V_a, (expressed in terms of volume of nitrogen gas at standard temperature and pressure) as functions of the pressure of nitrogen gas (expressed in terms of the fraction of the standard pressure, p/p_0) for two types of aluminophosphate solids at 77 K. Reproduced with permission of the Royal Society of Chemistry from *Incorporation of zinc in an aluminophosphate microporous phase*, G. C. Bond, M. R. Gelsthorpe, K. S. W. Sing and C. R. Theocharis (1985) *Journal of the Chemical Society, Chemical Communications*, 1056.

to the vertical axis of the diagram: the corresponding amounts of gas are considered to measure approximately the (dynamic) capacities of the corresponding monolayers. For the plot labelled (b), for example, the knee corresponds to a value of V_m of about $60 \, cm^3 \, g^{-1}$. Application of the ideal gas law with standard pressure $(1.013 \times 10^5 \, Pa)$ and temperature of 298 K indicates that the monolayer contains 1.5×10^{21} molecules of nitrogen, which occupy $1.5 \times 10^{21} \times 1.62 \times 10^{-19} = 2.4 \times 10^2 \, m^2$. Thus the specific surface area of the solid concerned in (b) is approximately $240 \, m^2 \, g^{-1}$.

For the purposes of this book it is unnecessary to develop BET adsorption isotherm theory further.

2.3.2 *Thermodynamic aspects of adsorption processes*

Adsorption is an exothermic process and the adsorbed molecule is usually bound to the surface by forces which are much stronger than those to which it is subjected in a fluid phase. The enthalpy change (ΔH) in adsorption is a negative quantity. Also, since adsorption converts a relatively free entity in a fluid phase into a localized entity attached to a surface, the corresponding entropy change (ΔS) will be negative. For an adsorption process to be feasible thermodynamically, the corresponding Gibbs (free energy) function change (ΔG) must be negative, specified by the familiar equation

$$\Delta G = \Delta H - T \Delta S$$

It might be supposed that a large part of the value of ΔS in any process involving firm attachment of a gas phase molecule to a solid surface will be governed by the general nature of the process. On this basis, values of ΔS might not be expected to vary too widely with changes in the identities of adsorbate and adsorbent when chemisorption occurs. On the other hand, values of ΔH are governed by the relative strengths of chemical bonds concerned and hence would be expected to be rather sensitive to the identities of adsorbate and adsorbent. Accordingly much of the interest in the thermodynamics of chemisorption tends to focus upon the enthalpy changes and the bonding strengths involved.

It is appropriate at this point to discuss the general types of chemisorption processes. The broadest division is between molecular chemisorption (in which all atoms linked in the original molecule remain linked in the chemisorbed form) and dissociative chemisorption (in which the original molecule gives rise to separated adsorbed fragments on the surface). Molecular chemisorption is usually restricted to molecules possessing multiple bonds: on the simplest view, abstraction of say two of the electrons from the multiple bond to form new bonds to the surface will not destroy the linkage between the atoms. An example is ethylene which, on adsorption on a platinum crystal face at temperatures below about 290 K, loses two π-electrons from its double bond to the σ-bonds which form between the carbon atoms and the platinum atoms at the surface. This process is accompanied by rehybridization at the carbon atoms to produce four tetrahedrally directed bonds corresponding to sp^3 hybridization. This chemisorption process is represented in Fig. 2.5. (It should be noted that π-bonded chemisorption of alkenic molecules to metal surfaces occurs under other circumstances (Section 6.1.2(a).) Dissociative chemisorption must occur generally for species with single bonds only. It may be illustrated by hydrogen adsorption on nickel. The adsorbed form of hydrogen concerned in catalytic processes on metals is atoms chemically bonded to

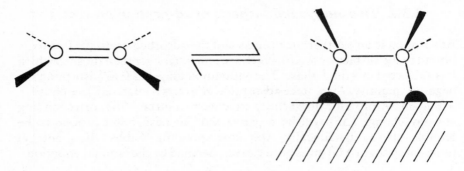

Fig. 2.5 Representation of the structural changes involved in the molecular adsorption of ethylene on a platinum surface. Open circles represent carbon atoms, filled half-circles represent platinum atoms on the surface, hydrogen atoms are not shown.

the surface. The key feature of the pathway followed by hydrogen undergoing dissociative chemisorption is that it represents the lowest potential energy possible at every distance from the metal surface, as represented in Fig. 2.6. This potential energy diagram is composed of two intersecting curves. That with the shallow well further from the surface corresponds to weak physisorption of molecular hydrogen. The much deeper well closer to the surface corresponds to chemisorbed atomic hydrogen. On the lowest energy pathway indicated, molecular hydrogen approaches the surface from the gas phase on the shallow curve before crossing over on to the atomic hydrogen potential curve and thus dissociating. The crossover point may be regarded as corresponding to a transition state in which the H—H bond is severely weakened and the Ni—H bonds are beginning to form.

From a purely thermodynamic point of view, the process represented by the right to left progression along the thick line in Fig. 2.6 may be regarded as

$$\tfrac{1}{2}H_2(g) + Ni_s \rightarrow H-Ni_s$$

where the subscript s denotes that the nickel atom is in the surface. The bond strengths indicated within Fig. 2.6 result in this process being exothermic by $46\,kJ\,(mol\,H)^{-1}$. The essential point of note here is that one bond in the hydrogen molecule gives rise to two nickel–hydrogen bonds after chemisorption, without affecting the bonding between the nickel atoms in the surface. Thus dissociative chemisorption always increases the total number of chemical bonds, which predisposes the process to being exothermic. The entropy change associated with the chemisorption of hydrogen on nickel is of the order of $-68\,J\,(mol\,H)^{-1}\,K^{-1}$. Thus

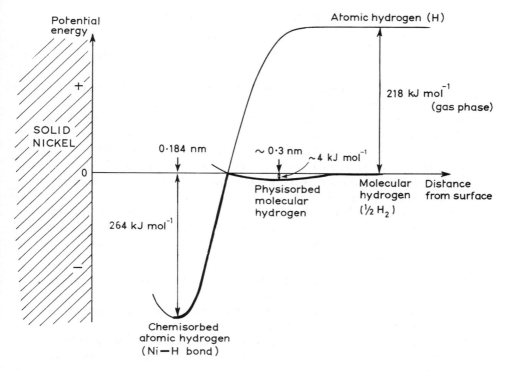

Fig. 2.6 Potential energy diagram (potential energy *versus* distance from the surface) representing the process of the dissociative chemisorption of hydrogen on a nickel surface. The actual pathway followed is indicated by the thickened portions of the curves. The numbers inserted refer to a nickel surface which is a perfect crystal face described by Miller indices (111) (see Section 4.1).

the Gibbs (free energy) function change at a temperature of 300 K is $\Delta G = -46 + (300 \times 0.68) = -26 \, \text{kJ} \, (\text{mol H})^{-1}$, which is substantial and negative as required for a feasible process.

A different type of chemisorption process occurs on the surfaces of acidic materials such as silica–alumina. These have labile protons (H⁺) which are transferred to the adsorbing molecule, producing an adsorbed cationic species held strongly by electrostatic forces. The adsorption of ammonia on such an acidic surface can be represented simply as

$$H^{+}{}_{s} + NH_{3}(g) \rightarrow NH_{4}^{+}{}_{s}$$

Materials such as silica–alumina have a wide range of sites in terms of the associated acid strength. The acidic hydrogens are in fact partially-bonded at the surface (H--S) and a hypothetical scheme may be used to consider the thermodynamics of the adsorption of ammonia, represented as

$$\text{H} \xrightarrow{\Delta H_1} \text{H}^+(\text{g}) \xrightarrow[+\text{NH}_3(\text{g})]{\Delta H_2} \text{NH}_4^+(\text{g}) \xrightarrow{\Delta H_3} \text{NH}_{4s}^+$$
$$\quad \text{S}^- \qquad\qquad \text{S}^- \qquad\qquad\quad \text{S}^-$$

The stronger is the initial acidic site, the lower will be ΔH_1. On this basis alone, the overall enthalpy change, $\Delta H = \Delta H_1 + \Delta H_2 + \Delta H_3$, will be more negative for the more strongly acidic sites i.e. more exothermic adsorption occurs on these. It should also be pointed out that acidic solids like silica–alumina also have other types of sites, which are able to accept a pair of electrons to form a coordinatively bound adsorbate. In the case of ammonia this process involves the donation of the lone pair of electrons on the nitrogen atom to this type of surface site.

It is appropriate here to turn attention to the experimental techniques which may be used to measure the energy changes concerned in adsorption processes. Three methods of major importance in this respect are summarized below.

1. Calorimetric measurement of the amount of heat evolved when a gas is brought into contact with an adsorbent.
2. Measurement of the variation of the amount of gas adsorbed on a particular surface as a function of temperature.
3. Measurement of the temperatures at which particular species, pre-adsorbed at lower temperature, desorb from a surface as its temperature is raised.

The calorimetric technique is often based on a Calvet-type micro-calorimeter, one design being shown in Fig. 2.7. The sample cell is located between two thermopiles, each of which incorporates 127 thermocouple junctions connected in series, creating a direct thermal link to the heat sink (aluminium) from the sample cell. This assembly constitutes a heat-conduction calorimeter in which the heat evolved within the sample cell is transferred quantitatively to the heat sink, which has effectively infinite capacity. The sample cell and the heat sink start in thermal equilibrium. This is upset when an amount of gas is introduced to the sample cell, generating heat in its adsorption. As a result heat flows to the sink until thermal equilibrium is restored: the integrated heat flowrate over time will equate to the total heat released by the adsorption process. At any instant the heat flux (dq/dt) is reflected in the potential difference (V) across a thermopile, both being proportional to the temperature difference between the sample cell and the heat sink. The integration of the entire time record of V (typically a rapid initial rise succeeded by a relatively slow decay) yields the integrated heat release (Q), through application of a calibration factor (α) commonly established using an electrical heating pulse.

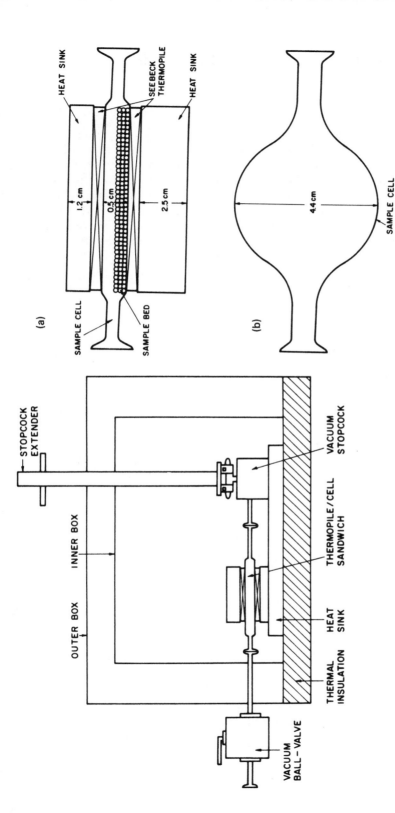

Fig. 2.7 A design of a microcalorimeter of the heat-flow type which has been used to measure the differential heats of adsorption of gases on high surface area solids. Left: side view exhibiting the double box design. Right: sample cell design, showing (a) a side view of the thermopile sandwich and (b) a top view of the sample cell. Reproduced with permission of the American Institute of Physics from *New microcalorimeter for the measurement of differential heats of adsorption of gases on high surface area solids,* M. O'Neil, R. Lovrien and J. Phillips (1985) *Review of Scientific Instruments,* **56,** 2314.

$$Q = \alpha \int_0^\infty V \, dt \qquad (2.6)$$

Calvet-type microcalorimeters offer high sensitivity: energy changes as small as 10^{-3} J can be measured. Moreover with a series of small additions of adsorbate gas to a sample of a solid adsorbent (typically a few grams), the heat of adsorption can be measured as a function of the accumulating amount (n) of adsorbate on the surface (i.e. the differential heat of adsorption). Figure 2.8 illustrates a typical profile of Q *versus* n for the adsorption of ammonia on a sample of silica–alumina. The form of the profile indicates the existence of a wide range of different strengths of

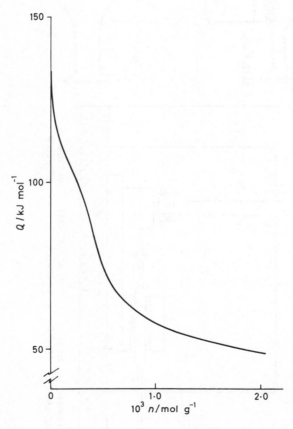

Fig. 2.8 Typical form of variation of the heat of adsorption (Q) of ammonia against the cumulative amount adsorbed (n) on fresh silica–alumina containing around 13% Al_2O_3 (w/w on dry basis) at ambient temperature.

acidity. The most acidic sites are neutralized first with the highest evolutions of heat. An alternative differential form of this type of plot appears in Fig. 5.9(b).

The second general method depends upon the measurement of the equilibrium pressure of an adsorbing gas above a surface as a function of temperature, when a fixed total amount of the gas is present. Equations (2.2) and (2.3) show that the variation of the amount adsorbed (proportional to θ) as the temperature varies will be governed by the ratio k_d/k_a and hence the corresponding $K^{\ominus}$ (assuming Langmuir adsorption isotherm behaviour). The Clapeyron–Clausius form of equation, derived from equation (2.4), then relates the variation to the enthalpy change involved in desorption

$$\left(\frac{\partial \ln K^{\ominus}}{\partial(1/T)} \right)_p = -\frac{\Delta H^{\ominus}}{R} \tag{2.7}$$

Instances of the arrays of experimental data required for this procedure are shown in Fig. 2.9 and 2.10. The general forms of these plots resemble the form shown in Fig. 2.2. Data at a particular pressure (p) for the various temperatures are used in equation (2.7) (i.e. in a linear plot of $\ln(p/p^{\ominus})$ *versus* $1/T$) to yield enthalpies of desorption (ΔH) of $120\,\text{kJ}\,\text{mol}^{-1}$ for carbon dioxide on zinc oxide (Fig. 2.9) and $142\,\text{kJ}\,\text{mol}^{-1}$ for carbon monoxide on the palladium surface concerned in Fig. 2.10 when the extents of surface coverage by adsorbed species are low (Section 4.1 to follow will explain the identification numbers).

The third general method is usually referred to as temperature-programmed desorption spectroscopy (acronym TDS). The principle is that the adsorbate is introduced to the surface at relatively low temperature, before the temperature is raised at a uniform rate; the desorption of the adsorbate as a function of temperature is recorded. The theory of TDS shows that the rate of desorption of the adsorbate is governed by the factor $\exp(-E_d/RT)$, a component of k_d in equation (2.2), where E_d is the activation energy for the desorption process. In most cases E_d will correspond closely in value with the enthalpy change for the desorption process.

An illustrative example is provided by the system in which ethylene is pre-adsorbed on alumina at ambient temperature, taken from the pioneering work on the TDS technique. When the temperature was raised at a typical rate of $16\,\text{K}\,\text{min}^{-1}$ with helium flowing at a constant rate over the solid, the record of the thermal conductivity of the emerging gas had the form shown in the inset in Fig. 2.11, showing an obvious first peak. The thermal conductivity here only changed when ethylene was being desorbed from the solid. Detailed theory (which cannot be developed here) predicts

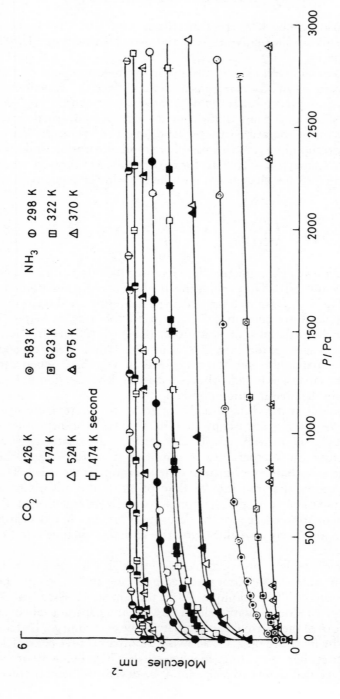

Fig. 2.9 Adsorption isotherms of carbon dioxide and ammonia (see key above diagram) on zinc oxide, as expressed by plots of the number of adsorbed molecules per unit area of surface against the equilibrium pressure (p) of the corresponding gas above the surface. The open symbols indicate adsorption and the closed symbols desorption in progression from one point to the next. Reprinted with permission from *Adsorption of water, ammonia and carbon dioxide on zinc oxide at elevated temperatures*, I. Yasumoto (1984) *Journal of Physical Chemistry*, 88, 4043. Copyright 1984, American Chemical Society.

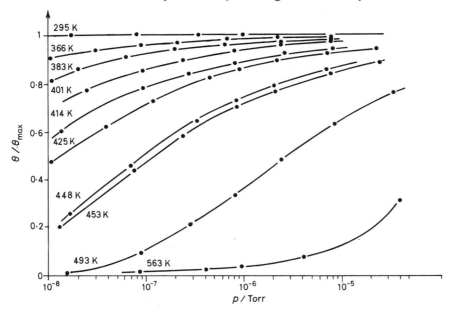

Fig. 2.10 Adsorption isotherms for carbon monoxide on the palladium crystal face identified by the Miller indices (111) (see Section 4.1) at various temperatures, as expressed by the variation of the ratio of actual surface coverage (θ) to the maximum (monolayer) surface coverage (θ_{max}) against equilibrium pressure (p, expressed in units of Torr: 1 Torr = 133 Pa). Reproduced with permission of Società Chimica Italiana from *Chemisorption on transition metal surfaces*, G. Ertl (1979) *Gazzetta Chimica Italiana*, **109**, 222.

that when the desorption rate is directly proportional to the surface coverage of the adsorbate (i.e. a first order process), equation (2.8) applies.

$$\frac{E_d}{RT_M^2} = \left(\frac{\nu_1}{\beta}\right) \exp\left(-\frac{E_d}{RT_M}\right) \qquad (2.8)$$

The parameter T_M is the temperature at which the peak maximum appears in the record, β is the uniform rate of temperature rise and ν_1 is the frequency factor in the Arrhenius form of the rate constant for the desorption process. There are then two approaches to obtaining the value of E_d. The variation of T_M values in experiments in which β is varied (say in the range 5 to 25 K min^{-1}) is measured. Equation (2.8) may be recast to obtain

$$2\ln T_M - \ln \beta = \ln (E_d/\nu_1 R) + (E_d/RT_M) \qquad (2.9)$$

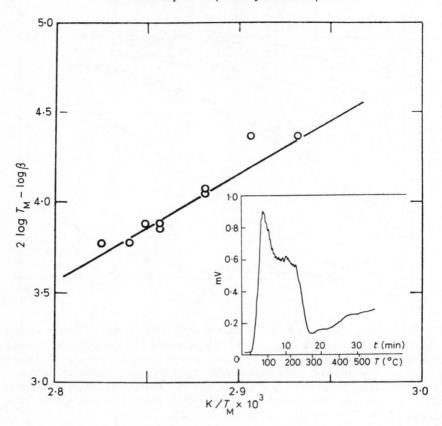

Fig. 2.11 Results of the temperature-programmed desorption of ethylene adsorbed on alumina (pretreated with air for 2 h and thereafter evacuated for more than 60 h, both at the temperature of 873 K). Inset plot: chart record of the signal corresponding to ethylene partial pressure in the flowing helium when the temperature of the adsorbent was increased at a rate (β) of 16.03 K min^{-1}. Main diagram: plot used to evaluate E_d (see text) for the first peak in the inset. Reprinted with permission from *Application of flash-desorption method to catalyst studies. I. Ethylene–alumina system*, Y. Amenomiya and R. J. Cvetanovic (1963) *Journal of Physical Chemistry*, **67**, 145, 146. Copyright 1963, American Chemical Society.

This predicts a linear plot of the left-hand side *versus* $1/T_M$ with gradient equal to E_d/R. The main part of Fig. 2.11 shows this plot for the first peak in the ethylene–alumina system. This plot yielded $E_d = 112$ kJ mol^{-1}. In these experiments the initial adsorption of ethylene on to the alumina was a rapid process, indicating that no significant activation energy was associated with it. This is the general condition required to allow equation

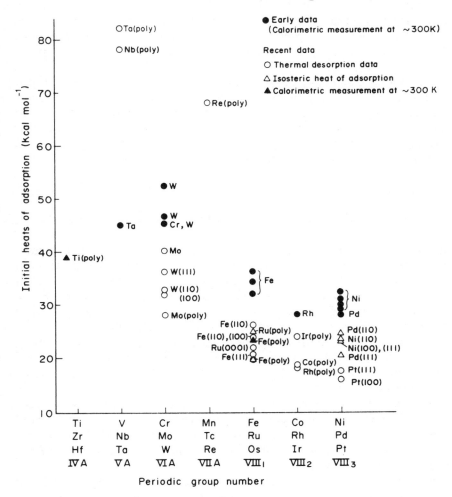

Heats of adsorption of H₂ on transition metals

Ti(poly) Ta Ti(poly) W Cr,W Mo W(111) W(110) (100) Mo(poly) Fe Ni Pd Rh

Fig. 2.12 Measured values of the initial heats of adsorption of hydrogen on transition metal surfaces (elements and periodic table group designations given below horizontal axis). Crystal faces are identified by Miller indices (see Section 4.1), polycrystalline metals are indicated as (poly). The inset key indicates the techniques used. On vertical scale, 1 Kcal mol⁻¹ = 4.184 kJ mol⁻¹. Reproduced from *Adsorption of H₂ on (110), (111) and stepped (111) iron single crystal surfaces*, K. Yoshida (1980) *Japanese Journal of Applied Physics*, **19**, 1882, with permission of the Publication Board.

of the enthalpy change associated with desorption to E_d. The alternative approach in TDS experiments is applied when only one value of T_M at a particular heating rate β is available. It is then necessary to assume a value of ν_1 in equation (2.8), predicted to be about $10^{13}\,\text{s}^{-1}$ by the theory of absolute rates. Further discussion of thermal desorption methods appears in Section 4.3.1.

The above discussion provides an introduction to the methods for obtaining enthalpies or heats of adsorption. Numerous measurements covering a wide variety of systems have been made. Figure 2.12 serves to illustrate the results which have become available for the initial (i.e. at low surface coverage) heats of dissociative chemisorption of hydrogen on particular surfaces of various transition metals (see Section 4.1).

2.4 Aspects of the kinetics of surface catalysed reactions

Relatively few catalytic processes are conducted industrially under conditions which make actual rates of reactions of major significance. In most cases rates are large enough to achieve essentially complete conversions. The syntheses of ammonia (Section 8.2) and methanol (Section 8.3) are perhaps the outstanding instances of catalysed processes in which kinetic factors are limiting in significant respects.

Kinetic investigation provided one of the few potential means of gaining some indication of the microscopic action involved in reactions on solid surfaces before the arrival of the sophisticated techniques which are now used routinely to identify surface species. Kinetic studies thus feature strongly in the less recent accounts of research in heterogeneous catalysis. However, the deduction of unambiguous mechanisms from the observed orders of reactions was rarely possible. Nowadays the study of the kinetics represents only a minor part of the overall thrust in research of surface catalysed reaction systems.

In the light of the above remarks, the approach here will be to set down only the most general principles governing the rates of reactions at surfaces. Exemplification of their application will be limited in the main to a few straightforward cases.

The general scheme for a surface catalysed reaction involves five stages, as indicated in Fig. 2.13 for the conversion of a reactant A into a product P. In general the rate of any one of these stages can create a bottleneck, such that the kinetic dependences of that stage are imposed on the rate equation for the overall process. In the most common case encountered, stage 3 is the rate-determining step in this way.

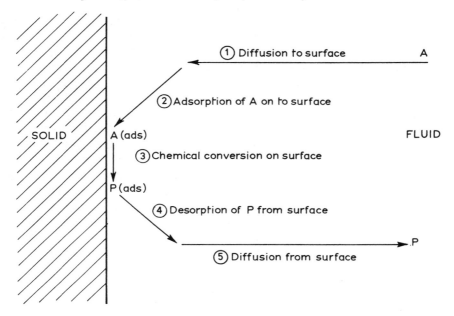

Fig. 2.13 Diagrammatic representation of the five stages involved in the conversion of a reactant A, initially in a bulk fluid phase, to a product P by a catalytic unimolecular reaction at a solid surface. Adsorbed species are indicated by (ads).

2.4.1 *Langmuir–Hinshelwood kinetics*

The Langmuir–Hinshelwood mechanism for a reaction at a solid surface applies when stage 3 in Fig. 2.13 is rate determining. The rate equation for the overall reaction is then predicted by application of the principle of mass action to this surface reaction in conjunction with the Langmuir adsorption isotherm. The former implies that the rate of reaction is proportional to the product of the fractional coverages (θ) of the reactant species, since these are proportional to the corresponding surface concentrations.

The simplest circumstance is a unimolecular reaction (corresponding to Fig. 2.13), in which the rate determining step can be written

$$A(ads) \rightarrow P(ads)$$

The rate is expressed by $k\theta_A$, when k is the effective rate constant. In the case of a bimolecular surface reaction written as

$$A(ads) + B(ads) \rightarrow Products(ads)$$

the rate is expressed by $k'\theta_A\theta_B$ similarly. Under circumstances when the product(s) of the reaction adsorb(s) significantly on to the surface, the Langmuir adsorption isotherm is also applied to this(these). Thus the Langmuir–Hinshelwood scheme assumes that species in the system are involved in adsorption/desorption equilibria which are preserved throughout the course of the reaction (i.e. the rates of adsorption/desorption are much larger than those of chemical reactions). Moreover the scheme demands that all species are adsorbed competitively on equivalent sites on the surface. The application of these postulates is now developed for general cases exemplified by particular reactions.

Consider a unimolecular reaction in which an adsorbed reactant A generates products X and Y. In the simplest case A will adsorb on a single site on the surface whilst X and Y are insignificantly adsorbed (i.e. once X and Y have formed on the surface they desorb rapidly and have negligible readsorption tendencies). In a gas phase system, when p_A is the partial pressure of A above the surface, the predicted rate equation (incorporating equation 2.3) is

$$\text{Rate}\,(R) = k\theta_A = \frac{kp_A}{(p_A + B)} \tag{2.10}$$

Equation (2.10) predicts various apparent orders of reaction (defined as the power to which p_A must be raised to be proportional to R), depending upon the relative sizes of p_A and B; the latter reflects the strength of adsorption of A. These are summarized in Table 2.6, in which the relevant sections of Fig. 2.2 are indicated. The fractional order (x) arises when p_A and B do not differ by several orders of magnitude: x increases as p_A decreases. A useful illustration of this type of kinetic variation is provided by data shown in Fig. 2.14. The values of x inserted at particular points are for the range within which *cis*-2-butene is said to be moderately strongly adsorbed. Many other unimolecular reactions on surfaces show this type of behaviour. The decomposition of stibine (SbH_3) on molybdenum can show almost the full progression from first to zero order as the partial pressure is increased across the accessible range.

In other unimolecular reactions, one of the products, say X, can be significantly adsorbed. Then there is competition between A and X for surface sites: the presence of X consequently inhibits (i.e. slows down) the rate by reducing the surface concentration of A. Let θ_A and θ_X and p_A and p_X represent the corresponding surface coverages and partial pressures respectively. Adsorption/desorption equilibria for A and X are then expressed by the equations (by analogy with equation 2.1)

$$K_A p_A (1 - \theta_A - \theta_X) = \theta_A \tag{2.11}$$

$$K_X p_X (1 - \theta_A - \theta_X) = \theta_X \tag{2.12}$$

Table 2.6 Apparent reaction orders corresponding to equation (2.10)

Strength of adsorption of A	Condition implied	Rate equation	Apparent order	Relevant section of Figure 2.2
Weak	$B \gg p_A$	$R = \dfrac{k}{B} p_A$	1	Below P
Moderate	None	$R = \dfrac{kp_A}{(p_A + B)} \approx k'' p_A^x$	$0 < x < 1$	PQ
Strong	$B \ll p_A$	$R = k$	0	Above Q

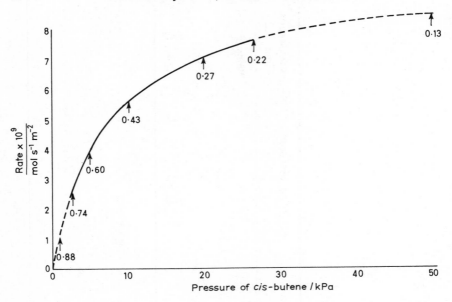

Fig. 2.14 Idealized plot of the initial rate of isomerization of *cis*-2-butene to *trans*-2-butene on a silica–alumina catalyst at a temperature of 358 K as a function of the pressure of *cis*-2-butene. The heavy line corresponds to the pressure range accessible in the experimental study (D. Ballivet, D. Barthomeuf and Y. Trambouze (1974) *Journal of Catalysis*, **34**, 423), the dashed extensions to extrapolation on the basis of the Langmuir adsorption isotherm. Apparent reaction orders (x) at various points are indicated.

The parameters K_A and K_X are of the nature of equilibrium constants, containing the ratio of the rate constant for adsorption over that for desorption of the species. The fraction of sites vacant (i.e. not occupied by either adsorbed A or X molecules) is $(1 - \theta_A - \theta_X)$. Application of the mathematical consequence of $m = n$ and $q = r$ that $m/q = n/r$ allows elimination of $(1 - \theta_A - \theta_X)$ between equations (2.11) and (2.12), yielding

$$\frac{K_A p_A}{K_X p_X} = \frac{\theta_A}{\theta_X} \quad \text{and} \quad \theta_X = \left(\frac{K_X p_X}{K_A p_A} \right) \theta_A \qquad (2.13)$$

Substitution of equation (2.13) into equation (2.11) and rearrangement yields

$$\theta_A = \frac{K_A p_A}{(1 + K_A p_A + K_X p_X)}$$

Thence the rate R will be expressed as

$$R = k\theta_A = \frac{kK_A p_A}{(1 + K_A p_A + K_X p_X)} \tag{2.14}$$

It is common for species of interest in catalytic reactions to be dissociatively chemisorbed, when the resultant fragments occupy two surface sites. Consider that this occurs for a diatomic molecule M_2, when the equation of rates of adsorption and desorption yields

$$K_M p_{M_2}(1 - \theta_M)^2 = \theta_M{}^2 \tag{2.15}$$

The factor $(1 - \theta_M)^2$ represents the probability that an impinging molecule arriving at a surface location finds two adjacent sites vacant, the prerequisite for dissociative chemisorption of M_2. The right hand side, θ_M^2, arises from application of the principle of mass action to the situation where two adsorbed M atoms must come together (effectively then a bimolecular process) to lead to desorption of M_2. When dissociative chemisorption of a product species, M_2, is in competition with molecular chemisorption of the reactant A, the analogous equations to (2.11) and (2.12) are

$$K_A p_A(1 - \theta_A - \theta_M) = \theta_A \tag{2.16}$$

$$K_M p_{M_2}(1 - \theta_A - \theta_M)^2 = \theta_M^2 \tag{2.17}$$

Following the procedure used to generate equation (2.10), with the additional stage of equating the square roots of both sides of equation (2.17) prior to elimination of $(1 - \theta_A - \theta_M)$, the resultant rate expression is

$$R = k\theta_A = \frac{kK_A p_A}{(1 + K_A p_A + K_M^{1/2} p_{M_2}^{1/2})} \tag{2.18}$$

An illustrative example of this type of kinetic behaviour is given in Table 2.7, in connection with nitrous oxide (N_2O) decomposition.

Bimolecular surface processes are more important in catalytic action on solids than are unimolecular processes in general. The various equations for expressing θ parameters in terms of partial pressures of species developed above may be applied as appropriate to generate rate expressions from the products of θ parameters for reactants. To be strictly within the compass of the Langmuir–Hinshelwood mechanism, these reactants must be competitively adsorbed on equivalent surface sites. Considering A and B as reactants which adsorb on single surface sites and assuming negligible adsorption of product species, the predicted rate expression takes the form

$$R = k'\theta_A \theta_B = \frac{k' K_A K_B p_A p_B}{(1 + K_A p_A + K_B p_B)^2} \tag{2.19}$$

Table 2.7 Examples of rate expressions for surface catalysed reactions and apparent interpretations according to the Langmuir–Hinshelwood scheme

Catalysed reaction	Catalyst	Expression proportional to rate	Apparent simplest interpretation
Thermal decomposition of nitrous oxide at low pressure ($N_2O \rightarrow N_2 + \tfrac{1}{2}O_2$)	Pt	$\dfrac{p_{N_2O}}{(1 + Kp_{N_2O} + K'p_{O_2}^{1/2})}$	Unimolecular decomposition, N_2O adsorbed molecularly, O_2 dissociatively adsorbed
Hydrogenation of cyclohexene (CH) in ethanol at 303 K ($C_6H_{10} + H_2 \rightarrow C_6H_{12}$)	Ni	$\dfrac{p_{H_2}p_{CH}}{(1 + Kp_{H_2} + K'p_{CH})^2}$	Bimolecular reaction, competitive adsorption of H_2 and CH
Deep oxidation of methanol with oxygen at 503 K ($CH_3OH + \tfrac{3}{2}O_2 \rightarrow CO_2 + 2H_2O$)	SmCoO$_3$ (Perovskite form)	$\dfrac{p_{O_2}^{1/2}p_{CH_3OH}}{(1 + Kp_{CH_3OH})^2}$	Bimolecular reaction, CH_3OH molecularly adsorbed, O_2 dissociatively adsorbed (weakly)
Selective oxidation of isobutene (B) by oxygen at 593–653 K ($B + 2O_2 \rightarrow CH_3COCH_3 + H_2O + CO_2$)	MoO$_3$/U$_3$O$_8$ on SiO$_2$	$\dfrac{p_B}{(1 + Kp_B)}\dfrac{p_{O_2}}{(1 + K'p_{O_2})}$	Bimolecular reaction, O_2 and B adsorbed separately on different types of site
Methanol synthesis at 562 K ($CO + 2H_2 \rightarrow CH_3OH$)	Cu/ZnO/Cr$_2$O$_3$	$\dfrac{p_{CO}p_{H_2}^2}{(1 + 5Kp_{CO} + Kp_{H_2})^3}$	Termolecular reaction, competitive adsorption with CO adsorbed five times more strongly than H_2

Although it is strictly outwith the Langmuir–Hinshelwood scheme, a situation in which reactants are separately adsorbed on different types of sites (usual on metal oxide surfaces) may be considered usefully at this point. Equation (2.20) expresses the predicted form of rate equation for this circumstance, involving independent adsorption/desorption equilibria for reactants A and B and no significant adsorption of products.

$$R = k''\theta_A \theta_B = k'' \left(\frac{K_A p_A}{(1 + K_A p_A)} \right) \left(\frac{K_B p_B}{(1 + K_B p_B)} \right) \qquad (2.20)$$

Apparent examples of kinetics corresponding to equations (2.19) (hydrogenation of cyclohexene) and (2.20) (selective oxidation of isobutene) are given in Table 2.7. But in fact these reactions do not proceed by the simple interactions of undissociated adsorbed species, as will become clear during Chapter 6. These examples then serve as cautionary illustrations of the difficulties which may be encountered in attempting to relate kinetic orders to microscopic events taking place on the surface.

Reactions of molecularities higher than two may also be dealt with using similar principles. In cases involving significant adsorption of two or more species on the surface, the relative K parameter values determined experimentally carry information on the relative strengths of adsorption of the corresponding species under the conditions concerned, if the Langmuir–Hinshelwood scheme is assumed to apply. This is illustrated by the methanol synthesis example appearing in Table 2.7. But again the actual mechanism of reaction belies the apparent simplicity of the rate expression, as will become clear in Section 8.3.

The overall point to be re-emphasized is that it is a comparatively rare circumstance when the rate expression found experimentally for a surface catalysed reaction can provide a definitive insight into the actual mechanism.

2.4.2 *Adsorption/desorption-limited kinetics*

A substantial number of catalytic processes at solid surfaces have rates which are governed by the rates of reactant adsorption or less commonly product desorption (stages 2 and 4 in Fig. 2.13 effectively). An important instance industrially is the synthesis of ammonia: in this it is the rate at which nitrogen is adsorbed on to the iron surface which is the rate determining step under normal operating conditions.

The main purpose in this subsection is to highlight two instances in which the observed kinetic dependences of the systems concerned reflect the true nature of the elementary processes which govern the overall rate.

The selective oxidation of propylene by oxygen on the catalytic surface presented by molecularly mixed SnO_2 and MoO_3 (1 : 1 in molecular proportions) provides a good example of an adsorption-limited process. At temperatures of around 670 K, the initial rate law took the form

$$\text{Rate} = kp_{O_2}^{1/2}$$

Significantly the reaction was zero order in propylene, which immediately rules out the possibility that propylene is involved in the rate determining step. Thus neither adsorption of propylene nor the surface reaction of adsorbed forms of propylene and oxygen can govern the overall rate. Rather the observed rate expression suggests that the limiting role is played by the dissociative chemisorption of oxygen on sites which are independent of those on which propylene adsorbs. This process may be represented

$$\tfrac{1}{2}O_2(g) \rightarrow O(ads)$$

The rate of this adsorption process would be expected to depend upon $p_{O_2}^{1/2}$ on the basis of the principle of mass action. It may be presumed that the adsorbed atomic oxygen (O(ads)) reacts thereafter with species created by the adsorption of propylene in processes which are not rate determining. In fact the surface coverage by atomic oxygen must be low to allow the adsorption process to proceed without significant occurrence of the reverse desorption. Further evidence will be given supporting the general features of this mechanism of selective oxidation of hydrocarbons on such mixed-oxide catalysts in Sections 5.2 and 6.2. To anticipate, the fundamental features are that the organic molecule is chemisorbed rapidly and thereafter reacts with oxygen derived from the solid itself (i.e. lattice oxygen). This precedes the rate-determining replenishment of the resultant vacancy with oxygen derived from the gas phase. Thus the observed rate law in this example provides a direct indication of this type of mechanism (often known as the Mars–van Krevelen type).

The dehydration reactions of the alcohols ethanol or 2-propanol over calcium phosphate surfaces show the kinetic characteristics of desorption-limited processes. The rates are independent of partial pressures (i.e. zero order kinetics) but the corresponding rate constants vary sharply with temperature with Arrhenius activation energy values well in excess of 100 kJ mol^{-1}. Zero order kinetics could in fact arise from a rate-determining unimolecular reaction with the reactant alcohol strongly adsorbed (see Table 2.6). But the activation energies are much larger than would normally be expected for this situation. However zero order kinetics can also arise when the desorption of a strongly bound product is the rate determining step. Indeed water is known to be very strongly adsorbed on solid phosphates which commends its identification as the crucial product. The overall rate of dehydration of the alcohol is then determined by the surface coverage of water, likely to be virtually complete under these circumstances, so that the rate is independent of the partial pressure of the alcohol. The process of reaction of an alcohol molecule may then be considered as follows in energy terms. In order to provide a site for adsorption of an alcohol molecule on the surface, energy must first be supplied to desorb the water molecule in residence. That accomplished, the dehydration of the adsorbed alcohol molecule proceeds rapidly and the alkene product desorbs readily, leaving the co-produced water molecule strongly adsorbed on the site. Thus the key energy term in respect of the observed activation energy is that required to desorb a water molecule: this could be viewed as activating the surface site rather than the reactant molecule as such.

2.4.3 *The kinetics of enzyme catalysed reactions*

The Michaelis–Menten mechanism provides useful basic interpretations of the kinetic behaviour observed in many reactions catalysed by enzymes. Using E and S to represent the enzyme and substrate (reactant) molecules respectively, this mechanism may be written as a sequence of three elementary steps

$$E + S \xrightarrow{k_1} ES \tag{1}$$

$$ES \xrightarrow{k_2} E + S \tag{2}$$

$$ES \xrightarrow{k_3} E + P \tag{3}$$

The symbols k_1, k_2 and k_3 denote corresponding rate constants and P represents the product(s).

In aqueous solutions, enzymes generally have very low solubilities on a molar basis, so that the total added concentration, $[E]_0$, of enzyme is very much less than concentrations of substrate, $[S]$, under all normal conditions. Accordingly the concentration of the enzyme–substrate complex, $[ES]$, will be very small compared to the concentrations of S and P throughout the observed course of the reaction. This circumstance allows the stationary state approximation to be applied through $d[ES]/dt \approx 0$. Following usual practice, the rates of the elementary steps are expressed using the principle of mass action and are combined to express the net rate of formation of ES, yielding the equations

$$\frac{d[ES]}{dt} = k_1[E][S] - k_2[ES] - k_3[ES] = 0$$

$[E]$ and $[ES]$ are not independent variables, so that $[E] = [E]_0 - [ES]$ is substituted to yield the equation

$$k_1[E]_0[S] - k_1[ES][S] - k_2[ES] - k_3[ES] = 0$$

This is rearranged to produce the expression for [ES]

$$[ES] = \frac{k_1[E]_0[S]}{(k_1[S] + k_2 + k_3)}$$

The overall rate (R) of reaction is expressed by the equations

$$R = \frac{d[P]}{dt} = k_3[ES] = \frac{k_1 k_3[E]_0[S]}{(k_1[S] + (k_2 + k_3))}$$

Division of numerator and denominator by k_1 yields

$$R = \frac{k_3[E]_0[S]}{([S] + (k_2 + k_3)/k_1)} = \frac{V_{max}[S]}{([S] + K_M)} \tag{2.21}$$

The right hand expression in equation (2.21) incorporates the conventional symbols used in connection with enzyme kinetics. V_{max} is the limiting (maximum) reaction rate (velocity) for a specified $[E]_0$ whilst K_m is referred to as the Michaelis constant (or sometimes the Michaelis–Menten constant); both apply for a particular enzyme–substrate system under defined conditions.

It should be apparent immediately that equation (2.21) for an enzyme catalysed process is of similar form to equation (2.10), the latter referring to a unimolecular reaction taking place on a solid surface (with partial pressure substituted for concentration). Thus the rate of the enzyme catalysed reaction will vary with [S] in a similar manner to the variation of rate with partial pressure shown in Fig. 2.14 for a unimolecular heterogeneous reaction. To pursue the tenet advanced in Section 2.2 to the effect that an enzyme molecule presents a true surface with a localized active site, this analogous behaviour is to be expected. Step (1) in the Michaelis–Menten mechanism is then to be recognized as the equivalent of adsorption, step (2) corresponds to desorption and step (3) will be the equivalent of chemical reaction on the solid surface when desorption of the product is easy. The requirement of the Langmuir–Hinshelwood mechanism that adsorption/desorption equilibrium is maintained for the reactant throughout the course of the reaction would carry forward to imply a condition in the Michaelis–Menten scheme that $k_2 \gg k_3$ i.e. that $K_m = k_2/k_1$. This condition can usually be regarded as achieved for practical purposes, when the mechanism could be written more logically as

$$E + S \rightleftharpoons ES$$
$$ES \rightarrow E + P$$

It may be remarked further that a system containing a particular enzyme offers a set of exactly equivalent sites for 'adsorption', since each enzyme molecule has an active site of the same configuration and structure. In the case of a solid surface, the Langmuir adsorption isotherm approach assumes that each individual adsorption site is equivalent. But on the usual solid catalyst, the adsorption sites will vary significantly in their characteristics and detailed configurations from one to another. Then the Langmuir adsorption isotherm approach averages across the range of properties of the set of adsorption sites: as a consequence it yields semiquantitative interpretations only, but these are of sufficient value under most circumstances unless a very detailed quantitative description of a heterogeneous catalytic system is sought. The point made here is to the effect that the enzyme–substrate system could actually be considered to represent one of the most quantitatively appropriate situations for proper application of the Langmuir adsorption isotherm.

Following the pattern shown in Fig. 2.2, a plot of the rate of an enzyme catalysed reaction *versus* concentration of substrate can be divided into sections. The lettering scheme used in Fig. 2.2 may be carried forward to labelling distinct regimes of kinetic behaviour, as summarized in Table 2.8 (c.f. Table 2.6). A typical instance of the variation of rate with [S] appears in Fig. 2.15.

In practice the middle section (PQ) represents the conditions under which enzyme catalysed reactions are usually conducted. The means of analysing kinetic data from these experiments is apparent if both sides of equation (2.21) are inverted to yield

$$1/R = 1/V_{max} + (K_m/V_{max})(1/[S]) \qquad (2.22)$$

The predicted linear plot of corresponding values of reciprocal rate *versus* reciprocal substrate concentration is often referred to as a Lineweaver–Burk plot. The intercept on the vertical axis corresponds to $1/V_{max}$ and the ratio of the gradient to the intercept is K_m. Enzyme systems are very

Table 2.8 Kinetic behaviour regimes corresponding to the Michaelis–Menten mechanism

Condition	Rate equation	Apparent order in S	Analogous section in Figure 2.2
$[S] \ll K_m$	$R = \dfrac{V_{max}[S]}{K_m}$	1	Below P
None	$R = \dfrac{V_{max}[S]}{([S] + K_m)} \approx k[S]^x$	$0 < x < 1$	PQ
$[S] \gg K_m$	$R = V_{max}$	0	Above Q

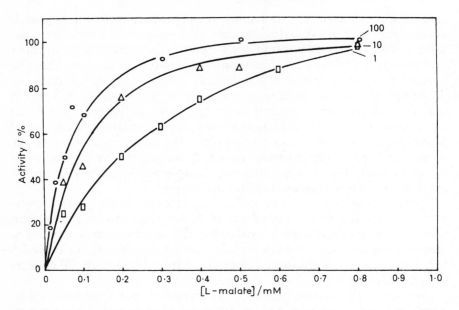

Fig. 2.15 Plots of activities (expressed as a percentage of the limiting rate of reaction) *versus* substrate (L-malate) concentration in systems containing the enzyme malate decarboxyoxidase at a temperature of 295 K. The data points and the corresponding curves represent results for systems with the enzyme present in homogeneous solution (○), immobilized in glutaraldehyde–bovine serum albumin film (△) and immobilized in polyurethane foam (☐). The numbers inserted in the top right-hand corner of the diagram express the relative values of the limiting rates when the same total amount of the enzyme is present. The horizontal scale is expressed in units of mM = 10^{-3} mol dm^{-3}. Reproduced from *Malic enzyme immobilization in continuous capillary membrane reactors*, G. Iorio, G. Catapano, E. Drioli, M. Rossi and R. Rella (1985) *Journal of Membrane Science*, **22**, 320, with permission of Elsevier Science Publishers B.V.

sensitive to the pH of the aqueous phase (see Section 7.2), so that the kinetic data used to construct a Lineweaver–Burk plot must be obtained at constant pH, in addition to constant $[E]_0$. Lineweaver–Burk plots have been used to obtain values of the parameters V_{max} and K_m for many enzyme catalysed reactions. Table 2.9 lists some illustrative values of the Michaelis constants and turnover numbers, the latter defined as $V_{max}/[E]_0$ and thus equivalent to the rate constant k_3 in the Michaelis–Menten mechanism. The turnover number of an enzyme has the same meaning as the turnover frequency defined for a solid catalyst in Section 1.2: both specify the number of reactant (substrate) molecules converted by an active

Table 2.9 Michaelis–Menten parameter values for some free enzyme–substrate systems at ambient temperature and approximately neutral pH

Enzyme	Substrate	$K_m/\text{mol dm}^{-3}$	$(V_{max}/[E]_0)/\text{s}^{-1}$
Alcohol dehydrogenase	Ethanol	5.5×10^{-4}	3.1
α-Chymotrypsin	N-ATME*	9.5×10^{-5}	28
Dextranase	Dextran	3.0×10^{-3}	39
Glucose isomerase	Glucose	0.16	480
Carbonate dehydratase	Bicarbonate	0.069	3.7×10^5
Catalase	Hydrogen peroxide	1.1	3.8×10^7

* N-acetyl-L-tryptophan methyl ester.

site in unit time. It is necessary to be cautious in detailed interpretation of apparent values of K_m and V_{max}. The actual mechanisms of enzyme catalysed reactions are often more complex than three elementary steps. A typical additional feature is the interposition of at least one configurational isomerization equilibrium between the initially formed complex, ES, and the appearance of products. Nevertheless most systems show variations of R with [S] which yield apparently linear Lineweaver–Burk plots. Accordingly, if full details of the mechanism are not known in any particular case, observed values of V_{max} and K_m cannot be related to the rate constant combinations indicated in equation (2.21). It is worth mentioning that a variety of advanced techniques are available for use in establishing full mechanisms and corresponding values of rate constants for elementary steps involved, but the description of these is beyond the scope of this book.

Attention may now be turned to systems in which the enzyme is not free (i.e. dissolved in an aqueous phase) but is attached to (immobilized on) an insoluble solid surface. This is the mode in which enzymes achieve practical significance as catalysts. Figure 2.15 shows data which illustrate the effect on kinetics of the immobilization of an enzyme. In general the effect of immobilization of an enzyme on the value of V_{max} is unpredictable. Significant changes in the apparent value of the Michaelis constant, K_m, are evident in Fig. 2.15, with a marked increase from a value of 6×10^{-5} mol dm^{-3} (0.06 mM) for the free enzyme system to 2×10^{-4} mol dm^{-3} (0.2 mM) for the enzyme immobilized in polyurethane foam. Frequently such an apparent change in K_m is more likely to reflect the relative inaccessibility of the enzyme molecules in the immobilized forms with respect to the substrate molecules than any alteration in the basic catalytic ability of the enzyme consequent upon its immobilization.

Consider a situation in which initially there is a homogeneous solution of the substrate extending from the bulk liquid phase to a solid surface upon which all of the enzyme molecules are immobilized. Then consider that the enzyme catalysed reaction which ensues consumes substrate molecules in the vicinity of the surface at a faster rate initially than that at which they can be replenished from the bulk solution by the process of mass transport (diffusion). The inevitable consequence is that after some time a concentration gradient of substrate will have developed close to the surface, as represented in Fig. 2.16. In a kinetic experiment, only the bulk concentration ($[S]_B$) can be measured and the rate equation is constructed in terms of this parameter. Let K_m and V_{max} be the Michaelis–Menten parameters for the free enzyme system and $K_m(app)$ and $V_{max}(app)$ be those measured for the immobilized enzyme system containing the same total amount of enzyme. The rate equation for the immobilized enzyme system should really be expressed in terms of the substrate concentration actually in contact with the surface ($[S]_E$ in Fig. 2.16) but practically it can only be expressed in terms of $[S]_B$

$$R = \frac{V_{max}(app)\,[S]_B}{[S]_B + K_m(app)} = \frac{V_{max}(app)}{1 + (K_m(app)/[S]_B)} \qquad (2.23)$$

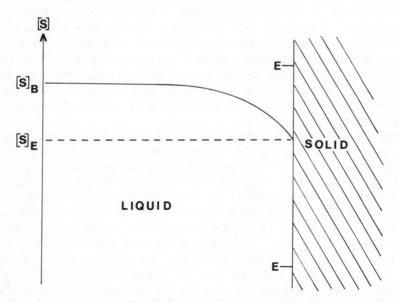

Fig. 2.16 Representation of a substrate (S) concentration gradient developed in the vicinity of a solid surface upon which enzyme (E) molecules are immobilized. The substrate concentration in the bulk solution is indicated as $[S]_B$, whilst the local concentration in contact with the enzyme molecules is indicated as $[S]_E$.

Suppose that the process of immobilization does not alter the true value of K_m, which would then appear as such if the denominator on the right-hand side of equation (2.23) were written as $1 + K_m/[S]_E$. It is then obvious that for the two denominators to produce equal effects when $[S]_E < [S]_B$, K_m must be less than $K_m(app)$. This accords with directions of variation of the apparent values of the Michaelis constants corresponding to Fig. 2.15. Thus increased apparent values of K_m accompanying the immobilization of an enzyme may arise simply from diffusional limitations: these would be expected to be most severe when an enzyme is immobilized within a porous or gel structure, through which the substrate molecules must diffuse.

The discussion above presumes that the chemical conversion process is rate determining. It simply regards the concentration gradient as inducing accelerated movement of substrate molecules towards the enzyme molecules localized at the surface.

2.5 Concluding remarks

This chapter might be said to have described many 'old fashioned' aspects of catalysis at surfaces. In covering the classifications, thermodynamic bases and simpler aspects of the reaction kinetics of catalytic actions, the content is restricted to phenomena which may be investigated experimentally using conventional methods and apparatus. In Chapter 4, the major topics will concern modern sophisticated methods which can yield direct information on the identity and roles of chemisorbed species involved in heterogeneous catalytic processes. As might be anticipated, the arrival of these techniques has resulted in an enormous extension of our knowledge of the mechanisms of reactions at solid surfaces. The main discussion of enzyme catalysis appears in Chapter 7.

3

The constitution of catalytic surfaces

At this stage of the development of the theme, it is appropriate to consider the physical structures of materials of significance in heterogeneous catalysis and the methods by which various types of catalytic surface may be produced.

3.1 Basic physical forms of catalytic surfaces

Three broad forms of catalytic surface can be distinguished on the basis of general physical structure. The most obvious is that offered by a non-porous bulk solid, as exemplified by the surfaces of a sheet of metal. On the other hand, a porous solid will have internal surfaces at the pore walls, in addition to external surfaces. A common example is charcoal, renowned for its high adsorptive capacity. The third general type of surface is presented by an active material dispersed over the surface of another solid (the support). The resultant covering may be discontinuous at the microscopic level, as is the case when platinum crystallites are supported on alumina. The above three types of surfaces are represented diagrammatically in Fig. 3.1. In other instances of supported material the coverage may be continuous, as can be the case for vanadia (V_2O_5) deposited on titania (TiO_2).

In the overwhelming majority of heterogeneous catalytic reactions, the chemical reaction is limited to the interface between solid and fluid phases, and the material of the bulk solid not in direct contact with the fluid phase is uninvolved. It is evident that this implies inefficient usage of the material, when only a small proportion of its constituent atoms is exposed at the

(a) (b) (c)

Fig. 3.1 Cross-sectional representations of (a) a non-porous, bulk-solid catalyst particle, (b) a porous, bulk-solid catalyst particle and (c) a supported catalyst with discontinuous coverage on the external surface of the particle of the support material. Black corresponds to the material possessing catalytic activity whilst barred white indicates support material.

surface. This situation provides a point of contrast with a dissolved homogeneous catalyst, every molecule of which is available for action. There is an improvement from left to right in Fig. 3.1 in terms of the ability of an amount of active material to offer exposed surface area. Equally there will be an enhancement of the exposed surface area per unit mass (i.e. the specific surface area) of a solid material when it is reduced to smaller particle sizes. Consider a non-porous solid of density ϱ which for simplicity

Table 3.1 Representative specific surface areas (A) for various solids

Type of material	Description	$A/\mathrm{m^2\,g^{-1}}$
Metals	0.1 mm thick platinum sheet	5×10^{-4}
	Platinum black	20
	Raney nickel	100
	Platinum finely dispersed on alumina	120
Non-porous solid	Cobalt oxide (Co_3O_4) with $\varrho = 6.07 \times 10^6\,\mathrm{g\,m^{-3}}$ and average $d = 33.5$ nm	30
Porous solids	Activated charcoals	$\leqslant 1120$
	X-type zeolite	900
	Y-type zeolite	900
	A-type zeolite	800
	Sepiolite (a clay mineral)	350
	Aluminium phosphate	250
	Silica–alumina	250
	Silica gel	200
	γ-alumina	180
	Kieselguhr (diatomaceous earth)	170

is in the form of uniform spheres of diameter d. The specific surface area is then expressed by $6/\varrho d$ and for a material with $\varrho = 2 \times 10^6$ g m^{-3} (roughly that of silica (SiO_2)), specific surface areas are 0.003 m^2 g^{-1} for $d = 1$ mm and 1.5 m^2 g^{-1} for $d = 2$ μm. The latter may be regarded as the realistic lower size limit for a solid which has been sieved to a fairly uniform particle size.

It is interesting to examine the list of some typical specific surface areas for various materials shown in Table 3.1. Total specific surface areas of solids are usually measured by application of the BET adsorption isotherm as described in Section 2.3.1.

3.1.1 *High surface area forms of metals*

Platinum blacks are finely divided powdered forms of the metal. These are prepared by chemical means which generally involve the reduction of an aqueous solution of chloroplatinic acid (H_2PtCl_6). Raney metals are effectively 'skeleton' forms resulting from the use of caustic solutions to leach out aluminium from the corresponding binary alloy. The procedure leaves microcrystallites of (say) nickel joined randomly to create spongy particles incorporating a large void volume within the intensive pore system so formed. It is clear from the data in Table 3.1 that porous solids can offer large specific surface areas, largely reflecting the availability of surfaces within the actual volume of the particles.

The entry in Table 3.1 for the supported metal emphasizes the large specific surface area created when a metal is highly dispersed, often in the form of particles characterized by dimensions of a few nm on a support surface. It is useful at this juncture to consider how the surface area presented by the metal may be measured and how the degree of dispersion may be described quantitatively. It is necessary to appreciate firstly that the physisorption involved in connection with the use of the BET isotherm cannot differentiate between different surface components. In order to isolate the area of surface presented by a dispersed metal, it is necessary to use a gas which chemisorbs only on the metal surface at a temperature which is high enough to make physisorption insignificant in comparison. For many of the metals in Group VIII of the periodic table (see labelling of Fig. 2.12) supported on materials like silica, alumina or titania, the use of hydrogen at ambient temperature satisfies the requirements. A monolayer of atomic hydrogen on the exposed metal surfaces is usually achieved at very small equilibrium pressures: consequently the amount of hydrogen required to cover the metal sites completely is measured directly using moderate pressures (1–25 kPa) of the gas. Each hydrogen molecule taken down from the gas phase is assumed to count two adsorption sites. Fig. 3.2

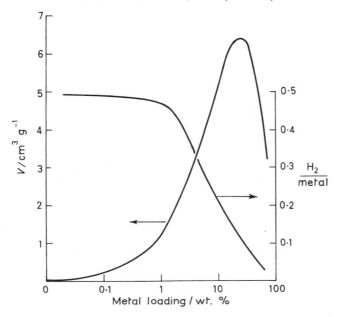

Fig. 3.2 Plots generated by data obtained for the chemisorption of hydrogen on a series of rhodium metal catalysts supported on silica at ambient temperature. The horizontal axis indicates the percentage of the solid material which is rhodium (dispersed on the surface). The left-hand vertical axis is the volume (V) of hydrogen adsorbed at NTP by unit mass of solid. The right-hand vertical axis (H_2/metal) is the number of hydrogen molecules adsorbed per rhodium atom present (surface and bulk), evaluated from the corresponding value of V. Based upon data given by J. H. Sinfelt (1979) *Reviews of Modern Physics*, **51**, 572.

shows some typical results. It is evident that at low metal loadings (below 1%) the value of the ratio on the right hand vertical axis approaches 0.5, which corresponds to one hydrogen atom per rhodium atom and indicates that almost all of the rhodium atoms are exposed at the surface.

The dispersion of a metal on an inert support is defined as

$$\text{dispersion}/\% = \frac{\text{Number of metal atoms exposed at surface}}{\text{Total number of metal atoms}} \times 100$$

As the metal particles become smaller (which usually accompanies lower loadings) the specific surface area which they present becomes larger, as does the dispersion. The data in Fig. 3.2 then indicate that the dispersion of the rhodium on the silica approaches 100% towards the left hand side of the diagram. In the same direction, the total amount of hydrogen chemisorbed (as expressed by the parameter V) tends towards zero, reflecting the decreasing number of rhodium atoms and hence chemisorption in total.

3.1.2 *Microporous solids*

Table 3.1 reveals that porous materials can offer extremely large specific surface areas. Pores are classified on the basis of their diameters, d: the smallest are *micropores* ($d < 2$ nm), intermediate are *mesopores* (2 nm $\leqslant d$ $\leqslant 50$ nm) and larger are *macropores* ($d > 50$ nm). Some materials, such as zeolites and many clay minerals, are entirely microporous. Others like charcoal and silica-alumina have irregular pores with widely variable diameters in a normal sample.

At later stages in the book it will be emphasized that the intracrystalline space in zeolites, which is commonly regarded as a system of micropores, offers most useful catalytic selectivity. At this point it is necessary to discuss the structures of zeolites and hence the origins of the microporosity.

Zeolites are aluminosilicate solids with structures based upon a three dimensional polymeric framework. The basic building block is a tetrahedron centred on either a silicon or an aluminium atom (often referred to as the T atom), with bonds to four oxygen atoms located at the corners. In turn each oxygen atom is bonded to two T atoms, i.e. shared between them. The manners in which numbers of these tetrahedral units, joined together through T—O—T linkages, form common zeolite crystalline structures are shown in Fig. 3.3. Key features here are the linking of four tetrahedra to form a square (with respect to the T atoms at the corners) and of six tetrahedra to form a hexagon. A basic substructural unit, the sodalite cage, is created by the combinations of squares and hexagons as shown: it has projecting oxygen atoms, available to form bonds to other sodalite cages, at the intersections. In the descending directions, the diagram indicates how three of the common types of zeolites (A, X and Y, the last two having the same basic structure) are generated by linkages of sodalite cages. The numbering in the diagram refers to the T atoms in the resultant *pore apertures*, eight in the A-type zeolite and twelve in X- and Y-type zeolites. These pore apertures are uniform throughout the entire structure of a particular zeolite. As a result, regular channels run through the pore apertures, linking between the larger void volumes known as *supercages*. In the A-type zeolite, the free (i.e. unobstructed) pore aperture has a diameter of 0.42 nm whilst the supercage has a diameter of 1.1 nm. In X- and Y-type zeolites, the free pore apertures have diameters of 0.74 nm whilst the supercage diameter is 1.3 nm. Figures 3.4(a) and (b) show space-filling models of these pore apertures: in the latter figure a similar model of the benzene molecule appears, aligned in the same plane

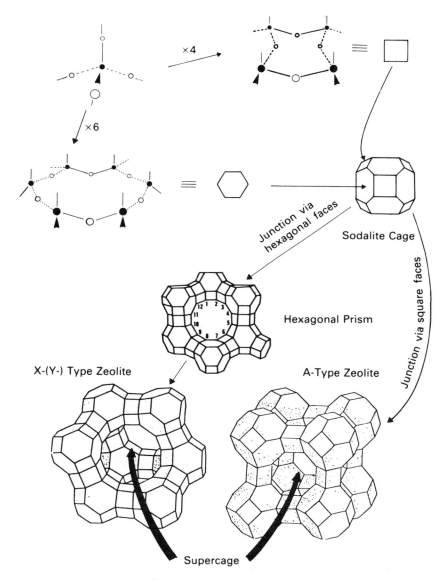

Fig. 3.3 Basic structural units and the modes of their combination in the common zeolites. T atoms (Si or Al) are denoted as ● in the simple structures and lie at the intersections of lines in the complex structures. Oxygen atoms are shown in the simple structures when they are represented as ○: in the complex structures an oxygen atom lies at the midpoint of each line. Reproduced from *Biomass, Catalysts and Liquid Fuels*, I. M. Campbell (1983) Holt. Rinehart and Winston Ltd, Eastbourne, p. 116, with permission.

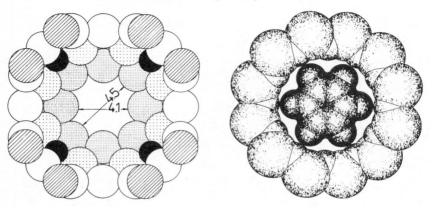

Fig. 3.4 Left: space-filling model representation of the pore aperture in an A-type zeolite. The black circles correspond to Na$^+$ cations (see Section 5.3) and all other circles represent oxygen atoms (the T atoms are 'buried'). The numbers are distances on a scale where 10 corresponds to 1 nm. Reproduced from J. Sauer and R. Zahradnik (1984) *International Journal of Quantum Chemistry*, **XXVI**, 799. Copyright ©1984 John Wiley and Sons Inc. Reprinted by permission of John Wiley & Sons Inc., New York.
Right: space-filling model representation of the pore aperture of an X- (or Y-) type zeolite. Within the aperture is a similar representation of a benzene molecule with the plane of the carbon atoms coinciding with the plane of the aperture. Reproduced with permission of the Royal Society of Chemistry from *The localization of benzene in a Y-zeolite*, A. N. Fitch, H. Jobic and A. Renouprez (1985) *Journal of the Chemical Society, Chemical Communications*, 285.

as the pore aperture. Both parts of Fig. 3.4 show that the wall of the pore aperture is actually formed by the oxygen atoms, with the smaller T atoms apparently hidden.

As a direct consequence of the extension of the channel system throughout zeolite crystals, up to half of the total volume defined by the external surfaces is in fact void and available for penetration by gas phase molecules. Comparison of the data in Table 3.1 for the non-porous cobalt oxide and the zeolites indicates that the internal surface areas of the latter will exceed the external surface area greatly, even for very small zeolite crystals. However, it is important to realize that this internal surface area will only be accessible to fluid phase molecules which are small enough to pass through the geometrical restrictions of the pore apertures. Here then there is what is termed *molecular sieve* action, when there is selective adsorption on the internal surfaces governed by the size and shape of the molecule concerned. For example, it is evident from comparison of Figs. 3.4(a) and (b) that benzene will be unable to penetrate through the pore aperture of an A-type zeolite and is thus excluded from adsorption on the internal surfaces. In fact, the largest molecules which are able to pass through the unobstructed A-type aperture are linear alkanes, whilst branched chain alkanes are excluded. Even at this early stage, it should be apparent that molecular sieve or size selective action by zeolites should be a very significant aspect of heterogeneous catalysis. Obviously it is the crystalline nature of zeolites which is vital in this respect. Amorphous porous materials, such as silica–alumina, will not usually have regular pore structures. Thus whilst silica–aluminas do offer high specific surface areas, they will not show size selective action.

3.1.3 *Supported liquid phase catalysts*

A porous solid on contact with a liquid phase will tend to absorb it through capillary action. Capillary pressures (directed inwards from the liquid phase) can correspond to several hundred times atmospheric pressure for very small pores. When the liquid phase concerned is essentially involatile under operating conditions, a supported liquid phase is created, with the liquid occupying part of the pore space and the solid serving effectively as its container. When this liquid phase is active catalytically, gaseous reactants can dissolve into the supported liquid phase and therein undergo microscopically-homogeneous catalytic conversion. The resulting products, if volatile under the conditions concerned, are eventually released to the gas phase. What has been created under these circumstances is a hybrid system which can retain the advantages of homogeneous catalysis (high selectivity and mild operating conditions) but simultaneously gains the advantages of solid catalysts (convenient handling and retention in the reactor, large interfacial areas for gas exchange processes). Table 3.2 lists some examples of supported liquid-phase catalysts and their applications.

3.1.4 *Immobilized and anchored catalysts*

Molecular catalysts, which might otherwise dissolve in a contacting liquid phase, can be bound to an insoluble solid, thus achieving what is termed *immobilization* or *anchoring*. The catalytic entities of main importance in this connection are enzymes, when the former term is used, and complex metal species, when the latter term is used conventionally. In either case the entity must be attached firmly enough to the macroscopic surface of the supporting material for it to be rather resistant to leaching under the conditions of its subsequent usage as a catalyst. The general process of

Table 3.2 Examples of catalytic systems based upon supported liquid phases

Reaction	Catalyst(s)	Liquid phase	Typical support
Oxidation of sulphur dioxide (production of sulphuric acid)	Vanadium ions	K_2SO_4/V_2O_5 melt	Kieselguhr
Polymerization of alkenes	H^+	Phosphoric acid	Kieselguhr
Ethylene hydrogenation	$RhCl(CO)(PPh_3)_2$*	Dioctylphthalate	α-alumina
Oxychlorination of alkenes	Copper ions	Melt of $CuCl_2/CuCl/KCl/$ rare earth halide	Silica gel
Selective oxidation of ethylene to acetaldehyde	Palladium/copper ions	Aqueous solution of $PdCl_2$ and $CuCl_2$	Kieselguhr

* $Ph = C_6H_5$.

attachment, particularly with regard to inorganic species, is sometimes described as the 'heterogenization of homogeneous catalysts'. Successful immobilization or anchoring results in a catalyst material which has the physical characteristics of a solid (making for easy retention in a reactor and separation of products) but which preserves the specificity in its catalytic action of the corresponding homogeneous catalyst. Additionally the activity which can be induced in a liquid, the bulk phase within which such catalysts are usually used, is not governed by the solubility of the catalytic entity in this medium (as is the case in homogeneous catalysis). The surface giving rise to the catalytic activity is then an inert underlay dotted with single catalyst molecules attached to it.

Examples of some usages of immobilized enzymes will be given in Section 3.2.4 in conjunction with discussion of the various modes of attachment. The principles of heterogenization can be illustrated now for some anchored inorganic catalysts. The major objective is to attach the entity to a solid surface in a manner which retains the detailed structure of the homogeneous catalyst as far as possible. One commonly used mode for anchoring a metal complex to a surface replaces the bond to one of its ligands with a chemical bond to the solid surface. This procedure usually demands that the support material has been *functionalized*, which means that potentially reactive groups have been created on its surface in a preliminary stage. An example is the anchoring of the homogeneous catalyst often referred to as the Wilkinson complex to a polystyrene (PS) support which has been functionalized with diphenylphosphino ($P(Ph)_2$) groups. The anchoring process is then represented:

$$\boxed{PS}-P(Ph)_2 + RhCl(P(Ph)_3)_3 \longrightarrow \boxed{PS}-P(Ph)_2RhCl(P(Ph)_3)_2 + P(Ph)_3$$

| (Functionalized support) | (Wilkinson complex) | (Anchored catalyst) | (Displaced ligand) |

In this process, the rhodium atom has one of its triphenylphosphino ligands replaced by one of the $P(Ph)_2$ groups bonded to the bulk polystyrene; this establishes a phosphino linkage between the polymer and the metal atom. The anchored complex preserves the ability of the Wilkinson complex to hydrogenate alkenes. In fact, the respective kinetic behaviours in the hydrogenations of linear alkenes or cyclohexene conducted in benzene solutions in the presence of either the free Wilkinson catalyst or its anchored form are very similar. This reflects the fact that the critical processes in each case can be described by the same mechanism.

Inorganic supports such as silica can be functionalized using the surface hydroxyl groups. An example of a tin-centred entity anchored to silica by a condensation process to form the Si—O—Si linkage is represented by the structure below:

$$\boxed{\text{SILICA}} - O - \underset{\underset{OCH_3}{|}}{\overset{\overset{OCH_3}{|}}{Si}} - \wedge\wedge - \underset{\underset{OCH_3}{|}}{\overset{\overset{C_4H_9}{|}}{Sn}} - OCH_3$$

This anchored species acts as a highly selective catalyst for the reduction of aromatic carbonyl compounds to alcohols. In the case of acetophenone, 1-phenylethanol is the only significant product.

Under some circumstances anchoring can be vital for the production of an active catalyst. Certain transition metal complexes in solution tend to form dimeric bridged species, thereby eliminating the vacant sites for coordinative bonding presented by the monomeric species. But when the initial complexes are anchored separately they are held apart and thus preserve the coordination vacancy which is essential for their catalytic action. For example, the free species $(C_5H_5)_2TiCl_2$ generates an active hydrogenation catalyst when it is treated with butyllithium. But in solution this resultant species dimerizes so rapidly that it cannot serve as an effective catalyst. However if the $(C_5H_5)_2TiCl_2$ species is anchored first to a polystyrene surface, subsequent treatment with butyllithium creates highly active hydrogenation sites which cannot engage in mutual destruction. The anchored form then provides a very effective hydrogenation catalyst.

Attractions between positive and negative electrical charges can be used to achieve anchoring in suitable cases, although the process can result in significant changes of the selectivity in catalytic action. The anion exchange resin, IRA 401, provides an effective support material for anchoring anionic complexes, such as $Pt_{15}(CO)_{30}^{2-}$. As a homogeneous catalyst, this complex is active in the hydrogenation of benzaldehyde to the products benzyl alcohol, benzene and methanol. Although the anchored complex is active in the same process, the selectivity is altered so that benzyl alcohol is the only significant product. In another instance, the cluster anion $Rh_5Pt(CO)_{15}^-$ in its free form is active for the hydrogenation of the aromatic rings of phenol, anisole, toluene, aniline or nitrobenzene. The activity of the form anchored on IRA 401 is however restricted to only the first three of these reactants under the same conditions. Again this illustrates that the anchored form is in some subtle respects different from the free cluster ion.

It is becoming clear that there is going to be enormous research effort in the field of anchored inorganic catalysts in the coming years. These catalysts offer the potential for achieving high activity under relatively mild conditions, with sometimes interesting and unusual selectivities. The processes for generating such catalysts, for investigating their detailed structures and for elucidating the mechanisms involved in their

Table 3.3 Examples of anchored inorganic catalysts and the reactions which are catalysed

Support	Linkage	Catalytic centre	Catalysed reaction
Phosphido–polystyrene	Phosphido	Pt(cyclo-octa-1,5-diene)Cl	Hydrogenation of benzene or toluene at 318 K
Aminated-polystyrene	Ethylenediamino	$Rh_6(CO)_{16}$	Water–gas shift $(CO + H_2O \rightarrow CO_2 + H_2)$
Polyacrylic acid	$-C \overset{O^{---}}{\underset{O^{---}}{\big\langle}}$	$Rh(P(Ph)_3)_x \quad (x < 3)$	Hydrogenation of alkenes
Silica	$\equiv Si-O-Ti \equiv$	Ti–Al bridged structure with Cl and C_2H_5 groups	Polymerization of alkenes (Ziegler-type process)
Poly-4-vinylpyridine	$=N \rightarrow Pd$	$N \rightarrow Pd$ chloride-bridged dimer structure	Hydrogenation of allyl alcohol
Silica	$\equiv Si-(CH_2)_5-S \big\langle$	$Rh(CO)(PC(CH_3)_3)$ centres linked through S and Cl	Hydroformylation of cyclohexene $(C_6H_{10} + CO + H_2 \rightarrow C_6H_{11}CHO)$
Alumina	Ionic	$H_3RuOs_3(CO)_{12}^-$	Isomerization of 1-butene
Sulphonated linear polystyrene	Ionic	Ru^{3+}	Fischer–Tropsch synthesis (see Section 8.4)
Anion-exchange resin (Amberlyst A-26)	Ionic	Co(II) *meso*-tetra-(4-sulphinatophenyl)porphine	Oxidation of thiols, selective isomerization of hydrocarbons

catalytic actions are at early stages of development as yet. To round off this limited account of anchored catalysts, some further examples are given in Table 3.3.

3.1.5 *Grafted catalysts*

An anchored catalyst is created by the binding of a species, without substantial change in its structure, to a solid surface. A grafted catalyst is produced when an initial structure bound to a surface is altered considerably by subsequent treatments. Here the initially bound species is not usually an active catalyst.

One example of the production of a grafted catalyst commences with the heating of a silica support to a temperature of 473 K in the presence of molybdenum pentachloride ($MoCl_5$) vapour. This induces a reaction with surface hydroxyl groups represented by the first step below:

$$
\underset{\boxed{\text{SILICA}}}{\overset{\text{OH}}{|}} + MoCl_5(g) \xrightarrow[(-HCl)]{473\ K} \underset{\boxed{\text{SILICA}}}{\overset{\text{OMoCl}_4}{|}} \xrightarrow[O_2]{773\ K} \underset{\boxed{\text{SILICA}}}{\overset{\displaystyle \overset{O}{\underset{\displaystyle Mo}{\|}}}{O\ \ O\ \ O}}
$$

With subsequent heating to 773 K in oxygen, the remaining chlorine atoms are driven off, establishing further bonds to the surface and producing a terminal Mo$=$O bond. This latter feature will be seen to be crucial in catalysts based upon molybdenum oxide which are active for selective oxidation (Sections 5.2 and 6.2). The final grafted catalyst above, in contact with methanol vapour and air at temperatures of around 500 K, induces the production of methyl formate with 90–95% selectivity.

A wide variety of highly active and selective catalysts can be prepared by grafting techniques commencing with the attachment of suitable organometallic species to a solid surface. The procedure may be extended ultimately to the production of highly dispersed, supported metal catalysts. However, with suitable treatments, the initially grafted species may give rise to a series of catalytically active materials. One example involves the generation of rhodium-centred structures attached to a titania (TiO_2) surface. The initially used species was a rhodium-η^3-allyl complex and grafting to the surface took place within 20 minutes on contact at 273 K. The various stages of treatment and the resulting structures are represented below:

$$Rh(C_3H_5)_3 + \boxed{\overset{\overset{OH}{|}}{TITANIA}\,\overset{\overset{OH}{|}}{}} \xrightarrow{273\,K} \boxed{\overset{\overset{\overset{C_3H_5}{|}}{\overset{Rh}{\diagup\,\diagdown}}}{\overset{O\quad\quad O}{|\qquad\quad|}}{TITANIA}} \xrightarrow[\,H_2\,]{293\,K}$$

(1)

$$\boxed{\overset{\overset{\overset{H}{|}}{\overset{Rh}{\diagup\,\diagdown}}}{\overset{O\quad\quad O}{|\qquad\quad|}}{TITANIA}} \xrightarrow[\,H_2\,]{473-773\,K} \overset{(Rh)_n}{\boxed{TITANIA}}$$

(2)   (3)

Both (2) and (3) above showed high activities for the hydrogenation of ethylene and for the hydrogenolysis of ethane (yielding methane), the latter process taking place readily at a temperature of 373 K (c.f. Section 6.1.2). The form (3) corresponds to small aggregates of 25 or more (n) rhodium atoms with mean particle diameters of around 1.4 nm. These are probably in the form of thin rafts to accord with the measured dispersion of close to 100%.

Figure 3.5 represents a series of grafted catalytic centres incorporating molybdenum and oxygen and supported on silica. Structure (1) results from contact between $Mo_2(\eta^3 - C_3H_5)_4$ with silica at 273 K over a period of 10 minutes, when the silica has been pretreated by heating to 773 K. Structure (4) has been shown to be active in the hydrogenation of ethylene at temperatures as low as 200 K. On the other hand, structure (5) catalyses selective oxidation of organic vapours in air: for example, at a temperature of 673 K it induces selectivities of 85% to acrolein ($CH_2{=}CH{-}CHO$) and 15% to acetaldehyde in propylene oxidation.

3.1.6 *Mixed-oxide surfaces*

There are many catalysts for which the activity depends upon the intimate (or chemical) mixing of solid oxides at the molecular level. As a consequence the activity is localized at particular microscopic sites at the surface by virtue of the detailed configuration of atoms there and the requirements of the catalysed reaction. There are two main types of catalyst incorporated under this subheading. The first arises from mixtures of

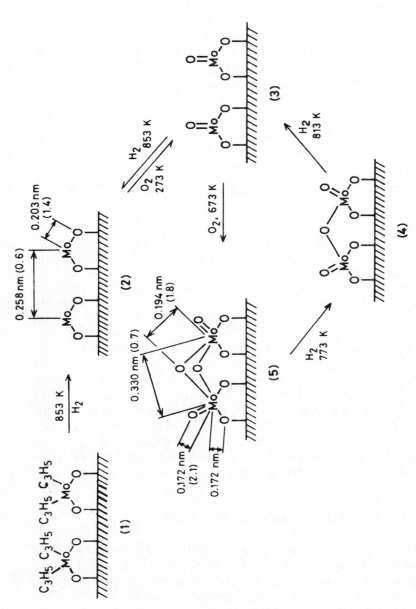

Fig. 3.5 Surface structures of molybdenum–oxygen species which may be prepared commencing with structure (1) on a silica support. Conversion conditions are indicated. Some bond lengths are given and associated numbers in parentheses are the co-ordination numbers of the molybdenum or oxygen atoms concerned. Reproduced with permission of the Royal Society of Chemistry from *New SiO$_2$-bound Mo dimers: active catalysts for selective oxidation of propene to acrylaldehyde*, Y. Iwasawa, N. Ito, H. Ishii and H. Kuroda (1985) *Journal of the Chemical Society, Chemical Communications*, 828.

oxides of transition metals (such as molybdenum or iron) and metalloids (such as bismuth or antimony) and act to induce redox reactions. These are dealt with in Sections 5.2 and 6.2. The second type of mixed oxide catalyst is one which has a strongly acidic nature. For example, silica and alumina mixed at the molecular level give rise to amorphous silica–alumina or crystalline aluminosilicates. Acidic catalysts induce conversions of hydrocarbons, such as isomerization of alkenes, which will be discussed in Sections 5.3 and 6.3. The activity at both of these types of surface will have an inherent patchiness: some microscopic sites will be highly active, others will be more weakly active and there may be parts of the surface which are inactive.

3.2 The creation of catalytic surfaces

The general principles underlying methods for preparing catalytically active solids and surfaces will be developed in this section. It should be evident now that many of the more important catalysts incorporate two or more distinct chemical substances. In some cases one material is deposited on to the pre-existing surface of another: in other instances two or more substances must be formed into a solid phase together. The account given here is concentrated upon the preparations of catalytic surfaces which demand more than straightforward production of a simple bulk material.

It will be useful at the outset to list the main categories of materials dealt with in the following subsections.

1. Solids created by mixing oxides at the molecular level.
2. Microporous crystalline solids.
3. Forms of metallic elements dispersed on support materials.
4. Immobilized enzymes and living cells.

The principles of preparing anchored and grafted catalysts have been developed in conjunction with the discussions of their natures in the preceding section.

3.2.1 *Mixed oxide catalysts*

Two general routes for producing an intimate mixture of oxides at the molecular level are based upon coprecipitation of forms of the corresponding elements from aqueous (or sometimes other) solutions or the melting (fusing) together of compounds at high temperatures.

Table 3.4 indicates the typical elements of interest for oxides used as catalysts and some suitable initial compounds for starting the

Table 3.4 Typical starting compounds for coprecipitative formation of mixed oxides

Oxide element	Ti	V	Cr	Mn	Fe	Co
Compound	$TiCl_4$	NH_4VO_3	$Cr(NO_3)_2$	$MnCl_2$	$Fe(NO_3)_3$	$Co(NO_3)$

Oxide element	Cu	Zn	Zr	Mo	Bi
Compound	$Cu(NO_3)_2$	$ZnCl_2$	$Zr(NO_3)_2$	$(NH_4)_2MoO_4$	$Bi(NO_3)_3$

Oxide element	Sn	Sb	U	Al	Si
Compound	$SnCl_2$	$SbCl_5$	$UO_2(NO_3)_2$	$Al(O\text{-}i\text{-}C_3H_7)_3$	$Si(OC_2H_5)$

Fig. 3.6 Representation of the general procedure used for the preparation of chemically mixed oxide catalysts.

coprecipitation procedures. Fig. 3.6 is a schematic representation of a typical general procedure suitable for most of the combinations of the elements concerned. The initially precipitating solid is often a complex mixture of hydroxylic compounds. These are subsequently decomposed to the oxides by heating in air, a process referred to as *calcination*. Obviously the composition of the final solid can be varied by changing the proportions of the components in the starting solution.

The fusion procedure commences with mechanical mixing of particles of suitable compounds of the elements concerned. With heating, the materials eventually form a melt within which intimate mixing occurs. On cooling, granulation and calcination, the mixed oxide results. Table 3.5 summarizes

Table 3.5 Typical routes based upon fusion to mixed-oxide catalysts

Starting compounds	Treatment	Result
Bi_2O_3, MoO_3	Melting at about 1200 K	Bi_2O_3–MoO_3 (Bi–Mo–O)
$Bi(NO_3)_3$, $(NH_4)_2MoO_4$	Ignition at 570–780 K	Bi_2O_3–MoO_3 (Bi–Mo–O)
CoO, MoO_3	Melting at 1273 K	CoO–MoO_3 (Co–Mo–O)
NH_4VO_3, $(NH_4)_6Mo_7O_{24}$	Heating in vacuo at 623 K	V_2O_5–MoO_3 (V–Mo–O)
Citrates of La and Ni	Heating at 1023 K in air	$LaNiO_3$

some typical procedures which have been used successfully. The conventions used to indicate these mixtures are to insert a bar between the chemical formulae of the oxides concerned (e.g. Bi_2O_3–MoO_3) or to simply write the element symbols with linking bars (e.g. Bi–Mo–O). These molecular mixtures are not to be regarded strictly as true chemical compounds. On the other hand, when an integral formula is given, as is the case for the last entry in Table 3.5, the formation of a true chemical compound characterized by a definite crystalline structure is implied. The material represented by the formula $LaNiO_3$ is a perovskite phase and has a similar lattice structure to that of the mineral perovskite, represented by the formula $CaTiO_3$.

3.2.2 Zeolites

Zeolites are outstandingly useful catalysts of a microporous nature. The basic structural features are indicated in Fig. 3.3. As would be expected for a crystalline material, the preparation of zeolites involves their slow appearance from the parent solutions. The precise type of zeolite formed is governed by the conditions during the synthesis, including the nature and concentrations of the dissolved species.

The typical starting materials are sodium aluminate and sodium silicate (or silicic acid). The syntheses are carried out at temperatures in the range 300–450 K, when the physical conditions may be described as moderately hydrothermal. Important parameters for control of the type of zeolitic solid which ultimately appears at the bottom of the synthesis container are reactant concentrations, the presence of particular species, temperature, pH and the time allowed. Significantly, zeolite phases are not thermodynamically stable in the full sense. The microporous structure, given sufficient time in contact with the overlying solution and suitable temperature and pressure conditions, would convert eventually into denser aluminosilicate phases. It is therefore an essential requirement that the synthesized zeolite is separated from the aqueous phase within a prescribed time scale and also that excess silicate is leached out from the material with thorough washing. Table 3.6 summarizes suitable synthesis conditions for the common types of zeolites. The entries in the last column reveal the differentiating feature of X- and Y-type zeolites.

As obtained initially, the zeolite pores retain considerable amounts of water, solvating the electrical charges within the structure. This water is driven off on heating, which provides the Greek origin of the name zeolite, literally meaning the stone that boils. Prior to various uses in connection with adsorption and catalysis, a zeolite must be thoroughly dehydrated by heating to temperatures of 600–700 K. Furthermore it is usually necessary

Table 3.6 Typical zeolite synthesis specifications at a temperature of 373 K

Type	Initial molar ratios in solution			Typical time/h	Si to Al atomic ratio in zeolite
	Na/Si	Si/Al	H_2O/Si		
A	0.5	1.0	17	3	1.0
X	0.9	1.5	48	8	1.0–1.5
Y	0.2	10	16	8	1.5–3.0

NaOH used to adjust the pH as required.

to exchange the cations (initially Na^+) which are located within the internal structure, in order to induce catalytic activity. The sodium ions can be exchanged for ammonium (NH_4^+) ions by immersing the solid in a hot and fairly concentrated (say 1 mol dm^{-3}) solution of ammonium nitrate for some time. Such exchange is used commonly in the course of the production of the acidic forms of the zeolites. Subsequent heating of the ammonium–zeolite to temperatures of the order of 700 K results in thermal decomposition of the ammonium ion, with ammonia being driven off, according to the representation

$$NH_4^+\text{–zeolite} \rightarrow NH_3 \uparrow + H^+\text{–zeolite}$$

The effective conversion of NH_4^+ into H^+ preserves the overall balance between positive and negative charges, keeping the microstructure stable whilst generating acidic sites. The acidic form of an X-type zeolite is often denoted by HX, for example.

Many other types of zeolite structures are known, not in nature generally but rather in solids synthesized under well controlled conditions. The type of zeolite obtained by hydrothermal crystallization of the aluminosilicate gel which emerges first from the solution is governed primarily by the composition of the gel and the temperature at which crystallization proceeds. It turns out that individual framework structures are favoured in the presence of specific cations, in particular those of an organic nature, which are larger in volume than the sodium ions present when A-, X- or Y-type structures form. These organic cations are believed to act as *templates* about which the aluminosilicate gel crystallizes to achieve the most 'comfortable' fit. There appear to be two key aspects to this. In the first place, the organic cations seem to influence the incorporation of aluminium into the forming aluminosilicate gel, so that there is a lower aluminium-to-silicon ratio therein than is the case in the common zeolites. The resulting solids are often referred to as high silica zeolites on the basis that the atomic ratios of silicon to aluminium exceed 2.5 and can be much higher. Secondly the organic cations seem to occupy positions within the pore apertures (or certainly close enough to them to govern their development) in the crystallizing aluminosilicate framework. This apparent templating action is manifested in the formation of pore apertures with unusual dimensions in comparison with the common zeolites. If the organic species makes a particularly good fit within a specific framework structure, then the same zeolitic product can be obtained from gel compositions extending over a wide range. On the other hand, if the organic species can be accommodated without much difficulty in a variety of zeolitic frameworks, the type of zeolite which appears will depend upon the gel composition, in particular its silicon-to-aluminium ratio.

The key novelty in the zeolite synthesis programme embarked upon by the Mobil Oil Corporation around 1970 was the incorporation of alkylammonium ions into the parent solutions. The tetrapropylammonium ion ($(C_3H_7)_4N^+$), physically much larger than Na^+, led to one of the most significant zeolites. The resulting structure had ten T atoms (Si or Al) in the pore aperture, intermediate between the eight of A-type and 12 of X- or Y-type zeolites. This zeolite is known by the acronym ZSM-5 (Zeolite Socony Mobil–number five in the series of materials produced in the programme). The sensitivity of the syntheses to the templating actions of the cations is revealed by the facts that the incorporation of different organic cations, tetramethylammonium or tetrabutylammonium, into the parent solutions led to other zeolites, typical forms known as offretite and ZSM-11 respectively.

A preparational procedure for ZSM-5 is as follows. The initial components added to the solution are sodium hydroxide, aluminium hydroxide gel, acid-washed precipitated silica and tetrapropylammonium hydroxide, the last obtained commonly as a 20% aqueous solution. Table 3.7 indicates the composition of the starting solution. The 'preferred' range is prescribed in the original patent for ZSM-5 whilst the entries in the row designated 'used' refer to a synthesis conducted in the author's laboratory. The resultant solution was sealed within strong Pyrex glass tubes (able to withstand internal pressure of at least 20 times atmospheric). These tubes

Table 3.7 Molar ratios of components in the initial solution for the synthesis of ZSM-5

	$(TPA^+ + Na^+)/$ Si	$TPA^+/$ $(TPA^+ + Na^+)$	$H_2O/$ $(TPA^+ + Na^+)$	Si/Al
Preferred range	0.20–0.75	0.4–0.9	10–300	5–20
Used by the author	0.54	0.71	37	11

TPA^+ represents the tetrapropylammonium cation.

were maintained at a temperature in the vicinity of 445 K for six days. On subsequent cooling to ambient temperature, a tube was observed to contain an upper (organic), light brown liquid layer and a lower (aqueous), colourless liquid layer overlying an off-white solid. When the seal on the tube was broken, some residual pressure escaped producing the characteristic odours of alkene and ammonia. After decanting off the liquids, the solid material was extracted, ground lightly to a coarse powder and washed thoroughly with large amounts of distilled water. The material was then dried in air prior to being calcined in flowing air at temperatures around 720 K for several hours. At this stage the material is heavily contaminated with sodium ions. The procedures of ammonium exchange and thermal decomposition to produce acidic forms have been described above. The final product in this case is designated HZSM-5 to indicate its acidic properties. It is an off-white powder and can be expected to be obtained in yields corresponding to around 20% of the combined masses of the solid reagents loaded initially.

Examination of ZSM-5 under an electron microscope reveals its microcrystalline nature. Fig. 3.7 shows a typical sample with

Fig. 3.7 Photograph taken using scanning electron microscope of crystals of ZSM-5 zeolite. The dimension across the photograph corresponds to 34 μm.

characteristically-shaped crystallites of the order of 6 μm across. The high-silica nature of ZSM-5 is shown by elemental analysis. Typically molar ratios, expressed in terms of SiO_2/Al_2O_3, in excess of 25 are found in the as-prepared material. A further characteristic is the large ratio of the internal surface area to the external surface area. For example, in the instance of a ZSM-5 sample with crystallite dimensions of the order of 10 μm, the image obtained by electron microscopy has been used to estimate an external specific surface area of 0.8 m^2 g^{-1}. The total surface area indicated by the BET isotherm (Fig. 2.4) for adsorption of nitrogen at a temperature of 77 K was 422 m^2 g^{-1}. The factor of over 500 by which the internal surface area exceeds the external surface area points to the relative insignificance of the latter.

It is not appropriate to discuss the detailed structure of ZSM-5 at this point. This has a particular relevance for the catalytic processes induced by this material and is thus reserved to Section 8.9.

There are many other solid materials which are microporous, as exemplified by aluminophosphates (Fig. 2.4), borosilicates and various clay minerals. These materials have not yet achieved the degree of significance gained by zeolites in catalysis and are only mentioned in passing therefore.

3.2.3 *Forms of metallic elements on supports*

The starting point for the preparation of all of the catalysts concerned in this subsection is a precursor species containing a metal atom existing in a fluid phase. The objective is to deposit this species by some means on to a solid surface so that, after various treatments, active sites based upon the metal or the metal atom in a particular oxidation state are generated. Evidently the supported metal catalysts discussed in Section 3.1.1 are one of the forms of interest here.

When the supporting solid is porous, it may be *impregnated* with a suitable solution of the precursor. Impregnation is the most general technique for the production of supported metal catalysts, but it is not without problems in many cases. Subsequently the solvent is evaporated off and the solute is left dispersed over the surface. For instance, an aqueous solution of chloroplatinic acid may be used as the precursor of a dispersion of platinum metal on alumina. Following impregnation and drying, the chloroplatinic acid left on the surface is reduced in flowing hydrogen, in summary represented as

$$n\text{H}_2\text{PtCl}_6 + 2n\text{H}_2 \xrightarrow[1-2\,\text{h}]{500-700\,\text{K}} (\text{Pt})_n + 6n\text{HCl}$$

$(Pt)_n$ indicates a surface aggregate containing a substantial number of platinum atoms, with n often of the order of hundreds or even thousands. This implies that the degree of dispersion of the metal achieved is limited by the tendency to aggregation accompanying reduction. Nevertheless the $PtCl_6^{2-}$ ions are initially adsorbed strongly on to separated sites on the alumina surface. It is also worth noting at this point that the use of chloroplatinic acid in conjunction with alumina results in the introduction of chloride to the surface, creating strongly acidic sites (as will be explained in Section 5.3). This acidification of the support may be avoided by the use of ammoniacal solutions of platinum diamminodinitrite $(Pt(NH_3)_2(NO_2)_2)$ to achieve the impregnation.

Other metal compounds may be used as catalyst precursors *via* impregnation, using their solutions in water or in organic solvents such as toluene. Figure 4.19 (in Section 4.4.5) will indicate the various stages involved in the production of cobalt metal supported on titania, for example. A selection of precursor compounds suitable for the methods indicated appears in Table 3.8.

In the case of metal carbonyl precursors, the vapour may be sublimed directly on to the support. Thereafter the deposited carbonyl molecules are decomposed thermally to yield the metal with evolved carbon monoxide.

The salt impregnation route to supported metals depends upon an ultimate reduction of the oxidation state of the metal to zero. This is accomplished readily with the precious metals (e.g. Pt, Pd, Ir, Ag) but tends to be incomplete with other metals such as chromium, molybdenum and tungsten. Evidently the metal is most likely to finish in the zero oxidation state if this is the state in the precursor, as in the carbonyls. Thus a good procedure for producing supported chromium, molybdenum or tungsten metals commences with impregnation of the carbonyls $(Cr(CO)_6$, $Mo(CO)_6$ or $W(CO)_6)$ into the support by sublimation, or by using their solution in toluene for instance. Thereafter, with heating under helium to

Table 3.8 Typical metal-containing catalyst precursors for impregnation

Method of impregnation	Typical compounds serving as precursors
via aqueous solution	$\left\{ \begin{array}{l} AgNO_3, RuCl_3, Pd(NH_3)_4Cl_2, RhCl_3, Ni(NO_3)_2, \\ H_2IrCl_6, NH_4VO_3, NH_4ReO_4, UO_2(NO_3)_2, \\ (NH_4)_6Mo_7O_{24} \end{array} \right.$
via organic solution	$\left\{ \begin{array}{l} \text{Metal carbonyls (e.g. } Fe(CO)_5, Mo(CO)_6) \\ \text{Metal acetylacetonates} \\ \text{(e.g. } VO(CH_3COCHCOCH_3)_2) \end{array} \right.$
via vapour sublimation	Metal carbonyls (e.g. $Co_2(CO)_8$, $Ir_4(CO)_{12}$, $W(CO)_6$)

temperatures of the order of 700 K, the deposited carbonyl molecules decompose leaving finely dispersed metal particles. In this procedure it is necessary to suppress any tendency for the support material to oxidize the metal, such as that originating from the presence of hydroxyl groups on an alumina surface. This potential problem is avoided if the alumina has been pre-calcined at temperatures of the order of 1100 K, when hydroxyl groups are removed in conjunction with the release of water vapour.

Grafting techniques can be used to produce highly dispersed, supported metals, as exemplified for rhodium on titania in Section 3.1.5.

When the metal concerned is inexpensive, a highly dispersed supported form can be produced by partial reduction of a coprecipitated oxide mixture. This technique is associated traditionally with nickel-on-silica catalysts, for which a preparational procedure is represented in Fig. 3.8.

Zeolites present a rather different type of surface compared to the other common supporting materials, such as forms of alumina, silica, titania and zirconia. The zeolite has cations at particular sites on the internal surfaces: in principle therefore a regular distribution of single precursor cations can be produced by ion exchange. Commencing usually with the sodium form of a zeolite, the introduction of another metal cation is accomplished by prolonged immersion of the solid in an aqueous solution of the metal salt (commonly acetate, chloride or nitrate) at temperatures of around 350 K. The precious metals are usually exchanged-in as ammonia-complexed ions, such as $Pt(NH_3)_4^{2+}$, $Pd(NH_3)_4^{2+}$ and $Rh(NH_3)_5Cl^{2+}$. In principle, the resultant cations separately distributed at localized sites within the zeolite should be capable on reduction of yielding highly dispersed metals. This is manifested by platinum in X- or Y-type zeolites when, even at high loadings, the metal is produced as separated small particles of almost uniform size. Figure 3.9 shows the image produced using an electron microscope of a platinum-loaded X-type zeolite. This material resulted from a 42% degree of ion-exchange of the sodium form, accomplished using an aqueous solution of $Pt(NH_3)_4Cl_2$: subsequently it was dried and thermally-treated at a temperature of 873 K for four hours under helium. The uniformity of the platinum particle size (about 5 nm across) is striking. This contrasts with the much wider variation of particle sizes achieved on amorphous supports such as silica or alumina.

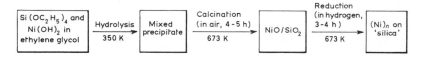

Fig. 3.8 Schematic representation of a procedure which has been used to produce nickel dispersed on silica.

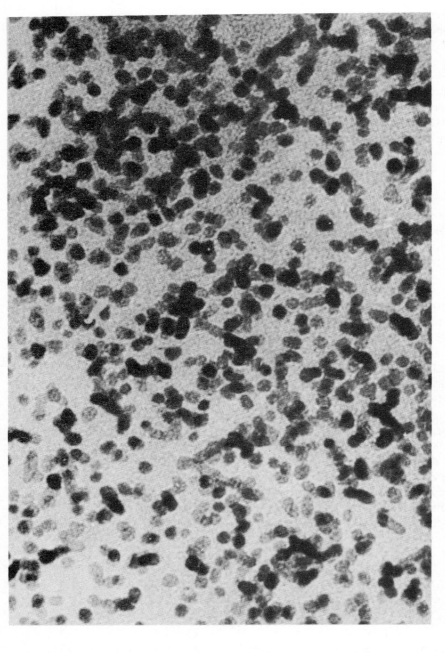

Fig. 3.9 Transmission electron micrograph (bright field) of platinum particles supported on an X-type zeolite. The dimension across the photograph corresponds to 240 nm. Reproduced with permission of the Royal Society of Chemistry from *Electron microscopy of Pt, Pd and Ni particles in a NaX zeolite matrix*, A. Kleine, P. L. Ryder, N. Jaeger and G. Schulz-Ekloff (1986) *Journal of the Chemical Society, Faraday Transactions I*, **82**, 208 (facing, plate 2).

However, many metal ions become very difficult to reduce to metal atoms when they occupy sites within zeolites. For example, Fe^{2+} ions in a Y-type zeolite cannot be reduced with hydrogen even at temperatures close to 1000 K. The resistance of such cations to reduction reflects the stability conferred by the microenvironment of the zeolite.

Particular treatments are required to produce very highly dispersed metals supported by zeolites. Even when reduction to the metal is possible, the conditions required tend to lead to some agglomeration (or sintering) of the particles formed and hence to poor dispersion in the final material. Direct reduction of a Y-type zeolite containing $Pt(NH_3)_4^{2+}$ cations with hydrogen at a temperature of 625 K results in poorly dispersed platinum. It seems that once the precursor species loses the positive charge the metal atoms have the ability to migrate across the surface to agglomerate together. When however the precursor species is decomposed in oxygen prior to reduction in hydrogen, almost 100% dispersion of the platinum can be achieved. Under the oxygen, the $Pt(NH_3)_4^{2+}$ ions are converted to platinum species which retain a cationic nature and thus remain bound to their lattice sites. In the course of the subsequent reduction by hydrogen, the platinum atoms never achieve sufficient mobility to become significantly agglomerated. A representative end-product of this procedure is a Y-type zeolite supporting platinum particles of diameters around 1 nm, these being located in the supercages.

The main alternative procedure to ion exchange for producing dispersed metals within zeolites commences with impregnation by metal carbonyls. For this an essential prerequisite is the complete dehydration of the zeolite, accomplished with heating to a temperature of approximately 700 K with evacuation. Subsequent to impregnation of the zeolite with the precursor species such as $Ru_3(CO)_{12}$ or $Fe(CO)_5$ from the vapour or the organic solution phases, the carbonyl species are decomposed on heating to around 700 K. Small metal particles result particularly when the decomposition is conducted under an inert gas (e.g. helium) rather than with evacuation; the former condition inhibits the mechanism of agglomeration via diffusion through the gas phase. It is interesting to note some experimental evidence for the dependence of the resultant metal loading on the vacant space within the supercages. When $Mo(CO)_6$ was introduced into HY–zeolite (acidic form), the amount of carbonyl taken in corresponded to one molecule per supercage. This implies that the supercage is not large enough to accommodate two carbonyl molecules. But, after decomposing the contained $Mo(CO)_6$ with removal of the bulky CO ligands, the space in the supercages was regenerated as indicated by the subsequent ability of the zeolite to take in more carbonyl. Evidently this cycle could be repeated to achieve further increased loadings of molybdenum in the zeolite.

Clay minerals, like zeolites to some extent, offer a porous structure with cationic sites distributed regularly over internal surfaces. Equally these materials undergo ion exchange when they are suspended in aqueous solutions of a metal nitrate (say 0.5 mol dm^{-3}) for a day. Thereafter the ion exchanged clay mineral is separated by centrifugation, thoroughly washed (or resuspended in deionized water and recovered again by centrifugation) and dried at temperatures of 310–350 K. Ion exchange of clay minerals can also involve the replacement of some of the aluminium ions in the layered structure, in addition to the other cations associated with these aluminosilicates.

The microenvironments within both zeolites and clay minerals create a much higher potency for catalytic action by contained metal species, as compared to the activities of corresponding species on amorphous supports. In fact the initial ion exchanged forms of some zeolites and clay minerals can serve as active catalysts in their own rights. Table 3.9 lists a few examples of catalytic actions illustrating this point. One view of the transition metal ions in zeolites or in clay minerals is that these cations are effectively complexed in anchoring. The solid framework would then be regarded as a mono- or poly-dentate ligand of the metal ion which is held by coordinating actions of lattice oxygens. The analogy is made then to the complexed metal cations which are active as homogeneous catalysts.

Most metal oxides of interest as commercial catalysts are relatively inexpensive and abundant materials. The main reasons for using these oxides in supported forms are not concerned with economical usage of material but rather the promotions of activities and selectivities (in comparison with those of the bulk oxides) which result in the reactions which they catalyse. For instance, V_2O_5 supported as a monolayer on the anatase form of TiO_2 is a much superior catalyst for the selective oxidation of many hydrocarbons compared to bulk V_2O_5. The general method for

Table 3.9 Processes catalysed by ion-exchanged zeolites and clay minerals

Cation incorporated	Support	Process catalysed
La^{3+} or Ce^{3+}	X-type zeolite	Hydrocarbon cracking
Ni^{2+} or Rh^{3+}	X-type zeolite	Oligomerization of alkenes
Co^{2+} or Cu^{2+}	Y-type zeolite	Ethanol oxidation to acetaldehyde
Fe^{3+} or Cr^{3+}	Montmorillonite*	Hydration of ethylene
Ti^{3+}	Hectorite*	Conversion of methanol to smaller alkenes

* Clay mineral.

Fig. 3.10 Schematic representation of a method for preparing a binary oxide (molybdenum–uranium) supported on silica.

producing supported oxide catalysts is the salt impregnation procedure described above, using compounds listed in Table 3.8. The supported oxide is in place after calcination. A binary-oxide supported catalyst can be prepared by successive impregnations, as illustrated schematically for a U–Mo–O catalyst on silica in Fig. 3.10. The resulting material is active as a catalyst for the selective oxidation of isobutene for example.

3.2.4 *Immobilized enzymes and living cells*

An enzyme molecule or a complete living cell (of bacteria or yeasts for examples) may be attached to or physically held at the surface of a solid material, when the catalytic entity is said to have been *immobilized*. The major advantages which follow are that the immobilized catalyst is easily removed from a liquid phase, allowing efficient recovery from batch reactors or retention within a zone of a flow reactor. Many enzymes are very expensive and only available in small amounts, so that immobilization can be regarded as a prerequisite for their usage in large-scale conversion processes.

Adsorption, polymer lattice entrapment and chemical bonding are the important modes of immobilization for commercial processes based on enzyme catalysis. This order represents that of increasing difficulty in the immobilization procedure involved.

In immobilization by adsorption, an aqueous solution of the enzyme is contacted with particles of a suitable insoluble solid. The suspension is agitated for a few minutes before the solid is separated by filtration and thereafter washed to remove any unadsorbed enzyme. The most widely used solids (carriers) in this connection are ion-exchangers, which are active for the adsorption of most proteins. Common examples are the anion exchanger DEAE- (diethylaminoethyl-) cellulose and the cation exchanger CM- (carboxymethyl-) cellulose. Oxides such as titania and clay minerals such as kaolinite can also be used. The binding forces are usually electrostatic in nature, acting between charges on the carrier and those associated with carboxylic and amino groups of amino acid residues at the external surface of the enzyme molecule (Section 2.2). Hydrogen bonds may also be involved to some extent. In concert these linkages provide quite strong attachment and the enzyme can be retained over substantial periods of usage. For instance, a glucose isomerase immobilized on DEAE-cellulose has been used in a flow reactor to catalyse the isomerization of glucose to fructose (see Section 7.4.1), with a half-life of around 200 h for leaching by the aqueous phase. In another instance, glucose oxidase was immobilized by adsorption on a cation exchange resin, to serve in the analysis of solutions for glucose content. The measurement technique concerned used the exothermicity of the oxidation to gluconic acid as manifested in the temperature increase of the flowing aqueous phase. Leaching of the enzyme occurred at a rate of 10% dm^{-3} with respect to the volume of the aqueous phase flowed over a period of several hours.

Polymer lattice entrapment may be used to immobilize both enzyme molecules and living cells. The basis of the method is that a gel with a three-dimensional network structure is induced to form in a solution of the enzyme or in a suspension of the cells. The large molecules or cells become enmeshed in the polymeric lattice and are physically confined by it. On the other hand, small substrate and product molecules can diffuse through the relatively open structure of the gel, allowing reactions catalysed by the trapped enzyme or cells to proceed.

There are two main routes to the formation of the gel around the catalytic entities. In the first, a gel material, such as κ-carrageenan, is dissolved in the warmed solution or suspension. The gel reforms on subsequent cooling, incorporating the enzyme or cells. The process of gel solution and reformation involved here is probably familiar in the making of a table jelly. Figure 3.11 represents the gel immobilization procedure and subsequent usage for the yeast *S. carlsbergensis*. Another variant of entrapment takes advantage of the ability of some enzymes to withstand suspension in organic solvents. In one instance the enzyme glucoamylase can survive suspension within a solution of polystyrene in benzene. A film of polystyrene containing trapped enzyme molecules is then created by casting on a sheet of glass. This procedure results typically in some 25% of the original amount of the enzyme being immobilized at the surface of the film and being active as a catalyst for the hydrolysis of soluble starch in an aqueous phase contacting the film. The remainder of the enzyme is buried more deeply within the film and is effectively lost.

The second major mode of lattice entrapment is based upon the synthesis of a cross-linked polymeric network from monomer species initially dissolved in the enzyme solution or the cell suspension. Acrylamide can serve in this role, being added to the aqueous phase together with a cross-linking agent, such as N,N'-methylenebisacrylamide. The polymer gel grows and extends its network throughout the aqueous phase, trapping the enzyme molecules or the cells. Silicic acid gels formed when solutions of

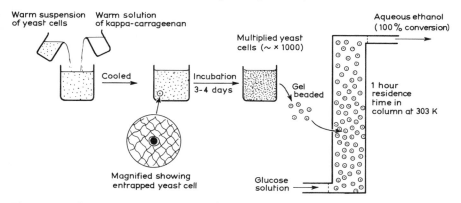

Fig. 3.11 Schematic representation of a procedure of polymer lattice entrapment of yeast cells and their subsequent usage in a reactor column effecting the fermentation of glucose to ethanol. Based upon a description of procedure given by I. Kolot (1980) *Process Biochemistry*, (Oct/Nov), 2.

sodium silicate are acidified have also been used for this mode of immobilization. Silastic resins (based upon silicone structures) are a third example of gels which are formed chemically to achieve entrapment. Polyurethane foams, grown from an initial aqueous phase, may also be used in this connection: an example of an enzyme so immobilized is concerned in Fig. 2.15.

Undoubtedly the most desirable general situation with regard to an immobilized enzyme is that in which a strong chemical bond provides the attachment to the support. The achievement of this chemical immobilization demands the formation of a covalent bond between non-essential groups of the enzyme molecule and suitable groups on the support material. The resultant immobilized enzyme will be immune to leaching and accordingly the system would be expected to retain its catalytic activity over long periods of use. The main problem in the procedures of chemical immobilization is that the reagents and conditions required to form the covalent bond can disrupt the delicate stability of the active site of the enzyme. It is not uncommon for trial procedures to fail completely by totally destroying the activity of the enzyme. Nevertheless many successful procedures of chemical immobilization have been developed, following which the enzyme retains at least partial activity. Here it is impractical to attempt to do more than to highlight a few examples which illustrate the principles involved.

Most carrier materials for chemical immobilization must be functionalized. This entails the attachment of groups amenable to the condensation reactions which are used generally to create the bond to the enzyme molecule. For example in the case of glass, functional groups can be

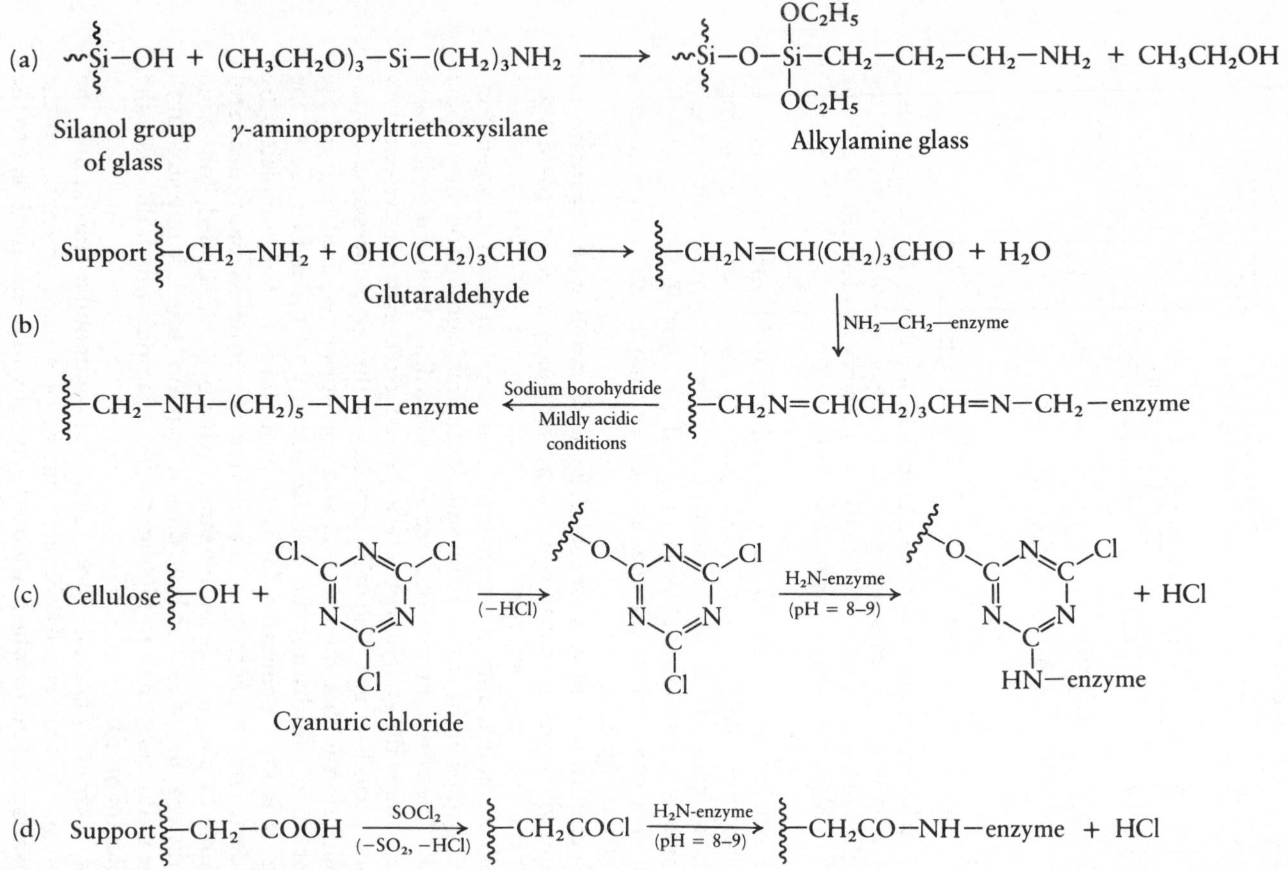

(a)

$$\sim\!\!Si\text{-}OH + (CH_3CH_2O)_3\text{-}Si\text{-}(CH_2)_3NH_2 \longrightarrow$$

Silanol group γ-aminopropyltriethoxysilane
of glass

$$\sim\!\!Si\text{-}O\text{-}\underset{\underset{OC_2H_5}{|}}{\overset{\overset{OC_2H_5}{|}}{Si}}\text{-}CH_2\text{-}CH_2\text{-}CH_2\text{-}NH_2 + CH_3CH_2OH$$

Alkylamine glass

(b)

$$Support\!\!\sim\!\!CH_2\text{-}NH_2 + OHC(CH_2)_3CHO \longrightarrow \sim\!\!CH_2N=CH(CH_2)_3CHO + H_2O$$

Glutaraldehyde

$$\Big\downarrow NH_2\text{-}CH_2\text{-}enzyme$$

$$\sim\!\!CH_2N=CH(CH_2)_3CH=N\text{-}CH_2\text{-}enzyme$$

$$\Big\downarrow \begin{array}{c}\text{Sodium borohydride}\\ \text{Mildly acidic}\\ \text{conditions}\end{array}$$

$$\sim\!\!CH_2\text{-}NH\text{-}(CH_2)_5\text{-}NH\text{-}enzyme$$

(c)

Cyanuric chloride

$$Cellulose\!\!\sim\!\!OH + \underset{\text{(Cyanuric chloride)}}{\text{(triazine ring with Cl, Cl, Cl)}} \xrightarrow{(-HCl)}$$

$$\text{(triazine ring: }O\!\!\sim, Cl\text{)} \xrightarrow[\text{(pH = 8–9)}]{H_2N\text{-}enzyme}$$

$$\text{(triazine ring: }O\!\!\sim, HN\text{-}enzyme\text{)} + HCl$$

(d)

$$Support\!\!\sim\!\!CH_2\text{-}COOH \xrightarrow[(-SO_2,\,-HCl)]{SOCl_2} \sim\!\!CH_2COCl \xrightarrow[\text{(pH = 8–9)}]{H_2N\text{-}enzyme} \sim\!\!CH_2CO\text{-}NH\text{-}enzyme + HCl$$

Fig. 3.12 Illustrative examples of processes used in chemical immobilization of enzymes. (a) Initial functionalization of glass support by grafting of an amino group. (b) The use of glutaraldehyde as a linking agent between a functionalized support and an enzyme. (c) Chemical immobilization mechanism for an enzyme on a cellulose support, using cyanuric chloride as the linking agent. (d) The use of thionyl chloride (SOCl₂) as a reagent for functionalizing a support with carboxylic acid groups for a

grafted on by reacting silane coupling reagents with the silanol (SiOH) groups on the surface. One instance leading to an alkylamine–glass is represented in Fig. 3.12(a). Silanes with other functional groups (such as —CH_2Cl, —CH_2OH, —CH_2SH and —CH_2CN) are available, providing the potential for chemical immobilization of almost any enzyme to a glass surface.

The reagents of wide applicability in the subsequent process of chemical attachment are those with potentially-reactive groups at each end of the molecule, as typified by glutaraldehyde. Here the coupling process usually involves the formation of a Schiff's base, with elimination of water. The mild conditions, including pH in the vicinity of 7, used in this procedure are compatible with the preservation of the activity of the enzyme. Figure 3.12(b) shows a representative course of immobilization using glutaraldehyde, in which the last step may be regarded as optional. Another commonly-used procedure, making use of the hydroxyl groups on cellulose in conjunction with the linking ability of cyanuric chloride, is represented in Fig. 3.12(c). Finally Fig. 3.12(d) indicates how thionyl chloride may be used to convert a carboxylic acid group on a support to an acyl group which can in turn be condensed with an amine group on an enzyme molecule. The examples given in Fig. 3.12 serve merely to provide insights into the general principles of methods of achieving chemical immobilization. In actuality, many functionalized support materials and indeed some chemically immobilized enzymes are available commercially.

To conclude this section, it should be pointed out that the cross-linking of enzyme molecules or living cells themselves using bifunctional reagents provides another mode of chemical immobilization. Some of these cross-linking agents (e.g. glutaraldehyde) directly cross-link the enzyme molecules or cells after reacting with protruding amine groups. Alternatively, others (e.g. hexamethylene diamine) effect cross-linking by reacting with protruding carboxylic acid groups which have been preactivated using carbodiimides. In general respects, the resultant materials from these procedures resemble those produced by lattice entrapment, except that the trapping mode is now chemical rather than physical in nature. One commercial example of a water insoluble material of this type is the immobilized glucose isomerase produced by Novo Industries of Denmark. In creating this, glutaraldehyde is used to effect chemical linking within an aqueous phase containing homogenized cells of *B. coagulans*, a bacillus species which contains the isomerase enzyme.

3.3 Concluding remarks

This chapter has been used to present a wide ranging survey of the broad natures of catalytic surfaces and the means by which these may be created.

Two general morphologies of solid substances, corresponding to porous and highly dispersed natures, are seen to offer very large surface areas for relatively small amounts of the material. Some microporous solids, such as zeolites, can be active catalysts in their own rights. Of wider significance is the advantage gained by using inert materials of a porous nature as high surface area supports upon which an active catalyst may be dispersed as very small particles. In many instances, the supported catalyst may be spread so thinly that one inherent characteristic of homogeneous catalysts is achieved, i.e. every potentially-active site is exposed to the catalysed process.

Profound advantages come from the attachment of molecular catalysts to supporting surfaces. The resultant material can be handled and used as a solid in whatever form is most convenient. At the same time, as a catalyst it may offer the high activity associated with heterogeneous systems combined with high selectivity more characteristic of homogeneous systems. In some cases, the active sites on the surface may be 'molecularly engineered' to produce essentially new catalysts which would not exist in the absence of the underlying support.

Until now in this book, various structures at surfaces, including those of chemisorbed species, have been introduced without indication of how these are elucidated experimentally. The techniques which may be applied to detect microscopic structures existing at surfaces form the major part of the next chapter.

4

The detection of adsorbates on solid surfaces

In this chapter interest is directed to the sophisticated techniques which may be applied to the detection and identification of adsorbed species and microscopic action of significance for catalysis at solid surfaces. The main development will proceed through a succession of the techniques which may now be regarded as applied almost routinely in many laboratories. The general principles underlying each of these will be indicated and examples will be given illustrating the type of information which may be obtained. In selecting the examples, some anticipation will be made of the catalytic processes which receive specific attention in later chapters.

Table 4.1 Techniques (acronyms) used to investigate phenomena at solid surfaces

---

Destructive techniques
   Temperature programmed reaction spectroscopy (TPRS)
   Secondary ion mass spectroscopy (SIMS)

Non-destructive techniques
   Low energy electron diffraction (LEED)
   (High resolution) electron energy loss spectroscopy ((HR)EELS)
   Auger electron spectroscopy (AES)
   Photoelectron spectroscopies $\begin{cases} \text{ultraviolet (UPS)} \\ \text{X-ray (XPS)} \end{cases}$
   Extended X-ray absorption fine structure (EXAFS)
   Infrared absorption spectroscopy
   Infrared reflectance–absorption spectroscopy (IRAS)

The techniques may be divided under the broad headings, destructive and non-destructive. The former type relies upon chemisorbed species being driven off the surface in the course of the procedure. The latter category is based upon the characteristics, generally of a spectroscopic nature, of species as they reside upon the surface. Table 4.1 lists the various techniques which will be discussed and indicates their acronyms which are used widely. Many other techniques have been developed, but a book of this length can only permit the discussion of the selection given in Table 4.1. It will be found however, as the rest of the book is explored, that these can provide a fairly comprehensive body of information for the catalytic reactions of main interest at the level concerned.

4.1 Crystal faces and cleaved surfaces of metals

The only surface which is entirely uniform at the microscopic level is a perfect crystal face composed of atoms of a single chemical element. Evidently this perfect crystal face provides the simplest type of surface for use as a heterogeneous catalyst. But it is evident that a real catalyst, used in a large scale process, will not have a regular microstructure at its surface. Therefore it is important to recognize immediately that observations made in a laboratory study using a crystal face as a catalyst may not of necessity have bearing on the corresponding real catalytic process. This caution stated, it is tempered by a reassurance that many valuable revelations of factors governing actual processes catalysed by metals in particular have come from systems in which the catalytic surface is a perfect crystal face or has highly regular microstructure.

At this stage it is necessary to describe conventional notations used to identify crystal faces and those surfaces created by cleavage of crystals in particular directions. Sets of numbers known as Miller indices are used to specify planes incorporating crystal faces. For each face of interest here, these numbers are equivalent to the reciprocals of the intersections of the particular plane with the x,y and z axes respectively, with the finite values reduced to the lowest set of integers. Thus, for example, one of the low-index faces of iron is identified as Fe(111): the corresponding plane makes intersections with the principal axes at points equally displaced from the origin. Another low-index face is Fe(110): this plane intersects the x and y axes at points equally displaced from the origin but is parallel to the z axis, so that the last element of the identification is the reciprocal of infinity, that is zero. The third basic face of iron is Fe(100), which corresponds to a plane parallel to that containing the y and z axes. Higher Miller index numbers identify planes specifying surfaces produced by oriented cleavage. These cleaved surfaces are composed of a repeating pattern of terraces and steps,

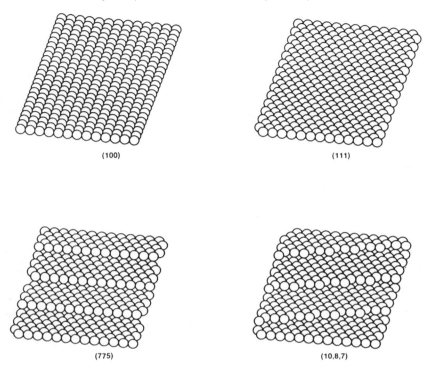

(100)

(111)

(775)

(10,8,7)

Fig. 4.1 Ball models of idealized atomic structures of the platinum (111) and (100) crystal faces, the stepped platinum (775) and kinked platinum (10,8,7) surfaces, all in the face-centred cubic (fcc) crystal form. Reproduced with permission of the Royal Society of Chemistry from *Molecular ingredients of heterogeneous catalysis*, G. A. Somorjai (1984) *Chemical Society Reviews*, **13**, 327.

which correspond themselves to discontinuous low index surfaces. Figure 4.1 shows ball models of two perfect faces and two higher index cleaved surfaces of platinum. In addition to terraces and steps, the (10,8,7) surface incorporates kinks, the discontinuities producing retreating edges along the steps.

Cleaved surfaces may be described more explicitly by an alternative notation (sometimes referred to as the TLK system). This indicates the widths of terraces and identifies the Miller indices of the component low index faces concerned. For example, one particular cleaved surface, which is designated as (533) on the basis of the plane corresponding to its overall orientation, is described as 4(111) × (100) in the TLK notation. This latter specification indicates that the terraces are four atoms wide and expose sections of the (111) basic face, whilst the intervening steps are single-atom

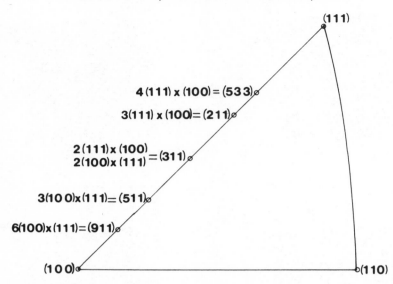

Fig. 4.2 Locations of various cleaved surfaces/crystallographic planes on the stereographic triangle. Cleaved surfaces are indicated by TLK notation and equivalent Miller indices. Reproduced from *Adsorption of hydrogen on stepped Pt single crystal surfaces*, B. Love, K. Seto and J. Lipkowski (1986) *Journal of Electroanalytical Chemistry*, **199**, 220 with the permission of Elsevier Science Publishers B.V.

deep exposures of the (100) face. Figure 4.2 indicates the location of the various planes/cleaved surfaces on what is termed the stereographic triangle. This diagram and the inserted TLK notations reveal how the succession of different cleaved surfaces down the side of the triangle linking (111) and (100) gradually switches over from terraces of (111) type with steps of (100) type to terraces of (100) type with steps of (111) type. The plane indicated by (311) in the Miller index system corresponds to the cross-over point for designation of terraces and steps in this respect.

The rates of some catalysed reactions conducted on different crystal faces of a metal can show large variations. This point may be illustrated for the low index faces of iron when they are used in turn to catalyse the synthesis of ammonia, according to the overall chemical equation

$$N_2 + 3H_2 \rightarrow 2NH_3$$

The disposition of the iron atoms at the surface is represented in the upper part of Fig. 4.3, whilst the lower part of this diagram indicates the corresponding rates of ammonia synthesis conducted in contact with these crystal faces under conditions approaching those of the industrial process

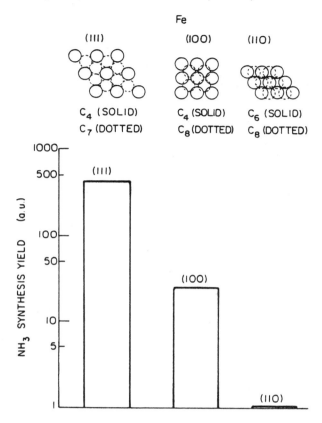

Fig. 4.3 Upper Part: idealized ball models, as viewed from above, of the atomic surface structure of the low index crystal faces (in the body-centred cubic form) of iron. Atoms in the topmost layer are shown as full circles and atoms in the next layer are shown as broken circles. The numbers appearing as subscripts to C are the coordination numbers of the iron atoms. Lower part: the yields of ammonia in a particular time resulting from contact of nitrogen/hydrogen mixtures under the same high pressure conditions when the catalytic surface is each of the low index faces of iron in turn. The synthesis yields (expressed in arbitrary units (a.u.)) are a measure of the rate of the reaction. Reproduced with permission of the Royal Society of Chemistry from *Molecular ingredients of heterogeneous catalysis*, G. A. Somorjai (1984) *Chemical Society Reviews*, **13**, 325.

(Section 8.2). A general explanation is that different spatial separations and coordination numbers of the iron atoms allow a reactant to be accommodated more comfortably on one face than on another in some respect affecting the rate determining step. Kinetic responses to changes in the identity of crystal faces of metal catalysts are observed generally for reactions in which carbon–carbon, nitrogen–nitrogen or carbon–oxygen bonds are broken or formed: accordingly such reactions are described as being *structure sensitive*. Further exemplification is found in the hydrogenolysis of ethane (C–C bond scission) represented by

$$C_2H_6 + H_2 \rightarrow 2CH_4$$

The rate achieved on a Ni(111) face is considerably less than it is on Ni(100) under the same conditions. On the other hand, reactions involving only the scission or creation of carbon–hydrogen, hydrogen–hydrogen or oxygen–hydrogen bonds have rates which are independent largely of the identity of the particular metal crystal face which induces the catalytic action.

Many surface catalysed reactions are favoured strongly by the presence of microscopic defects. Carbon monoxide shows little tendency to decompose when contacting low index faces of nickel at temperatures up to 450 K. In contrast, extensive decomposition of carbon monoxide occurs when the gas contacts cleaved or polycrystalline nickel surfaces at a temperature of 400 K (see Figure 4.5). Hydrocarbons also tend to decompose on stepped surfaces but not on low index crystal faces of nickel or platinum at relatively low temperatures. For instance, cleaved faces of these metals catalyse the dehydrogenation of cyclohexene to benzene at ambient temperature. However, substantial elevation of temperature is required to induce this reaction to occur on the low index crystal faces of these metals. The origin of such effects will be discussed in Section 5.1.

4.2 The effects of pressure on surface phenomena

Many of the techniques used for the detection of the species existing on solid surfaces operate only at very low pressures. Often the chamber in which the experiments are conducted must be evacuated to ultrahigh vacuum (UHV), a condition which corresponds to pressures below 10^{-7} Pa (of the order of 10^{-12} of atmospheric pressure). Under these circumstances the mean free pathlengths of electrons or ions in the gas phase are very long and are orders of magnitude larger than the distances of travel of these particles within the experimental systems to be described. Thus electrons which impinge on to a target surface or reach detectors therefrom may be presumed not to have lost energy in collisions with gas phase molecules. Equally ions may be presumed to be immune to chemical reactions in the gas phase. Thus under UHV conditions, all observed effects may be ascribed to conversion processes in the surface layers of the solid target.

The association of observations made under low pressure conditions with the mechanisms of related catalytic processes conducted at atmospheric pressure or above involves a considerable extrapolation. One relevant consideration is the effect that a change of pressure of perhaps 14 orders of magnitude may have on the position of equilibrium in a catalytic reaction system. Any reaction which involves a net decrease in the number of gas phase molecules will be subject to a movement of the position of chemical equilibrium towards the reactants as the pressure is lowered. This is likely to imply that such reactions will not generally be observable if conducted under UHV conditions. The cyclotrimerization of acetylene to benzene

$$3C_2H_2 \rightarrow C_6H_6$$

on palladium provides an almost unique example of a reaction of this type which occurs under both UHV and atmospheric pressure conditions. On the other hand, reactions which lead to an increase in the number of gas phase species will be promoted under UHV conditions. Thus processes such as dehydrogenation and decomposition of hydrocarbons will be enhanced.

Experimental systems have been designed to bridge across the gap from the conditions of real catalytic reactions to the UHV conditions required to investigate the surface involved. The basic principle is to allow the surface to achieve its steady state coverage of adsorbed species under the high pressure conditions before bringing it to UHV conditions. One arrangement used is the equipment of the UHV chamber with an internal cell which can enclose the surface, isolating it from vacuum and forming part of a closed loop batch reactor which can be pressurized to about 3 MPa. Reactions within this sealed cell can then proceed with product monitoring by conventional means. Thereafter the gases are pumped away and on opening the cell the surface is exposed to UHV conditions for the analysis of the remaining surface species. In this it is justifiably presumed that chemisorbed species formed during the exposure to reactants do not escape from the surface significantly on the time scale of subsequent measurements made under UHV conditions. The desorption rates of species bound by strong chemical bonds would be expected to be small at ambient temperatures (Section 2.3.2). The attraction of such systems lies in their potential to relate the detailed chemical nature of the surface (as revealed by techniques applied under UHV) to the kinetic behaviour and product yields observed under working catalytic conditions.

4.3 Destructive techniques for surface investigation

4.3.1 *Thermal desorption methods*

The underlying principle of these methods can be stated as follows. Subsequent to the adsorption of species at a relatively low temperature, the temperature of the surface is raised at a uniform rate and a record corresponding to the desorptions of particular species into the gas phase as functions of temperature is obtained. The simplest situation, in which the originally adsorbed species desorbs unchanged, has been discussed in Section 2.3.2. Now the main interest is in the technique known as temperature-programmed reaction spectroscopy (TPRS) in which the species which desorb are the result of chemical conversions of the initially adsorbed species on the surface. The usual detection method applied in TPRS is mass spectrometry. The typical experimental system will be evacuated to total pressures below 10^{-5} Pa, with a relatively high pumping rate used in conjunction with a temperature rise rate of the order of $10 \, \text{K s}^{-1}$. Under these conditions the record of the mass spectrometer signal corresponding to a particular product as a function of time (temperature) will show a maximum or peak. Product evolution begins generally at a temperature which is just sufficient to allow the relevant surface reaction(s) to proceed with a significant rate. Thereafter, with the temperature rising steadily, the rate of evolution passes through a maximum value, before it begins to diminish as the corresponding reactant coverage on the surface becomes depleted substantially. The rate of evolution of a particular product from a surface, when this rate is controlled by the rate of the generating reaction on the surface, is usually expressed by first- (equation 4.1) or second- (equation 4.2) order kinetic equations

$$-\frac{dn}{dt} = v_1 \, n \exp\left(-E_d/RT\right) \qquad (4.1)$$

$$-\frac{dn}{dt} = v_2 \, n^2 \exp\left(-E_d'/RT\right) \qquad (4.2)$$

In these equations, n is the number of molecules of reactant adsorbed per unit area of the surface, v_1 and v_2 are kinetic frequency factors and E_d and E_d' are the respective activation energies of the reaction steps controlling the rates on the surface. For a peak appearing in the experimental record, the rising signal approaching the peak reflects the increasing values of the exponential terms in equations (4.1) and (4.2) as T increases. The falling part of the profile after the peak is the response to the depletion of n at higher temperatures when the surface coverage of reactant is decreasing rapidly. Theory (the details of which are beyond the present scope) predicts that the peak in the record corresponds to the maximum rate of desorption of the product concerned. The temperature (T_M) at which this maximum appears in the recorded profile is independent of the initial coverage by reactant species for a first order surface reaction (equation 4.1) but decreases with increasing initial coverage for a second order process (equation 4.2). A series of experiments using different amounts of initial adsorbate will therefore allow determination of the order concerned.

When a chemical conversion takes place on a surface prior to easy desorption of the product(s), basic points can be drawn as follows.

1. The values of T_M indicate relative rates of reaction on the surface, with higher values of T_M corresponding to higher activation energies.
2. Integrated areas under the recorded profile for a species are proportional to the amount of that product formed.
3. Different species which evolve with the same value of T_M and matching peak profiles originate from a common rate determining reaction on the surface.
4. There is an empirical proportionality between T_M and E_d which translates in a reasonable approximation as $T_M/K \approx 3.8\ E_d/\text{kJ mol}^{-1}$.

The application of these principles and the general method are illustrated through several examples.

Figure 4.4 shows the record obtained from an experiment in which formic acid (HCOOH) is adsorbed initially at a temperature of 200 K on to a copper (110) surface. The temperature is then raised at a rate of

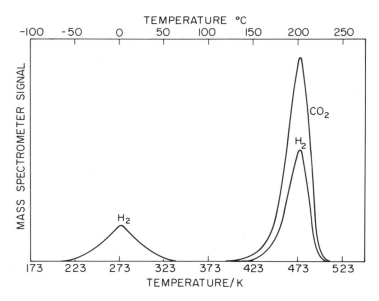

Fig. 4.4 Temperature-programmed reaction spectrum of formic acid adsorbed on copper (110) crystal face. Reproduced with permission of Academic Press Inc. from *Thermal desorption study of formic acid decomposition on a clean Cu(110) surface*, D. H. S. Ying and R. J. Madix (1980), *Journal of Catalysis*, **61**, 49.

approximately $10 \, K \, s^{-1}$. Two products are evolved: hydrogen gives two peaks, that at the higher temperatures matching the peak of carbon dioxide. Similar patterns of peaks have been observed in TPRS experiments with formic acid adsorbed on crystal faces of other metals, including gold, silver and platinum. The record shown in Fig. 4.4 appears to be explained by the mechanism below

$$\left.\begin{array}{l} HCOOH(ads) \rightarrow HCOO(ads) + H(ads) \\ \quad\quad 2H(ads) \rightarrow H_2(g) \end{array}\right\} \quad 275 \, K \, peak$$

$$\left.\begin{array}{l} 2HCOO(ads) \rightarrow CO_2(g) + H(ads) \\ \quad\quad 2H(ads) \rightarrow H_2(g) \end{array}\right\} \quad 475 \, K \, peaks$$

As before (ads) is used to indicate chemisorbed species. The hydrogen and carbon dioxide peaks centred on the temperature of 475 K are identical when normalized. This points to the generation of H_2 and CO_2 from the reaction of a common adsorbed precursor, evidently the formate species HCOO(ads). In other words it is the thermal decomposition of HCOO(ads) which is the rate determining step for the evolution of carbon dioxide and the second phase of hydrogen evolution. The rate of this reaction, according to Fig. 4.4, becomes significant when the copper surface reaches a temperature of about 400 K and becomes a maximum at about 475 K. It is easy to demonstrate that the actual desorption processes of hydrogen and carbon dioxide are not limiting kinetically. When these gases themselves are adsorbed on to the copper surface, they give rise to thermal desorption peaks at temperatures much lower than 475 K. At this point it is appropriate to anticipate the abilities of other techniques to identify species at surfaces by virtue of their spectroscopic characteristics. When the electron energy loss (EELS) technique (Section 4.4.2) was applied to the copper surface concerned here at temperatures between ambient and 400 K, the pattern of loss peaks observed corresponded to that expected of the formate species. Furthermore formate adsorbed on the Cu(110) surface has also been identified by infrared reflection absorption spectroscopy (IRAS) (Section 4.4.6): this revealed that the formate species is bonded to the surface through its two oxygen atoms in a bidentate or bridged form (i.e. with the two oxygen atoms in equivalent positions relative to the surface) and with its molecular plane essentially perpendicular to the surface. All of these experiments then confirm the postulate implied by the above mechanism that the formate species is stable on the Cu(110) surface in the temperature range between the two hydrogen peaks shown in Fig. 4.4. Equally they support the postulate that formic acid is dissociatively chemisorbed on Cu(110), with cleavage of the oxygen–hydrogen bond, at temperatures just above 200 K.

A second example of the application of the TPRS technique concerns the interactions of carbon monoxide with nickel surfaces, a (111) crystal face and a cleaved surface $5(111) \times (110)$ or $(7,9,11)$. Carbon monoxide was the only species desorbed and Fig. 4.5 shows three records of experiments conducted with temperature rise rates of $16 \, \text{K s}^{-1}$. Using the perfect crystal face (Fig. 4.5(a)), a single peak is observed: this can only correspond to desorption of carbon monoxide which has been chemisorbed molecularly, preserving the carbon–oxygen linkage. This experiment may be regarded as producing a thermal desorption spectrum (Section 2.3.2). Such a peak is termed the α peak conventionally. In Fig. 4.5(b), a second peak appears at higher temperature. The effect of subjecting adsorbed carbon monoxide to bombardment by electrons is partial dissociation with the generation of chemisorbed carbon atoms and oxygen atoms. The energy supplied by the

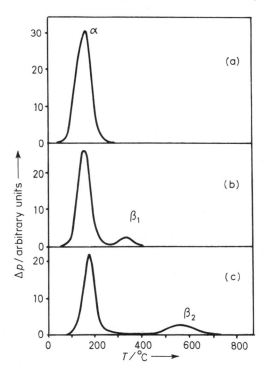

Fig. 4.5 Profiles corresponding to the desorption of carbon monoxide (measured by Δp) as a function of temperature (T) from nickel surfaces: (a) Ni(111), (b) Ni(111) when the initially dosed surface has been subjected to an electron beam ($150 \, \mu\text{A}$ for 10 minutes over an area of $1 \, \text{mm}^2$) and (c) a cleaved nickel surface. $T/^\circ\text{C} = T/\text{K} - 273$. Reproduced from *Thermal desorption of CO on a stepped Ni surface*, W. Erley and H. Wagner (1978) *Surface Science*, **74**, 337 by permission of Elsevier Science Publishers B.V.

electrons is used to overcome an activation energy barrier between molecularly adsorbed carbon monoxide and the dissociatively chemisorbed state. The interpretation of the second (β_1) peak is that this evolution of carbon monoxide originates from the association of the chemisorbed atoms on the crystal surface: this process is characterized by a larger activation energy than that governing desorption of molecularly adsorbed carbon monoxide. The stepped nickel surface concerned in Fig. 4.5(c) gives rise to the α peak and a second peak (β_2), the latter displaced to considerably higher temperatures than the β_1 peak in (b). Carbon monoxide is evidently dissociatively chemisorbed to some extent on the stepped surface, in contrast to its completely non-dissociative chemisorption on the crystal face in (a). This provides direct evidence of the point made in Section 4.1 concerning the promotion of heterogeneous chemical activity by surface defects. The desorption process corresponding to the β peaks can be represented generally as

$$C(ads) + O(ads) \rightarrow CO(g)$$

The temperature difference between the β_1 and β_2 peaks must then be interpreted in terms of atoms being chemisorbed at different types of surface sites. Since the β_1 peak in (b) corresponds to atoms chemisorbed on a perfect crystal face, the β_2 peak in (c) must originate from atoms of carbon and oxygen adsorbed more firmly at sites other than those within the terraces (111) of the stepped surface. Inevitably this leads to the conclusions that sites associated with the steps promote dissociative chemisorption of carbon monoxide and that the chemisorption bonds to the resultant atoms are relatively stronger at these sites. These observations then bear out the point made in Section 4.1 that defects on surfaces are often the main sites of catalytic action.

The last example in this section also centres on carbon monoxide, illustrating important promotional effects induced by the presence of alkali metals, typically potassium on transition metal surfaces. Figure 4.6 shows thermal desorption spectra of carbon monoxide (initially adsorbed at ambient temperature) on a platinum crystal face upon which potassium has been deposited to varying extents. The peak in the lowest spectrum ($\theta_K = 0$) is evidently an α peak. Within the lower range of values of θ_K, the α peak moves to higher temperatures as θ_K increases (e.g. from 520 K ($\theta_K = 0$) to 550 K ($\theta_K = 0.3$)). This indicates a significant increase in the strength of bonding between molecularly chemisorbed carbon monoxide and the platinum surface as the amount of potassium thereon rises. The interpretation of this effect will be discussed in Section 5.1. The sharp peak appearing to the right of the α peak at the higher values of θ_K is thought to reflect the formation of surface complexes (of type CO–K–Pt) when the potassium creates an effective surface phase.

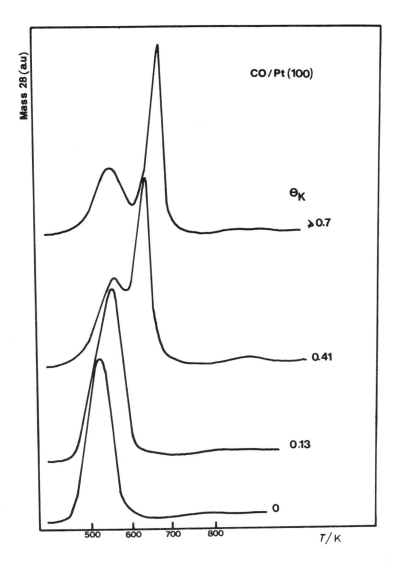

Fig. 4.6 Thermal desorption spectra of carbon monoxide, measured mass spectrometrically at mass 28 (atomic units (a.u.)), on a platinum (100) crystal face upon which potassium has been pre-adsorbed to a surface coverage of θ_K. In each case a constant exposure to carbon monoxide at a temperature of 300 K has been made prior to the programmed temperature rise. The experiments were performed in a UHV chamber working at pressures in the 10^{-8} Pa range. Reproduced from *The influence of potassium and the role of coadsorbed oxygen on the chemisorptive properties of Pt(100)*, J. C. Bertolini, P. Delichère and J. Massardier (1985) *Surface Science*, **160**, 536 by permission of Elsevier Science Publishers B.V.

It is clear that thermal desorption methods may provide useful information in themselves. But their greatest power is achieved when they are used in conjunction with techniques which identify directly the species existing on the surface concerned.

4.3.2 *Secondary ion mass spectrometry (SIMS)*

The principle of this technique is that when a surface is bombarded with an energetic beam of primary ions, fragments of the uppermost layers are detached from the surface in the form of secondary ions. These are identified by mass spectrometry. The SIMS technique is thus inherently destructive of a layer produced by chemisorption. Evidently the experimenter would wish the rate at which the chemisorbed species are stripped off to be reasonably slow, in order to allow sufficient time for full investigation. Accordingly in what is termed the static secondary ion mass spectrometry (SSIMS) method, the intensity of the primary beam is low enough to allow a surface monolayer to be gradually depleted over times of the order of several hours. The typical primary ions are argon (Ar^+) with kinetic energies in the range 500 to 3000 eV. In a typical SSIMS experiment, the intensity of the primary ion beam would correspond to an electrical current of the order of 10^{-9} A and it would impinge on a surface area of 10^{-4} m^2 for a period of 10^2 to 10^3 s. Under these conditions the extent of removal of a chemisorbed layer is insignificant. The chamber in which the experiments are conducted must be evacuated to pressures below 10^{-5} Pa and more generally to UHV levels. A quadrupole mass filter provides a convenient detection facility, the limiting sensitivity extending down to of the order of 10^{-17} kg of secondary ions in some cases.

One interesting example of the application of SSIMS concerns the reaction of carbon monoxide and hydrogen on a nickel crystal face (111). This was performed using a crystal transference system. The clean Ni(111) surface was exposed to a carbon monoxide–hydrogen (deuterium) mixture under conditions which induced the catalytic methanation reaction

$$2CO + 2H_2 \rightarrow CH_4 + CO_2$$

The nickel crystal was then cooled to ambient temperature and was mechanically-transferred using a valveless mechanism to a UHV chamber within which the SSIMS investigations were made. Figure 4.7 shows the resultant mass spectra. These spectra reveal directly the presence of the CH_x species, chemisorbed on the nickel atoms at the surface as manifested in spectrum (b); these are considered to be the key intermediates in catalysed methanation over nickel (Section 8.4). Spectrum (c) shows the deuterated forms which confirm that the parent surface species form from the reactant gases. A similar experiment with labelled ^{13}CO yielded $Ni^{13}CH_x^+$ cluster ions, again confirming that these species form from reactant gases and not from any contaminant sources. The variation of the signals corresponding to each CH_x species as the reactor temperature was

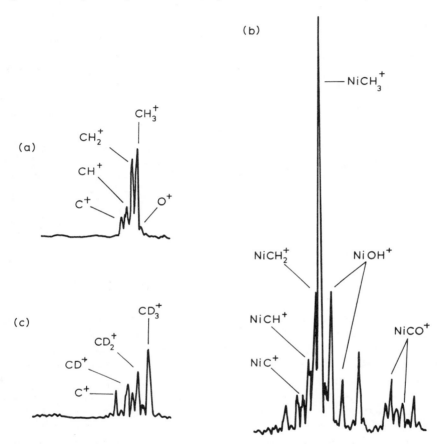

Fig. 4.7 SSIMS spectra obtained from bombarding a nickel(111) surface with an argon (Ar^+) ion beam (3000 eV, $<5 \times 10^{-9}$ A) under UHV conditions after transference from a batch reactor in which it catalysed the reaction of CO + H_2 (D_2) (1 : 4 v/v) mixtures at temperatures in the range 473–573 K and total pressures of 6–13 kPa for 30–60 minutes, forming CO_2 and CH_4. Mass spectra (signal intensity *versus* mass number) are shown for (a) the low mass region (CO + H_2), (b) the high mass region (CO + H_2) and (c) the low mass region (CO + D_2). Reprinted with permission from *Direct SIMS observation of methylidene, methylene and methyl intermediates on a Ni(111) methanation catalyst*, M. P. Kaminsky, N. Winograd, G. L. Geoffroy and M. A. Vannice (1986), *Journal of the American Chemical Society*, **108**, 1315. Copyright 1986 American Chemical Society.

varied also proved to be interesting. The CH_2^+ ion signal decreased in intensity above 411 K, the CH_3^+ ion signal remained constant below 443 K, the CH^+ ion signal only decreased above 483 K while the C^+ ion preserved almost constant signal intensity over the temperature range 340 to 523 K. These observations suggest that CH is the CH_x species which is most tightly bound to the nickel and that C^+ arises mainly from a highly stable, graphitic form of carbon formed on the surface in the course of the methanation reaction. Nevertheless the observation that CH, CH_2 and CH_3 chemisorbed species have surface concentrations of the same order of magnitude suggests that these species have not very different stabilities on the nickel surface.

One of the major problems in the interpretation of results from SSIMS techniques is the necessity for back tracing to establish the relationship of a detected secondary ion to species actually present on the surface. On many occasions this is not straightforward. Thus although SIMS provides in principle one of the most sensitive methods for the detection of chemisorbed species, its application has in fact been rather limited in comparison with the other techniques discussed in this chapter.

4.4 Non-destructive techniques for surface investigation

4.4.1 *Low energy electron diffraction (LEED)*

Electrons are diffracted, on account of their associated wave nature, when they enter ordered surfaces. The electrons which are elastically scattered (i.e. without loss of energy) as a consequence carry information on the arrangements of atoms at the surface. It was in 1970 that the LEED technique became fully developed for the analysis of surface structures. Before then, experimental and theoretical bases were not available to relate fully diffraction patterns to the nature of species adsorbed on a surface.

One key factor in the use of electrons as probes of surface structure is the ease with which they are scattered by atoms. Figure 4.8 shows the average depths below surfaces from which electrons may escape as a function of their energies. The inserted points for various chemical elements suggest an insensitivity of the escape depth to the chemical nature of the material providing the surface. The average escape depth in the minimum region of the diagram is approximately 0.4 nm, corresponding to roughly three atomic layers. Thus for electrons having any energy in the range 10 to 1000 eV, if they penetrate into (or, under circumstances relevant to other techniques, are generated within) a surface at depths corresponding to five or more atomic layers, they will not emerge from the surface. Such electrons are trapped and lost to the electron cloud within a bulk metal.

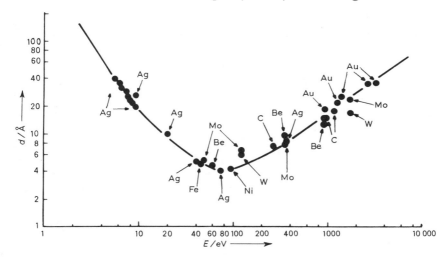

Fig. 4.8 Average escape depths (*d*) of electrons from elemental surfaces as a function of their energy (*E*) (1 Å = 0.1 nm). Reproduced from *Elementary processes at gas/metal interfaces*, G. Ertl (1976), *Angewandte Chemie (International Edition)*, **15**, 392 with permission from VCH Verlagsgesellschaft Verlagsleitung, Weinheim.

Another key factor for electrons is that their scattering coefficient (corresponding to the optical absorption coefficient appearing in the familiar Beer–Lambert equation for light) in a metal is some six orders of magnitude greater than the scattering coefficient for X-rays. This means that electrons are very highly sensitive to surface structures, to the extent that they can provide quantitative information for a small fraction of a monolayer of an ordered adsorbate. But equally this high sensitivity also requires that the surface must be substantially free of contaminant species. For LEED, the target surface must be pre-cleaned at the atomic level, an operation now performed routinely by procedures such as ion bombardment and annealing under UHV conditions. It is also apparent that LEED experiments must be conducted under UHV conditions to avoid scattering of electrons in the gas phase.

The incident beam in LEED experiments consists of monoenergetic electrons. The energy (*E*) of these electrons is dictated by the corresponding wavelength (λ) according to the de Broglie equation incorporating electron mass (*m*) and linear velocity (*v*).

$$\lambda = \frac{h}{mv} = \frac{h}{(2mE)^{\frac{1}{2}}} \tag{4.3}$$

(*h* = Planck's constant = 6.625×10^{-34} J s)

For E equivalent to 150 eV, the corresponding wavelength is 0.10 nm, similar to interatomic distances in surface structures. Thus diffraction is expected for these low energy electrons, with back scattered electrons carrying structural information on the surface layers.

The experimental arrangement for the LEED technique resembles that used in the Laue method for X-ray diffraction in basic respects. A collimated electron beam (replacing the X-ray beam in the Laue method) impinges on to the target surface. Electrons undergo back scattering in those directions which satisfy the Laue conditions regarding lattice periodicity (i.e. waves in phase with one another). In addition to the elastically scattered electrons, electrons with lower energies also emerge, the results of inelastic scattering and secondary processes: these are stopped by a gauze–grid system which sets up suitable electrical potential gradients. Finally the elastically scattered electrons are accelerated on to a fluorescent screen by a potential of several thousand volts, when they produce bright spots of light which are clearly visible and can be photographed. The magnitude and distribution of the intensity within a spot may be determined photometrically: alternatively the fluorescent screen can be replaced with a movable electron collecting device, which allows the current in specified directions to be measured. The basic features of a LEED system are represented in Fig. 4.9.

The full theoretical analysis of LEED patterns of spots requires application of the dynamical theory of diffraction, incorporating multiple scattering effects. In principle this can relate both the positions and intensities of spots in a diffraction pattern to parameters in the surface structure. The details of this type of analysis are beyond the scope of this book. In outline, the angular directions of the diffracted beams indicate the nature of the adsorbed species whilst the spot intensities can be related to

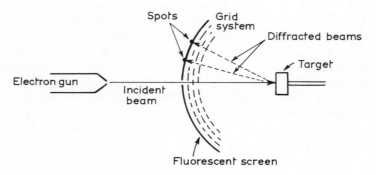

Fig. 4.9 Representation of the arrangement of the basic components of a LEED system, all of which are contained in a UHV chamber.

Table 4.2 Bond lengths measured by the LEED technique and predictions for covalent bonds

Surface–Adsorbate	Bond length/nm	
	Predicted	Measured
Ni(111)–H	0.160	0.184
Fe(100)–O	0.208	0.208
W(100)–N	0.222	0.224
Ni(100)–S	0.235	0.219
Cu(100)–Cl	0.235	0.238
Rh(110)–S	0.250	0.239

Reproduced from *Analysis of Surface Bond Lengths Reported for Chemisorption on Metal Surfaces*, by K. A. R. Mitchell, *Surface Science* (1985) **149**, 93–104 by permission of North-Holland Physics Publishing, Amsterdam.

interatomic distances. It is usual practice to devise trial models of adsorbed structures and to vary parameters in these until a match is obtained between the predicted and experimental LEED patterns. The ultimate proving of a specific model is the maintenance of agreement between these patterns when the experimental parameters such as energy and angle of incidence of the electron beam are varied. At present, the large majority of cases for which detailed analysis has been achieved are those for atomic species chemisorbed on low index faces of metals. The degree of complexity rises sharply when the adsorbate is molecular. Carbon monoxide adsorbed molecularly on nickel crystal faces provides one of the few instances in which the microscopic superstructure on the surface has been established with confidence.

Table 4.2 shows a selection of bond lengths which have been determined for atoms chemisorbed on low index faces of metals. These measured values are compared with predicted values, evaluated using Slater hard sphere radii for both atoms concerned. The reasonably close agreement between experimental and predicted values implies that the bonds to the surfaces are largely covalent in nature.

Most often in studies of interest from the viewpoint of catalysis, the LEED technique is used in a diagnostic mode. Adsorption on a surface is marked by a change in the pattern of spots when a gas is contacted with a clean surface. Different adsorbed species give rise to different patterns of spots. One instance of this mode of application commences from the patterns of diffraction spots represented in Fig. 4.10. These diagrams show that the different crystal faces of the metal give rise to characteristic spot

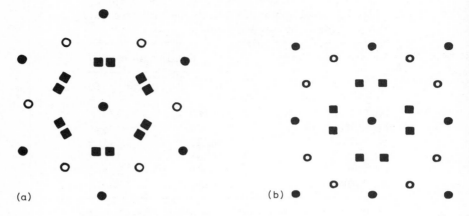

Fig. 4.10 Diagrams representing the patterns of diffraction spots obtained in LEED experiments on rhodium crystal faces before and after contact with carbon monoxide at temperatures just below ambient. The symbols used to locate the relative positions of the diffraction spots are as follows: ● = spot originating from the rhodium surface, ○ = spot originating from a carbon monoxide overlayer, ■ = double spot (overlapping spots) originating from both rhodium and carbon monoxide lattices. (a) Rh(111) surface using 71 eV electrons, (b) Rh(100) surface using 59 eV electrons. Reproduced from *LEED and thermal desorption studies of small molecules* (H_2, O_2, CO, CO_2, NO, C_2H_4, C_2H_2 *and* C) *chemisorbed on the rhodium (111) and (100) surfaces*, D. G. Castner, B. A. Sexton and G. A. Somorjai (1978) *Surface Science*, **71**, 529, 531, by permission of Elsevier Science Publishers B.V.

patterns. When carbon monoxide is chemisorbed molecularly, its presence on the rhodium surfaces gives rise to indicative spots. The diagnosis was made on the basis that these carbon monoxide spots appeared also when carbon dioxide was contacted with the surfaces concerned, providing clear evidence for its dissociative chemisorption.

The LEED technique can also be applied to slightly imperfect surfaces, containing defects such as steps. The key feature in this connection is the shape of the diffraction spots as manifested by their intensity profiles. When the surface microstructure may be described as an arrangement of units with some regularity (such as islands of adsorbed species at steps, separated by bare intervening terraces), the spot shape can be matched by predictions from models; the procedure uses relatively low levels of computational resources. A basic set of predicted profiles of spots for various simple microstructural features can be created, so that extrapolation can be made to more complex situations by way of combinations of the basic profiles. Further details of how a LEED diffraction pattern can be used to elucidate defect structures on surfaces are beyond our present scope.

The LEED technique is usually applied in conjunction with other techniques to obtain information on surfaces of interest in catalysis. Combination of the various types of information would then be expected to lead to a secure interpretation of mechanisms involved in catalytic reaction *via* the intermediate species identified.

4.4.2 *Electron energy loss spectroscopy (EELS)*

EELS may be regarded as the technique complementary to LEED. In LEED it is the elastically scattered electrons which are of interest. In EELS it is those electrons which have lost energy in inelastic scattering which are investigated to provide information on species existing at the surface. Over the past decade or so, the energy resolution which is possible with respect to both the incident and scattered electrons has been improved markedly. The present EELS technique is often referred to accordingly as high resolution electron energy loss spectroscopy (HREELS).

Basically the EELS technique relies upon quantitative energy conversion, in which a small part of the kinetic energy of the incident electrons becomes vibrational energy in the bonds existing at the surface. In some respects EELS is analogous to optical Raman spectroscopy in which the result is the conversion of a small part of the energy of a photon of light into excitation within the internal modes of a molecule. In HREELS systems, a beam of monoenergetic electrons (energy in the range 1 to 10 eV with a spread about the mean of at most 0.01 eV) is directed on to the target surface, usually a crystal face. At these low energies, the impinging electrons achieve interaction with the chemical bonds at the surface through phenomena involving both long- and short-range forces: the details of these need not be of concern here. As a consequence, some of the electrons which are back scattered from the surface have suffered energy losses of the order of 0.1 eV, corresponding in size to the separations of quantized vibrational levels of adsorbed species on the surface. The energy spectrum of inelastically scattered electrons will therefore show distinct features corresponding to characteristic vibrational frequencies (or wavenumbers) of species existing at the surface, allowing their detection and identification.

Not only does HREELS give direct information on the nature of species adsorbed at surfaces, but it is also a highly sensitive technique having the ability to respond to of the order of 10^{-3} of a monolayer of carbon monoxide for example. The resolution which may in fact be obtained in HREELS systems (equivalent to 30 to 40 cm^{-1} on the conventional

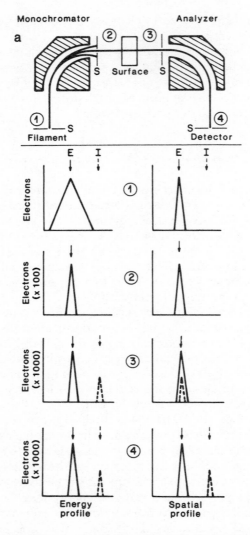

Fig. 4.11 Schematic diagram of a conventional high-resolution electron energy loss spectroscopy (HREELS) system. The lower panels show both the energy and spatial profiles of the electron beam at the points (1) monochromator entrance, (2) monochromator exit (note the action of the slit S), (3) analyser entrance (dashed line represents inelastically-scattered electrons (I), full line represents elastically-scattered electrons (E)) and (4) the detector. The vertical scale changes as the electrons traverse the spectrometer, with losses due to selection by slits (S) and to the low reflectivity of most surfaces. Reproduced with permission from *Time-resolved electron energy loss spectroscopy*, T. H. Ellis, L. H. Dubois, S. D. Kevan and M. J. Cardillo (1985) *Science*, 230, 258. Copyright 1985 by the AAAS.

wavenumber scale) is low in comparison with that obtainable in infrared spectroscopy. However HREELS offers the much better sensitivity, in particular in the region of low vibrational frequencies below 1.5×10^{13} Hz (500 cm^{-1} in wavenumber) which are found in many adsorption situations.

The chambers in which EELS measurements are made must be evacuated to UHV conditions, both to maintain uncontaminated surfaces and to eliminate significant scattering of electrons by gas phase molecules. Figure 4.11 is a schematic representation of the central features of HREELS systems; in addition it represents energy and spatial distribution

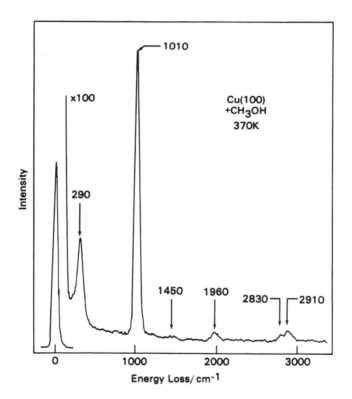

Fig. 4.12 HREELS spectrum of a copper (100) face upon which a monolayer of oxygen and then excess methanol have been adsorbed at a temperature of 100 K before the temperature is raised to 370 K. The electron beam energy was 5 eV. The numbers labelling peaks in the diagram are wavenumbers/cm^{-1} corresponding to selective energy losses. Reproduced with permission of Springer Verlag Inc. from *Identification of adsorbed species at metal surfaces by electron energy loss spectroscopy*, B. A. Sexton (1981) *Applied Physics*, A 26, 13.

profiles of the elastically (E) and inelastically (I) scattered electrons at the locations indicated by the inserted numbers. The hemispherical electron monochromator and analyser rely for their operation upon the dependence of the deflection force produced by an electrical field (created by application of a voltage) in the curved channels upon the velocity and hence the kinetic energy of the electrons. The voltage applied across the analyser is changed steadily to reveal the spectrum of energy losses as a function of the kinetic energies of inelastically scattered electrons.

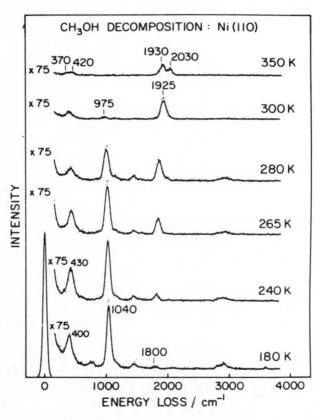

Fig. 4.13 HREELS spectra of a nickel (110) face upon which methanol (CH_3OH) has been adsorbed at a temperature of 80 K. The surface was heated to the temperature indicated at the right of each trace and then cooled to 80 K prior to recording the spectrum. Reproduced from *Characterization of the adsorption and decomposition of methanol on Ni (110)*, S. R. Bare, J. A. Stroscio and W. Ho (1985) *Surface Science,* **150**, 412 with permission of Elsevier Science Publishers B.V.

The value of the HREELS technique in gaining information relevant to the mechanisms of catalytic reactions is now illustrated for two systems pertinent to methanol oxidation. In the presence of oxygen at temperatures of the order of 450 K, methanol is partially oxidized to formaldehyde over a copper surface but is completely (or deeply) oxidized over a nickel surface. Figure 4.12 shows the spectrum of the intensity of energy losses obtained when oxygen and then methanol are adsorbed onto a copper (100) surface. Figure 4.13 shows a series of EELS spectra which were obtained when methanol was initially contacted with a nickel (110) surface at a temperature of 80 K and the surface was heated thereafter to the temperatures indicated. Table 4.3 lists the assignments of the observed loss peaks corresponding to chemisorbed methoxy (CH_3O) species in Fig. 4.12 (at 370 K) and in Fig. 4.13 (at 180 K).

Figure 4.13 shows that methoxy exists on the surface of nickel at temperatures of 180 K and 280 K, but also that significant changes occur as the temperature rises across this range. The growing peak in the wavenumber range 1800–1930 cm^{-1} corresponds to the C—O stretching vibration of molecularly adsorbed carbon monoxide. At temperatures above 280 K, this carbon monoxide peak appears rather than the spectrum of methoxy, indicating the instability of the latter. But the basic point to be taken from Fig. 4.12 is that methoxy is a stable adsorbed species on a copper surface at temperatures up to 370 K under UHV conditions. Other observations have shown that on copper(100) at higher temperatures, methoxy becomes unstable leading to the evolution of formaldehyde (HCHO) and hydrogen into the gas phase. The corresponding conversion

Table 4.3 Assignment of loss peaks in HREELS spectra of adsorbed methoxy species

Figure 4.12 Surface Cu(100) Temperature 370 K			Figure 4.13 Surface Ni(110) Temperature 180 K	
Loss-peak wavenumber /cm^{-1}	Energy loss /meV	Loss-peak assignment*	Loss-peak wavenumber /cm^{-1}	Energy loss /meV
290	36	metal–O	400	50
1010	125	C–O	1040	129
1450	180	CH_3 deformation	1440	179
2830	351	C–H (symmetric)	2790	346
2910	361	C–H (antisymmetric)	2910	361

* Stretching modes unless otherwise indicated.

process would be represented by the chemical equation

$$2CH_3O \text{ (ads)} \rightarrow 2HCHO(g) + H_2(g)$$

There is a significant item of additional information of relevance to this process. It has been found that when formaldehyde is adsorbed on a copper(110) face, for example, the activation energy for cleavage of one of its C—H bonds is 92 kJ mol^{-1}. In fact this exceeds considerably the surface binding energy of chemisorbed formaldehyde, evaluated as 54 kJ mol^{-1}. Thus, when it is formed on copper surfaces, formaldehyde will tend to desorb intact rather than to undergo dehydrogenation. On the other hand, Fig. 4.13 indicates that adsorbed methoxy is only stable on a nickel surface at temperatures below ambient. When the temperature of the Ni(110) surface is raised above 240 K, the EELS spectrum begins to change indicating that a surface dehydrogenation process is occurring which may be represented by the equation

$$CH_3O(\text{ads}) \rightarrow CO(\text{ads}) + 3H(\text{ads})$$

On nickel surfaces therefore it may be presumed that any formaldehyde formed is subject to dehydrogenation and is unlikely to desorb intact, in evident contrast to the situation on copper surfaces.

These observations suggest that the partial oxidation of methanol to formaldehyde, dependent upon the stability of the methoxy radical and the desorption of formaldehyde, will be promoted on copper surfaces. But on nickel surfaces at normal temperatures for oxidation, methanol simply serves as a source of adsorbed carbon monoxide and hydrogen, the subsequent oxidations of which complete the deep oxidation of methanol. This rationalization supports the view that observations made under UHV conditions can be highly significant for real catalytic processes.

4.4.3 *Auger electron spectroscopy (AES)*

Highly energetic electrons are involved in AES and also in the photoelectron spectroscopic techniques to be described in the next subsection. In the AES technique, the target surface is subjected to a beam of monoenergetic electrons, with typical energy in the range 1000 to 3000 eV. The result is the emission of secondary electrons with energies typically in the range 100 to 500 eV. It is indicated in Fig. 4.8 that the mean free pathlengths of these in the solid surface are in the range 0.4–0.8 nm. Thus the emitted electrons carry information on the topmost atomic layers of the surface.

The primary electrons cause ionization within the target material by inducing the ejection of electrons from core orbitals, generally the K or L shells, of atoms. The resultant electron holes are repopulated by electrons falling from higher orbitals in the atom. The energy liberated as a result of one such electronic transition can be transferred non-radiatively to another bound electron in the atom concerned: this is ejected subsequently as a secondary electron, the so-called Auger electron, and its kinetic energy reflects the nature of the parent atom and its microenvironment. Also the rate of emission of the Auger electrons with a particular kinetic energy is proportional to the number of source atoms in the target surface when the intensity of the primary electron beam is held constant. Thus the AES technique can serve as a means for obtaining both qualitative and quantitative information on the nature of surfaces.

The area of surface investigated at one instant in an AES experiment is governed by the absorption characteristics for the primary electrons; it is typically of the order of $1 \, mm^2$. Of necessity the technique is applied under UHV conditions. Moreover the high sensitivity of AES detection means that contaminant species must be removed from the target surface prior to an experiment; ion-bombardment and annealing can be used for this purpose. The technique is potentially destructive but it can be applied so that significant damage is not produced in the structures on the surface within the time required to make a series of AES measurements. For this reason the electron flux densities in the primary beam are restricted usually to the equivalent of current densities of the order of $0.1 \, A \, m^{-2}$. It may be remarked that physisorbed or weakly chemisorbed species are rather susceptible to beam damage and are not investigated by AES methods generally.

The experimental arrangements for AES investigations usually incorporate an electron gun to generate the primary beam. The spectrum of Auger electrons as a function of their kinetic energies may be revealed using an electron beam analyser of the type shown in Fig. 4.11. Alternatively the type of system shown in Fig. 4.9 (in connection with LEED) may be adapted by the replacement of the fluorescent screen with an electron collecting concave surface, using the grids (typically four in number) in a retarding-field analysing mode. AES spectra are often obtained in the differential form, displaying the first derivatives (dN/dE) of profiles of the number (N) of Auger electrons as a function of their energy (E). The resultant derivative profile (dN/dE *versus* E) has the effect of sharpening features in the spectrum and thus aids the detection of small amounts of species on surfaces. Figure 4.14(a) shows the full AES spectra recorded for an iron(110) crystal face as the target, 'clean' (labelled (A)) and after contact with a mixture of carbon monoxide and hydrogen (labelled (B)). The higher resolution section of the latter spectrum shown as Fig. 4.14(b) indicates there are different microenvironments of the carbon atoms (i.e. different carbonaceous phases) when contact times and temperatures are varied. The phases indicated as I and II are believed to be adsorbed CH_x species (c.f. Fig. 4.7) and a carbidic–carbon layer with bonded hydrogen respectively. Such species are likely to be significant as intermediates in the syntheses of hydrocarbons from carbon monoxide–hydrogen mixtures, which are usually conducted on iron catalysts (Section 8.4).

AES spectra 'fingerprint' particular species in the sense that sharp features appearing at particular energies in the spectra will correspond for the atoms of one chemical element contained within the same

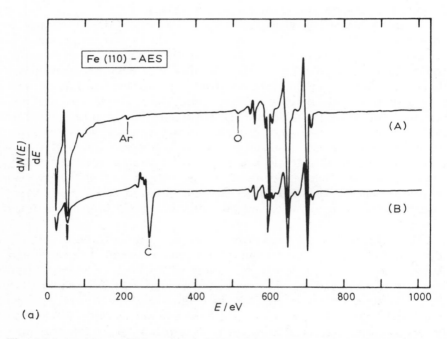

(a)

Fig. 4.14 (a) Auger (AES) spectra of iron (110) face (A) nearly clean with small peaks due to residual argon and oxygen and (B) after exposure to a carbon monoxide/hydrogen mixture (1 : 20 v/v) at a temperature of 615 K for 90 minutes. $N(E)$ is the number of Auger electrons emitted with energy E. The C peak indicates the presence of carbonaceous phases on the surface. (b) Carbon Auger electron spectra of the three carbonaceous phases formed on the iron (110) face after contact with a carbon monoxide/hydrogen mixture (1 : 20 v/v) at a pressure of 1 bar for times (t) at a temperature (T) as follows. Phase I: $T = 565$ K, $t = 15$ s. Phase II: $T = 615$ K, $t = 15$ s. Phase III: $T = 615$ K, $t = 90$ min. Reproduced from *On the chemical nature of the carbonaceous deposits on iron after* CO *hydrogenation*, H. P. Bonzel and H. J. Krebs (1980) *Surface Science*, **91**, 502, 501 with permission from Elsevier Science Publishers B.V.

microenvironment but on different surfaces. This point can be illustrated for systems in which nitric oxide (NO) is chemisorbed on crystal faces of various metals. On ruthenium at a low temperature of 83 K, the introduction of NO gave rise to several sharp features in the part of the AES spectrum corresponding to emission of Auger electrons from a nitrogen atom. Similar features are encountered in the AES spectrum of gaseous NO, which implies that the NO was molecularly chemisorbed on ruthenium at 83 K. In contrast, a very different set of features appeared in the AES spectrum when nitric oxide contacted the same ruthenium surface

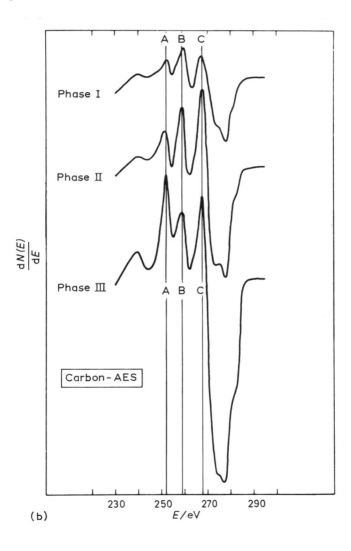

(b)

at the much higher temperature of 468 K. This set of features resembled those found when NO was adsorbed on the tungsten(110) face at ambient temperature. There is considerable evidence (obtained using other techniques) that nitric oxide is dissociatively chemisorbed on tungsten surfaces at similar temperatures, so that these AES spectral features can be assigned to chemisorbed nitrogen atoms. The inevitable conclusion is that nitric oxide is dissociatively chemisorbed on ruthenium at 468 K. These observations bear out the fact that the Auger electrons emerging from the atoms are very sensitive to the bonding state of these atoms at the surface concerned.

The AES technique may be used to investigate the spatial distribution of chemical elements on the surfaces of actual catalysts. An illustrative example is based on an ammonia synthesis catalyst prepared from magnetite (Fe_3O_4) fused with small amounts of the oxides of potassium, aluminium and calcium prior to its reduction. Table 4.4 lists compositional data for this so-called promoted catalyst, with the data for the surface compositions obtained using AES. This Table reveals the tendency for the surface of the material to be enriched strongly with the elements which are minor components in the bulk solid. Even more remarkable features of the surface are elucidated by moving the primary electron beam across the solid (termed the scanning AES mode), when the distributions of iron and potassium are revealed. Prior to reduction of the oxide, the potassium atoms are found to be congregated in islands on the surface. But following reduction, the potassium atoms are found to be spread rather uniformly across the iron surface. This led the original investigators to postulate that the active catalytic surface for the synthesis of ammonia was metallic iron covered typically with between 20% and 50% of a monolayer incorporating the elements potassium and oxygen. The origin of the resultant high activity for ammonia synthesis will be discussed in Section 5.1.

Table 4.4 Elemental compositions (atoms %) of a promoted iron catalyst

Phase	Element				
	Fe	K	Al	Ca	O
Bulk	40.5	0.35	2.0	1.7	53.2
Surface before reduction	8.6	36.1	10.7	4.7	40.0
Surface after reduction	11.0	27.0	17.0	4.0	41.0

Reproduced with permission of the American Institute of Physics from *Primary steps in catalytic synthesis of ammonia* by G. Ertl, *Journal of Vacuum Science and Technology (1983) A* **1**(2), April–June, 1247.

4.4.4 *Photoelectron spectroscopies (UPS, XPS)*

When a surface is subjected to very high energy radiation, electrons are ejected from the orbitals of constituent atoms generally. As in the AES technique, the kinetic energy of an emitted electron reflects the immediate surroundings of the parent atom. The binding energy (BE) of the electron in the parent atom is defined as equal to the difference between the initial photon energy ($h\nu$, where ν is the frequency of the monochromatic radiation used) and the maximum kinetic energy (KE) possessed by the electron when it is ejected:

$$BE = h\nu - KE \qquad (4.4)$$

There are two general variants of photoelectron spectroscopy, distinguished by the type of radiation used. In that termed ultraviolet photoelectron spectroscopy (UPS), short wavelength ultraviolet radiations (commonly the helium lines designated He I (21 eV energy, 59 nm wavelength) or He II (41 eV, 30 nm)) are used to cause the emission of electrons in the outer (valence) orbitals of species at the surface. In X-ray photoelectron spectroscopy (XPS), X-ray radiations (commonly Mg Kα (1254 eV, 0.98 nm) or Al Kα (1487 eV, 0.83 nm)) are used to eject inner electrons in the core orbitals of atoms in the target. In UPS the binding energies concerned are of the order of 10 eV, so that the kinetic energies of the emitted electrons (equation 4.4) are expected to be in the range 10–30 eV. In XPS both the binding and kinetic energies are expected to be of the order of hundreds of electron volts. Reference back to Fig. 4.8 shows that these electrons can only emerge from within the surface layers of the target without suffering inelastic scattering and thus having maximum kinetic energies. Under normal circumstances, about a third of the photoelectrons emitted without loss in energy originate from the outermost atomic layer, whilst the overwhelming majority of the remainder come from the next three atomic layers of an adsorbate–surface system.

Photoelectron spectroscopic experiments on surfaces must be conducted under UHV conditions, to avoid both attenuation of the radiation and scattering of electrons in the gas phase. A collimated beam of radiation from a helium discharge source (for UPS) or from an X-ray source (for XPS) is directed on to the target surface. The energy distribution of the emitted electrons may be measured using an analyser unit of the type shown in basic design in Fig. 4.11.

The situations created when carbon monoxide is contacted with an iron surface may be used to provide the first illustration of the investigative abilities of photoelectron spectroscopies. Figure 4.15(a) shows the XPS spectral features which result from the photoejection of electrons in the 1s orbital of the carbon atom (C(1s)), when the surface is subjected to the

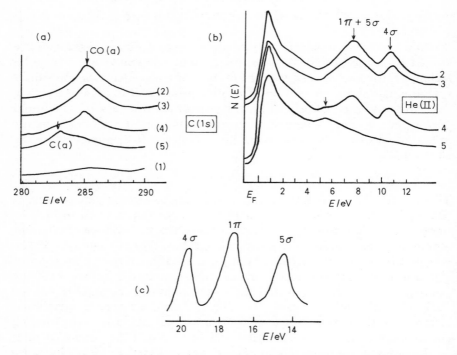

Fig. 4.15 (a) X-ray photoelectron spectra (plots of the number of photoelectrons *versus* binding energy) originating from the ejection of carbon (1s) electrons from a surface created initially by the adsorption of carbon monoxide on a polycrystalline iron film (atomically clean) at a temperature of 80 K. Al $K\alpha$ radiation is used. The spectra refer to the following conditions: (1) the clean iron surface, (2) after adsorption of CO at a temperature of 80 K, (3) and (4) during warming to the temperature of 300 K achieved in (5). (b) The corresponding ultraviolet photo-electron spectra obtained using He II radiation, with the orbitals of carbon monoxide from which the ejected electrons originate indicated. E_F locates the energy of the Fermi level of iron. (c) The ultraviolet photoelectron spectrum of gaseous carbon monoxide obtained using He II radiation. The horizontal scale represents the binding energy of electrons prior to ejection. Reproduced from *New approaches to surface chemistry*, M. W. Roberts (1982) *Science Progress Oxford*, **68**, 69 with permission of Blackwell Scientific Publications Ltd.

procedures indicated in the legend. Figure 4.15(b) shows the corresponding set of UPS spectral features, these resulting from the photoejection of various valence electrons of carbon monoxide from molecular orbitals designated as 4σ, 1π and 5σ. In Fig. 4.15(b), the binding energy scale is expressed relative to the so-called Fermi level (see Section 5.1 for definition) of iron and does not therefore give the actual binding energies directly. Figure 4.15(c) shows a UPS spectrum of carbon monoxide gas on a true binding energy scale. About 8 eV should be subtracted from the energies indicated to afford a comparison with the energy scale of Fig. 4.15(b). Figures 4.15(a) and (b) reveal immediately that the form in which carbon monoxide (CO) adsorbs on iron changes dramatically between temperatures of 80 K and 300 K. The only likely form at 80 K is molecularly adsorbed CO. Other evidence (for instance Fig. 4.14) indicates that at higher temperatures dissociative adsorption of CO occurs on iron surfaces. Thus the shift in the XPS peak in Figure 4.15(a) from the position marked as CO(a) to that marked as C(a) is the response to a change in the microenvironment of the carbon atom from molecularly adsorbed CO to the chemisorbed carbon form produced following cleavage of the carbon–oxygen bond. Figure 4.15(b) reveals the corresponding disappearance of the molecular orbital structure of CO in the UPS spectra, (2) to (5). Comparison of the UPS spectrum labelled (2) (corresponding to molecularly adsorbed CO) with that for gas phase CO in Fig. 4.15(c) shows that the relative energies of molecular orbitals are changed by the process of molecular chemisorption, as would be expected. Discussion of the molecular orbitals of CO and their involvement in bonding to metal surfaces will appear in Section 5.1. For the present the basic point to be drawn from Fig. 4.15 is the sensitivity of the photoelectron spectra to the nature of the species chemisorbed on the surface.

The second example is chosen to illustrate the ability of the XPS technique to measure parameters which enable the postulates of the Langmuir–Hinshelwood mechanism to be confirmed directly (Section 2.4.1). Carbon monoxide and oxygen undergo a catalysed reaction on iridium surfaces, represented as

$$CO + \tfrac{1}{2}O_2 \rightarrow CO_2$$

Oxygen would be expected to be dissociatively chemisorbed on transition metal surfaces (Section 2.3.2). On this basis the rate determining surface reaction in a Langmuir–Hinshelwood mechanism would be

$$O(ads) + CO(ads) \rightarrow CO_2$$

Application of the principle of mass action to a bimolecular process of this type would lead to a rate (R) proportionally expressed as

$$R \propto \theta_O \, \theta_{CO} \qquad (4.5)$$

where θ parameters represent the fraction of the surface covered by the subscripted species. The XPS spectral peaks corresponding to the ejection of electrons from oxygen $1s$ orbitals of these reactants appeared at different binding energies, near 532 eV for CO(ads) and near 530 eV for O(ads) on the iridium(111) crystal face used. Now the relative numbers of photoelectrons within particular peaks in XPS spectra taken using the same operational parameters are proportional to the number of the parent atoms present on the target surface. The number of incident X-ray photons absorbed by a particular type of atom will depend evidently upon the proportion of the photons impinging thereon, which in turn depends upon the corresponding surface concentration or coverage (θ) of the species concerned. Thus at a defined value of θ, a particular adsorbed species will induce the conversion in effect of a fixed proportion of the incident photons to ejected photoelectrons with the characteristic kinetic energy. Half of a monolayer of an adsorbed species would give rise therefore to a corresponding XPS peak one half of the size of that which would arise with the full monolayer. Thus in the example concerned, when carbon monoxide and oxygen were brought into contact with the iridium(111) surface, the sizes of the peaks near 532 eV and 530 eV could be related directly to the corresponding values of θ_{CO} and θ_O respectively. In this way corresponding values of surface coverages and the rate of reaction were obtained over ranges of gas phase partial pressures and temperatures. These conformed to equation (4.5) and thus confirmed the applicability of the Langmuir–Hinshelwood mechanism to this reaction system.

A third example illustrates the value of the XPS technique in quantitative investigations of adsorption isotherms (Section 2.3.1) by virtue of its ability to yield directly the surface concentrations of particular adsorbates. The surface used resulted from the vaporization of iron and its subsequent deposition on to a silica surface, performed under vacuum conditions. A preliminary point of interest is that the XPS peaks corresponding to the ejection of $2p$ electrons from the iron atoms on this surface appeared at the same binding energy as those from a metallic iron target. This reveals that the silica was acting simply as a physical support for the deposited iron and there was no chemical interaction between the iron and the support. The main interest concerned the adsorption of nitric oxide (NO) on this supported iron surface. Two peaks corresponding to the ejection of nitrogen $1s$ electrons appeared at binding energies of 396.7 eV and 400.6 eV in the resultant XPS spectrum at ambient temperature. The 396.7 eV peak was assigned to atomic nitrogen bound to the iron surface on the basis that a corresponding peak appeared in the XPS spectrum of iron nitride. The significance of this peak for the NO system is that it indicates dissociative chemisorption of the gas. The 400.6 eV peak originated from molecularly chemisorbed NO: it appeared in the XPS spectra of other systems in which NO was known to be adsorbed without dissociation. When nitric oxide was contacted with the iron supported on silica at elevated temperature (473 K), only the peak corresponding to dissociative chemisorption appeared in the XPS spectrum. This exemplifies a general point that dissociative chemisorption is more likely at higher temperatures, which is also apparent in connection with Fig. 4.15(a).

If a clean surface is contacted with a specified pressure of an adsorbing gas for a defined time and subsequently the adsorbed amount of this gas is retained when the surface is taken to UHV conditions, the number of molecules bound to the surface during the exposure may be deduced from the size of the corresponding XPS peak. The exposure concerned may be defined quantitatively as the pressure of the gas multiplied by the time of contact with the adsorbent surface. A unit used commonly for expressing exposure is the Langmuir (L), defined as equivalent to 1.33×10^{-4} Pa s. Figure 4.16 shows the variation of the size (relative intensity) of the XPS peak at 396.7 eV as a function of nitric oxide exposure on various supported iron surfaces at a temperature of 473 K. The form of these

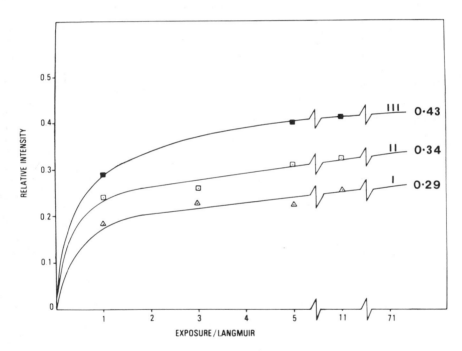

Fig. 4.16 Plots of the intensity of the XPS peak at a binding energy of 396.7 eV (corresponding to adsorbed atomic nitrogen) as a function of exposure to nitric oxide at a temperature of 473 K of iron-on-silica. Iron/silicon ratios increase in the order I, II, III. Reproduced from *Interactions of NO and SO₂ with iron deposited on silica*, R. V. Siriwardane and J. M. Cook (1985) *Journal of Colloid and Interface Science*, **104**, 254 with permission of Academic Press Inc.

curves evidently resembles the expectations of the Langmuir adsorption isotherm (Fig. 2.2). On the basis of equation (2.3) (substituting p_{NO} for p_A) and assuming that adsorption/desorption equilibrium is in fact achieved during each exposure, the vertical axis of Fig. 4.16 will be proportional to surface coverage (θ) while the horizontal axis will be proportional to p_{NO}. The form of the curves suggests that this assumption is reasonably justified in these instances. The limiting relative intensity values (appearing as numbers inserted on the right in the diagram) correspond to monolayers and can be obtained by extrapolation to infinite exposure using the form of equation (2.3). Thus these XPS measurements indicate not only the forms of the adsorption isotherms but also identify the nature of the adsorbed species. In this nitric oxide-on-iron system, the adsorption/desorption equilibrium at the temperature of 473 K can be represented as

$$NO(g) \rightleftarrows N(ads) + O(ads)$$

A final example of the XPS technique demonstrates its ability to yield information on the state of aggregation of a supported catalyst, say a metal (M) on an inert support (S). The ratios of the sizes of peaks corresponding to the ejection of electrons from atoms in M and S (I_M/I_S) can be measured as a function of the extent of loading of M. Figure 4.17 shows two general types of variations commonly observed. The key point is that the photoelectrons detected emanate from shallow depths, down to about

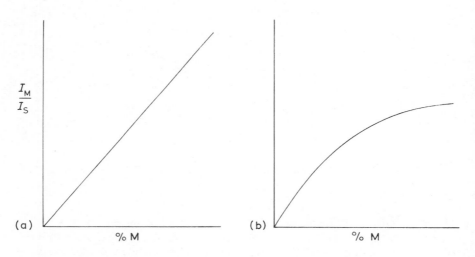

Fig. 4.17 Forms of plots of the ratio of XPS peak intensities (I) for a metal (M) on an inert support (S) as functions of the percentage loading of the metal (%M) which may be obtained from X-ray photoelectron spectroscopic measurements on supported metal catalysts (see text).

1 nm (see Fig. 4.8). Thus if the metal particle is larger than some 2 nm across and the size increases with further metal loading, no increase in the size of the corresponding XPS peak will be observed: the number of M atoms effectively 'hidden' within the aggregates on the surface of S increases as they grow. But, on the other hand, if the metal particles remain small and the effect of increased metal loading is to increase the number rather than the size of the particles, all of the metal atoms remain 'visible'. The XPS response of the atom in the support is not altered significantly by the degree of metal loading. Figure 4.17(a) shows the linear plot of I_M/I_S *versus* metal loading which is expected when the metal particles remain small (i.e. all M atoms visible). Figure 4.17(b) shows an initially linear plot (small particles) which gives way to a curved form corresponding to less efficient detection of metal atoms (the response to growth in size of existing particles) at higher metal loadings. This latter form is typical of metals such as manganese and iron supported on medium surface area (of the order of $200 \, m^2 \, g^{-1}$) silica or alumina. The basic deduction from obtaining a plot of type (b) is that the metal tends to exist as aggregates rather than in a highly dispersed form on the support.

The examples which have been chosen to illustrate this subsection highlight the power of photoelectron spectroscopy in the investigation of surface phenomena. Further examples will be mentioned at the appropriate points in following chapters.

4.4.5 *Extended X-ray absorption fine structure (EXAFS) techniques*

In recent years, synchrotrons which generate intense and spectrally continuous radiation in the X-ray region have become available. In conjunction with monochromators, these have allowed the determination of absorption coefficients of atoms in targets as functions of the energies of the incident X-ray photons. The absorption act involves the ejection of a core electron and this is identified by the conventional letter (K,L,M etc.) indicating the atomic orbital from which this electron is removed. In principle any process which reflects the rate of absorption of the radiation can be used to produce the EXAFS spectrum. The creation of a hole in the core orbital will give rise to Auger electron emission: the major elastic Auger channel produces an electron at a far higher energy than that of the direct photoelectron, so that the total secondary electron yield is dominated by this process. The yield of secondary electrons provides a parameter proportional to the absorption coefficient of the target atom. When the absorbing atom is part of a solid, a modulation is imposed upon the profile of the absorption coefficient as a function of photon energy, appearing on the high energy side of the absorption threshold or edge. This edge represents the condition that the photon energy matches the energy required to eject the electron. The fine structure of the modulation reflects the nature and spatial arrangements of other atoms in the microscopic vicinity of the absorbing atom. The effect originates in the wave nature associated with the outgoing electron, as expressed quantitatively by the de Broglie equation (4.3). There is interference between the primary electron wave and components which have been scattered back from atoms in the vicinity of the source atom. This interference is manifested in the modulated structure of the absorption coefficient profile.

It may be helpful to understanding of the effect to mention a macroscopic situation which offers some analogy. Consider a pond with a few large stones protruding above the surface. A pebble is dropped into the water to generate ripples. On encountering the projecting stones, parts of these outward-travelling ripples are reflected to generate a complex disturbance pattern. Different arrangements of the stones and different cross-sectional shapes at the waterline would give rise to different ripple patterns. In principle then, it would be possible to analyse a particular ripple pattern to deduce the arrangement and shapes of the stones. This indicates the simple basis of EXAFS techniques.

The modulated fine structure may extend for more than 1000 eV above the energy corresponding to the absorption edge. The frequency and amplitude of the modulations provide information about the nature, number and spatial locations of atoms close to the atom which actually absorbs the X-ray photons. EXAFS is specific for chemical elements: by varying the energy of the X-rays, investigations can be switched from the atoms of one element to those of another and the respective micro-environments can be probed. It is important to realize that the technique is not dependent upon the existence of long range crystallographic order in the material, so that EXAFS can be applied to such diverse situations as metals dispersed on supports and the metal centres within enzyme molecules.

The EXAFS technique may be used in a diagnostic manner, in which the basic principle is that matching modulation structures will be obtained for atoms in the same microenvironment. This allows identification of the natures of species existing on surfaces by comparison of the EXAFS spectra with those of materials of known structures. Figure 4.18 illustrates this. Cobalt atoms create the absorption edge concerned. The left part of this Figure shows a set of EXAFS spectra of the materials obtained at various stages during the preparation of cobalt supported on titania, using impregnation by cobalt nitrate in aqueous solution as the initial procedure (Section 3.2.3). The right part of this Figure shows the EXAFS spectra of reference forms of cobalt. Visual matchings of modulated structures yield various identifications. Comparison of (B)(left) with the spectrum of Co₃O₄ on the right indicates that calcination of the impregnated material induces the formation of a bulk-like Co₃O₄ phase on the titania. Also there is a strong resemblance between (C)(left) and the spectrum of the compound

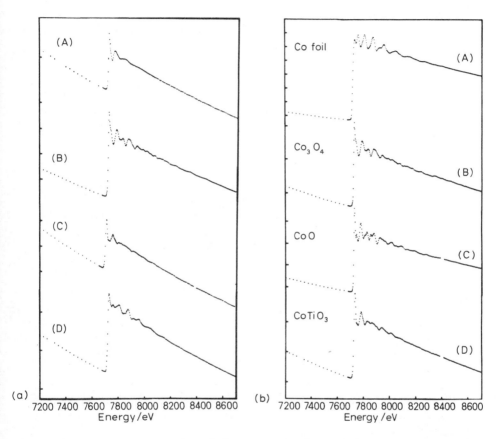

Fig. 4.18 (a) EXAFS spectra of the materials obtained during the course of preparation of cobalt metal catalyst supported on titania (TiO₂) *via* the impregnation method starting with aqueous cobalt nitrate. (A) Sample dried at a temperature of 383 K overnight. (B) Sample calcined in air at 723 K for 4 h. (C) Sample calcined in air at 973 K for 4 h. (D) Sample calcined at 723 K for 4 h and then reduced under hydrogen at 973 K for 4 h. (b) EXAFS spectra of reference compounds: (A) Co metallic foil, (B) Co₃O₄, (C) CoO and (D) CoTiO₃ powder. Reprinted with permission from *Catalyst preparation procedure probed by EXAFS spectroscopy. 2. Cobalt on titania*, K. Tohji, Y. Udagawa, S. Tanabe, T. Ida and A. Uedo (1984) *Journal of the American Chemical Society*, **106**, 5173, 5174. Copyright 1984 American Chemical Society.

CoTiO$_3$ on the right. This suggests that exposure of the impregnated material to the temperature of 923 K induces a solid state reaction between the oxides of the two metals resulting in the production of CoTiO$_3$ on the surface. Finally in connection with Fig. 4.18, the close correspondence between (D)(left) and the spectrum for cobalt metal foil on the right indicates that after reduction the prepared material consists of cobalt metal particles supported on titania. In combination these spectra substantiate the sensitivity of the phenomenon concerned in EXAFS to the microenvironment of the absorbing atoms.

At a considerably more sophisticated level, there are procedures for the detailed analysis of EXAFS spectra. At the level of this book, the underlying theory can only be developed in outline. The fine structure associated with a particular absorption edge is extracted by the use of what is termed the EXAFS function

$$\chi(\kappa) = (\mu - \mu_0)/\mu_0 \qquad (4.6)$$

The parameters μ and μ_0 are atomic absorption coefficients, corresponding to the total absorption and the monotonic atom-like absorption (or the absorption without interference effects) respectively. Equation (4.6) assumes that there is no background absorption from atoms not of interest. κ here is the wave vector defined by the fundamental equation

$$\kappa = \{2\pi \, (2mE)^{1/2}\}/h = 2\pi/\lambda \qquad (4.7)$$

in which m is the electron rest mass, E is the kinetic energy of the electron ejected in the primary act and h is Planck's constant. The relationship to the associated wavelength (λ) comes from equation (4.3). A modified EXAFS function, expressed as $\kappa^n \chi(\kappa)$, with $n = 1, 2$ or 3 arbitrarily, is often used to achieve amplification of the fine structure. $\chi(\kappa)$ will be affected by an unknown number of coordination shells in the microenvironment of the atom which absorbs the photon. The Fourier transform technique is applied to resolve the effects of these different shells. The Fourier transform of the modified EXAFS function, denoted by $\theta_n(r)$, may be expressed in the integral form

$$\theta_n(r) = \frac{1}{\sqrt{2\pi}} \int_{\kappa'}^{\kappa''} \kappa^n \chi(\kappa) \exp(2iKr) \, dK \qquad (4.8)$$

Here r is the interatomic distance parameter and the limits of integration, κ' and κ'', coincide with nodes in $\chi(\kappa)$. The function $\theta_n(r)$ shows peaks when plotted against r: the corresponding values of r are related to the average distances between the absorbing atom and the neighbouring atoms in particular coordination shells.

The general method for analysing EXAFS spectra in connection with catalytic materials is based upon matching the profile to that predicted by a model. This procedure involves computing the forms of $\theta_n(r)$ *versus* r plots for a series of models, in which the interatomic distances and number and identities of neighbouring atoms are varied until a match is obtained with the experimental profile. Strong indications of the structure to be incorporated into the model can be provided by straightforward comparison of the raw EXAFS spectra (as indicated in Fig. 4.18) or its Fourier transform function for the material being investigated with EXAFS spectra of the same element in its forms and compounds with known structures.

Figure 4.19 shows EXAFS spectral data for rhodium at high dispersion on an alumina support. Comparison of parts (a) and (b) of this Figure shows the effect on χ ($\chi(\kappa)$) resulting from the adsorption of carbon monoxide on to the rhodium. Part (c) shows the Fourier transform functions (FT$' = \theta_3(r)$) corresponding to the profile shown in part (b). As a consequence of matching with corresponding functions derived from models, the peaks, labelled A and C in part (c), were shown to originate from the existence of a species $Rh(CO)_2$ at the surface, with distances of 0.18 nm and 0.30 nm separating its rhodium and carbon atoms and its rhodium and oxygen atoms respectively. The peak B resulted from direct bonding between rhodium and oxygen atoms; its presence indicated that the $Rh(CO)_2$ surface group was attached to the alumina support through three oxygens with equal Rh—O bond lengths of 0.212 nm. This distance is rather significant in that it is slightly longer than that of the Rh—O bond in the compound Rh_2O_3. This accords with a view that the rhodium in the $Rh(CO)_2$ surface species is in its oxidation state of one (i.e. Rh(I) or Rh^+) rather than the metallic state (Rh(0)). It is worthwhile commenting upon the greater extension of the fine structure (to $K \approx 12\,\text{Å}^{-1}$) in Fig. 4.19(a) as compared to the restriction (to $K \approx 6\,\text{Å}^{-1}$) in Fig. 4.19(b). This points to a conclusion that each rhodium atom has more rhodium atom neighbours prior to the adsorption of carbon monoxide than after: in other words the rhodium particles are disrupted considerably during the course of the adsorption of carbon monoxide

The above is a brief discussion of a highly sophisticated technique for the revelation of microscopic structures. Some variants may be encountered. XANES (X-ray absorption near-edge structure) focuses upon the spectral region in the vicinity of an absorption edge, extending to a displacement of about 50 eV. Multiple scattering effects are important in XANES and the modulated spectral profile contains chemical information about the central X-ray absorbing atom in terms of its valence, site symmetry, coordination geometry, ligand type as well as bond distances. The technique referred to as SEXAFS (surface extended X-ray absorption fine structure) generally is concerned with X-ray photons having energies corresponding to more than 50 eV above that representing the absorption edge. In this spectral region

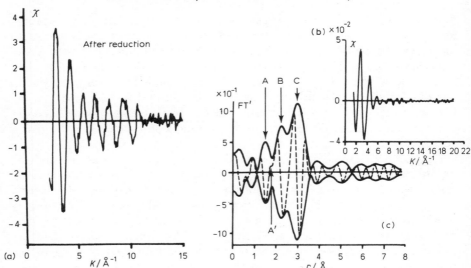

Fig. 4.19 EXAFS spectra obtained at the rhodium K-edge from a rhodium (0.57% w/w) on γ-alumina catalyst at 77 K. (a) Primary plot of the EXAFS function (χ) against the wave vector (K) when the material has been reduced at a temperature of 593 K in the presence of 100 kPa of hydrogen. (b) Corresponding plot to (a) after carbon monoxide has been adsorbed on the reduced material at ambient temperature under a pressure of 100 kPa of carbon monoxide. (c) The K^3-weighted Fourier transform (FT′) plot derived from (b) after normalization and smoothing, using limits of $K_{max} = 8.4$ Å^{-1} and $K_{min} = 3.24$ Å^{-1}, showing real (full line) and imaginary (dashed line) components. (1 Å = 0.1 nm). Reprinted with permission from *Structure of rhodium in an ultradispersed Rh/Al₂O₃ catalyst as studied by EXAFS and other techniques*, H. F. J. van't Blik, J. B. A. D. van Zon. T. Huizinga, J. C. Vis, D. C. Koningsberger and R. Prins (1985) *Journal of the American Chemical Society*, **107**, 3142, 3144. Copyright 1985 American Chemical Society.

only single-scattering effects are important: analysis of the modulated structure allows the determination of interatomic separations concerned in adsorption systems with higher accuracy than any other technique presently used. SEXAFS probes only the local structure around adsorbate atoms and is thus the technique of choice for the study of disordered surface phases.

4.4.6 *Infrared absorption spectroscopy*

The techniques under this heading might be regarded as having wider application potentially than the others described in this chapter in that they do not demand UHV conditions.

Low energy electrons have typical depths for penetration of a surface of the order of 1 nm. The penetration depths for infrared radiation are much larger generally, say of the order of 1000 nm. Thus infrared radiation cannot be used in a similar manner to electrons to provide information on species existing at surfaces. Thin wafers of many ceramic materials, such as silica–alumina, transmit near-infrared radiation effectively. When a species is adsorbed on such a wafer and the adsorbed forms have characteristic absorption bands of significant optical density, the resultant spectrum may be used for identification and quantification. In addition to adsorption on ceramic materials themselves, adsorption phenomena on highly dispersed metals supported on ceramic materials can also be investigated by infrared absorption spectroscopy. The absorption cells used in this straightforward type of study are fitted with end windows of infrared transmitting materials, such as sodium chloride or calcium fluoride. The wafers of ceramic material, formed by mechanical pressing, are mounted within the cell. The operations for introducing the adsorbate to the wafer may be carried out using conventional vacuum systems, capable of achieving pressures in the 10^{-4} Pa range. The infrared spectrometers used commonly are double beam instruments, incorporating gratings or prism grating combinations to achieve spectral resolution.

Illustrative examples of the infrared absorption spectra which may be obtained using silica–alumina wafers are shown in Fig. 4.20. Assignments of the significant absorption bands have been made as shown in Table 4.5. The demonstrated coexistence of pyridinium ions and coordinatively bound pyridine immediately provides the information that there are two types of acidic sites (which interact with the organic base) on the surface of silica–alumina (as discussed in Section 5.3). Physisorbed pyridine is driven off the surface by prolonged evacuation at a temperature of 423 K, as is revealed by comparison of (B) and (C) in Fig. 4.20(a) showing the disappearance of the corresponding broad structure around 3000 cm^{-1}. However it is evident that the other forms of adsorbed pyridine are not removed by this treatment. Also apparent in Fig. 4.20(b) is the ability of water vapour to convert sites associated with coordinatively bound pyridine (i.e. Lewis acid sites) into those associated with the pyridinium ion (i.e. Brønsted acid sites). (See the features at 1545 and 1450 cm^{-1} in (B) and (C).)

Infrared absorption spectroscopy can also be applied to continuous metal surfaces, when it is used in the infrared reflectance-absorption spectroscopy (IRAS) mode. Here the optical arrangement is such that the incident beam impinges on to the surface at a small angle (typically about 2° with respect to the surface plane). Grazing incidence is achieved consequently, when the beam is reflected with some degree of transmission through the adsorbed layer at the surface. One illustrative instance of the application of IRAS concerns carbon monoxide adsorbed on a stepped platinum surface, for which the sequence of spectra shown in Fig. 4.21 was generated. A stepped surface of a metal will offer two general types of site for molecular chemisorption, at steps and within terraces. Two distinct bands are apparent in the spectra corresponding to intermediate coverages. As indicated in other experiments (see Fig. 4.5 for example), step sites

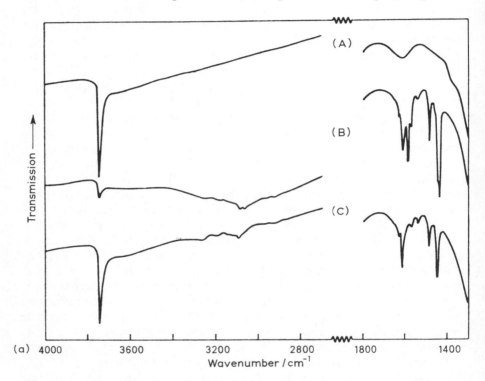

Fig. 4.20 (a) Infrared transmission spectra of silica–alumina (A) calcined and evacuated at a temperature of 773 K, (B) exposed to a pressure of 2.3 kPa of pyridine at 423 K for 1 h followed by evacuation for 1 h at 423 K and (C) evacuated for an additional 16 h at 423 K. (b) Infrared transmission spectra of silica–alumina (A) as in (C) (a), (B) with additional exposure to a pressure of 2.3 kPa of water vapour at 423 K for 1 h followed by evacuation at 423 K for 1 h, (C) with additional exposure to water vapour at a pressure of 2.0 kPa at 298 K for 1 h followed by evacuation for 1 h at 298 K and (D) with evacuation for an additional 16 h at 423 K. Reprinted with permission from *The nature of the acidic sites on a silica–alumina. Characterization by infrared spectroscopic studies of trimethylamine and pyridine chemisorption*, M. R. Basila, T. R. Kantner and K. H. Rhee (1964) *Journal of Physical Chemistry*, **68**, 3200, 3204. Copyright 1964 American Chemical Society.

achieve preferential adsorption compared to terrace sites in general. This view extends to the present instances to suggest that the spectral band at the lower frequency, which is observed at low surface coverages, reflects carbon monoxide chemisorbed at step sites. Correspondingly, when occupation of terrace sites is expected to come in at higher surface coverages, the apparent shift of peaks towards the right in the Figure as the surface coverage increases is a real effect on this account. There is also superimposed an effect of increasing interactions between adsorbed carbon monoxide molecules as they pack together more closely on the surface.

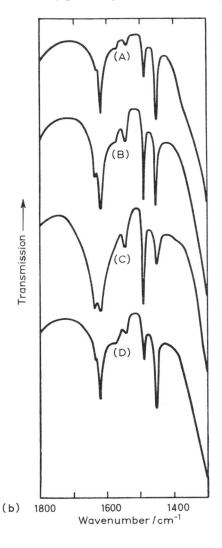

Table 4.5 Assignment of bands for pyridine adsorbed on silica–alumina

Nature of species	Adsorbed structure	Wavenumber/ cm^{-1} of characteristic bands
Pyridinium ion	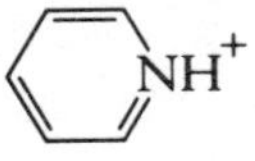 NH^+	3260, 3188, 1638, 1620, 1545, 1490
Coordinatively-bound pyridine	 $N:$	1620, 1577, 1490, 1450
Physisorbed pyridine	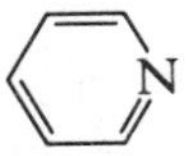 N	Broad feature centred on 3000

4.5 Concluding remarks

This chapter should convince the reader of the enormous impact made upon surface chemistry by the development of the modern techniques discussed. Comparison of the level of information which is obtainable on intermediates involved in catalytic actions with that accessible using the 'old-fashioned' methods (Sections 2.3 and 2.4) should explain immediately the rapidity of the advances in knowledge of heterogeneous reactions over the last 20 years or so.

The next two chapters attempt to create the framework for basic interpretation of the courses of reactions induced at solid surfaces. Chapter 5 concentrates attention on the chemisorption processes and Chapter 6 extends this to discussion of mechanisms of surface catalysed reactions.

Fig. 4.21 Infrared reflection–absorption spectra in the carbon–oxygen bond stretch region from the system of carbon monoxide adsorbed on a platinum (533) or 4(111) × (100) surface at a temperature of 85 K, at the percentage surface coverages (θ) by the adsorbate indicated on the right of each spectrum. Reproduced from *An infrared study of the adsorption of CO on a stepped platinum surface*, B. E. Hayden, K. Kretzschmar, A. M. Bradshaw and R. G. Greenler (1985), *Surface Science*, **149**, 399 with permission of Elsevier Science Publishers B.V.

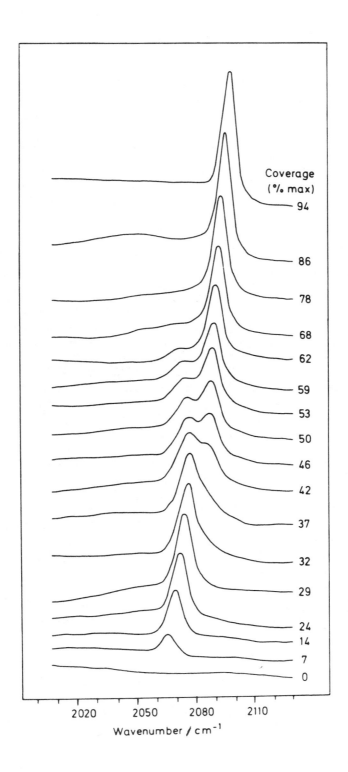

Coverage
(% max)
94

86

78

68

62

59

53

50

46

42

37

32

29

24

14

7

0

Wavenumber / cm⁻¹

5

Chemisorption processes
at solid surfaces

The main thrust of this chapter is to gain understanding of how chemisorptive attachments to various types of solid surfaces come about. Processes of chemisorption will be seen to depend upon redistributions of electron densities or on some occasions upon the effective transfer of a proton (H^+) to the molecule concerned. The particular nature of the surface determines how chemisorption is achieved. This chapter will therefore be developed as a progression through broad categories of the solids which are of most general importance as catalysts, in order transition metals, redox oxides and acidic materials.

The theoretical approach for metals will be different from that for the other two categories. The properties of the surface of a metal cannot be divorced from those of its bulk: the valency electrons are delocalized and thus cannot be considered to be associated with any particular metal atom, be it in the surface or within the bulk. Moreover the surface of a pure metal is composed of only one type of atom. On the other hand, redox oxides and solids characterized by strong acidity have surfaces composed of more than one kind of atom and thus present a variety of sites at which chemisorption may take place. Furthermore the chemical nature of these surfaces can change without the effect being transmitted into the bulk of the material. Accordingly the approach for redox oxides and acidic solids will focus upon the isolated and localized nature of the chemisorption sites on the surfaces.

5.1 Transition metal surfaces

Reference back to Table 2.1 exemplifies the fact that the large majority of catalytically active metals belong to transition series rather than to main groups in the periodic table. This suggests immediately that valency electrons of *d* nature are of fundamental significance for catalytic actions of metal surfaces. Chemisorption on metals involves the formation of bonds of a substantially covalent nature (Table 4.2). If the process is regarded as based upon the sharing of electron density from covalent bonds in the species being adsorbed, then molecular chemisorption can be exemplified by considering benzene on nickel. On nickel crystal faces (111 or 110), benzene preserves its identity in chemisorption at low temperatures, the adsorbed species having the six carbon atoms in a plane parallel to the surface (see Fig. 5.6(a)). On the basis of the temperatures at which benzene desorbs from these nickel faces in thermal desorption experiments (Sections 2.3.2 and 4.3.1), the binding energy involved is of the order of 120 kJ mol^{-1}. Only one simple view of electronic interaction appears to accord with these features, the overlap of π-electron density of the benzene ring with electron density associated with the nickel surface. Similarly ethylene chemisorption on a nickel face might be based on overlap between π-electron density from the adsorbate and electron density derived from the metal. But the situation for ethylene is more flexible than that for benzene. The rehybridization of orbitals at the carbon atoms, represented in Fig. 2.5, may occur. In fact, molecular chemisorption of ethylene is restricted to temperatures below ambient. At temperatures between 290 K and 450 K approximately, ethylene chemisorbs dissociatively on to nickel faces to yield chemisorbed hydrogen atoms and chemisorbed ethylidyne ($\equiv$C—CH$_3$). Dissociative chemisorption is in fact the basic feature of many systems of interest for catalysis by metals, when atoms and radicals appear as chemisorbed intermediates.

It is not necessary to achieve a detailed understanding of the bonding between adsorbed species and metal surfaces at the level of this book. But the strength of the chemisorption bond is an important parameter in connection with the rationalization of catalytic activity at metal surfaces: the fundamental aspects of this may be considered usefully at a fairly elementary level. The delocalized valency electrons move through the metallic lattice with ease, as is manifested by the high electrical conductivity of metals. Mobile electrons experience a varying potential field associated with the positively charged lattice sites created by the nuclei with their core electrons. This implies that a range of allowed energy levels, constituting a band, must be available to the valency electrons within a bulk metal. This situation contrasts with the discrete energy levels associated with the potential field in an isolated atom.

The electronic theory of bulk metals postulates that there are very large numbers of allowed energy levels, densely crowded within an electronic band. Each band is designated by the orbital specification of the corresponding electrons in the isolated atom (e.g. 3*d*, 4*s* etc.). The number of energy levels within a particular band is equal to the number of corresponding atomic orbitals which would result if all of the metal atoms were separated from one another. Consider a sample of a metal of the first transition series composed of N atoms, where N is a very large number, say of the order of 10^{23}. Each atom if isolated, would have five $3d$ valency orbitals. In this instance the $3d$ band of the bulk metal sample would incorporate $5N$ individual energy levels.

Figure 5.1(a) is a diagram representing the allowed energy levels of valency orbitals in the isolated atom and the density of energy levels ($N(E)$) within bands in a bulk sample of the same first transition series metal. Figure 5.1(b) indicates how the limits and electronic population of the $3d$ band change along the series. The density of levels in the $3d$ band is much

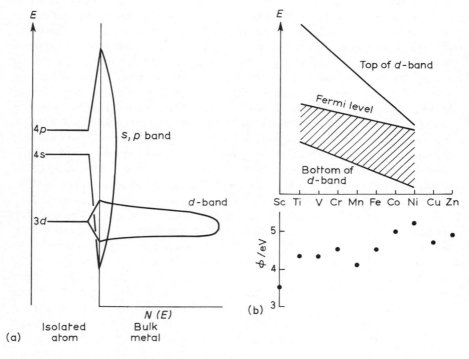

Fig. 5.1 (a) Representations of the variations of energy level densities $N(E)$ in the valency bands of a bulk sample of a first transition series metal as a function of binding energy (E), compared with the orbital energies of the corresponding isolated atom on the left. (b) (above) Variation of the energies (E) associated with the $3d$ band along the elements of the first transition series (barred section denotes the extent of filling by electrons). (b) (below) Variation of work function values (ϕ) along the first transition series. After R. Hoffmann, S. D. Wijeyesekera and S-s. Sing (1986) *Pure and Applied Chemistry*, **58**, 481–494.

larger than that in the overlapping $4s,4p$ band: the former extends over a narrower range (typically 4 eV) than the latter (20 eV). The average energy and the width of the $3d$ band decrease along the series. Just as is the case for individual atomic orbitals, each energy level in the band can be occupied by two electrons. The *Fermi level* separates the filled and empty energy levels and it decreases gradually in energy along the series. This is roughly paralleled by the increasing trend of *work function* (ϕ) values, these corresponding to the energy gap between the Fermi level and a free electron, along the series, as indicated in the lower panel.

Profound differences in the chemical properties of isolated metal atoms and clusters of metal atoms have been demonstrated experimentally. A flowing system, with an inert gas acting as the carrier, has been used in a demonstration of this point. At the upstream end, the beam from a laser was focused on to a rod of cobalt metal: the resultant vaporization dispatched clusters (Co_n, $n = 1,2,3,...$) downstream. In a specific case of interest, deuterium (D_2 or $^2H_2$) was introduced downstream of the cluster source and upstream of a zone in which an excimer laser was applied to ionize species for detection using a mass spectrometer. A schematic diagram of the experimental arrangement is shown in Fig. 5.2. When deuterium becomes chemically attached to a Co_n species, the mass peak associated with this species (inclusive of all species represented as $Co_n D_{2x}$) is spread upwards, depleting the mass peak corresponding to bare Co_n. Atomic cobalt (Co_1) and Co_2 peaks showed no significant changes with the addition of deuterium to the system, whereas peaks for larger Co_n species showed large depletions and spreading. The evident interpretation is that atomic cobalt does not interact chemically with deuterium (hydrogen) but the larger clusters chemisorb deuterium. This constitutes one clear illustration of the very different properties of metallic entities as compared to isolated metal atoms.

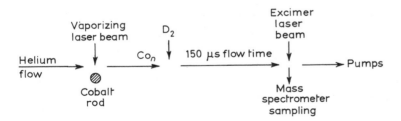

Fig. 5.2 Schematic representation of the experimental arrangement in an experiment for detecting the chemisorption of deuterium on cobalt clusters (Co_n). Further details may be obtained from *Journal of Chemical Physics* (1985), **83**, 2293–2304 *et loc. cit.*.

Table 5.1 Ionization potential (IP) and work function (ϕ) values for some transition metals

	Metal			
	Ni	Cu	Pd	Pt
IP/eV	8.3	7.7	7.6	9.0
ϕ/eV	5.2	4.7	5.4	5.6

Further manifestations of the different electronic properties of isolated atoms and bulk forms of the same metal are found in comparison of the energies required to free an electron (the ionization potential and the work function respectively). Table 5.1 compares values of these for representative transition metals. These data imply that metal surfaces are better electron donors than are individual metal atoms, allowing their stronger interaction with vacant orbitals of an adsorbate.

The determination of chemisorption bond energies was discussed in Section 2.3.2. It is appropriate at this stage to examine series of mean values of single bonds between common atoms and the surfaces of metals of the first transition series. These are shown in Fig. 5.3: more detailed data for hydrogen appeared in Fig. 2.12. The general trends are clear; the strengths of chemisorption bonds decrease with progression along the transition series. The detailed electronic theory of bonding between adsorbed species and metal surfaces is highly complex and it is inappropriate to pursue this here. But the key factor for an adsorbate (A) with an unpaired electron is that it has a singly occupied orbital which has an energy E_A which lies below the energy (E_F) of the Fermi level. In the process of chemisorption of A on the metal surface, significant transfer of electron density takes place between these two levels, which results in the appearance of the difference $E_F - E_A$ (as a squared term in fact) in the quantitative equation for the strength of the chemisorption bond. Thus as E_F decreases along the transition series, $E_F - E_A$ and hence the bond strength decreases consequently. It is unnecessary to go further than this with the theory for present purposes. The main approach adopted is simply to attempt to rationalize observed phenomena taking place on transition metal surfaces in terms of the general trends of Fig. 5.3. These trends also pertain for multiple bonds between adsorbed species and metal surfaces.

Figures 4.12 and 4.13 presented evidence (from HREELS investigations) that chemisorbed methoxy (CH_3O) was far more stable on copper than on nickel surfaces. Also in connection with Fig. 4.4, evidence from TPRS experiments shows that chemisorbed formate (HCOO) is relatively stable

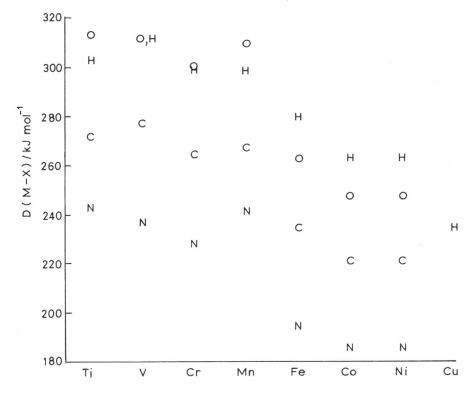

Fig. 5.3 Plot of single-bond energies of metal-adsorbed atom systems (D(M–X)) along the first transition series of the periodic table, where the adsorbed atom concerned (X = O, H, C or N) is indicated by the symbol at the appropriate point. Based upon data tabulated by E. Miyazaki (1980) *Journal of Catalysis*, **65**, 84.

on copper surfaces: this stability is also observed on surfaces of silver and gold, the end members of the second and third transition series respectively. For both of these adsorbates the most likely course of decomposition appears to be hydrogen abstraction by the surface, to produce a chemisorbed hydrogen atom. Now the weaker is the prospective bond between the metal surface and the hydrogen atom, the less likely it would seem that the adsorbed species is to decompose. The stronger bonding to hydrogen found towards the middle of the transition series would be expected to make species like adsorbed methoxy rather unstable, as is the case on nickel and platinum. This may not be the only factor involved but for present purposes it provides a reasonably simple rationalization.

Carbon monoxide is chemisorbed molecularly on some transition metals but dissociatively on others at moderate temperatures. An important general consideration is that an approximate borderline can be drawn through the periodic table from nickel ($3d^8$ in terms of the valency electrons in the atom) in the first transition series, through ruthenium ($4d^6$) in the second to rhenium ($5d^5$) in the third. Metals to the right of this borderline (such as copper ($3d^{10}$), palladium ($4d^8$) and platinum ($5d^8$)) tend to chemisorb carbon monoxide molecularly under usual catalytic reaction conditions. Those to the left, such as iron ($3d^6$) and molybdenum ($4d^4$), chemisorb carbon monoxide dissociatively. Figures 4.21 (for platinum) and 4.14 and 4.15 (for iron) bear out this difference. The enthalpy changes involved in dissociative chemisorption, represented in hypothetical stages as

$$C\equiv O(g) \rightarrow C(g) + O(g) \rightarrow C(ads) + O(ads)$$

offer some insight into the origin of this borderline. The strengths of the chemical bonds attaching the atoms to the surface (C(ads) and O(ads)) decrease to the right in the periodic table. Thus the favourability of dissociative chemisorption decreases in the same direction on the basis of the overall exothermicity of the process above. This simple view must be tempered by the fact that significant activation energies exist in the actual pathway between molecularly and dissociatively chemisorbed carbon monoxide, as mentioned in connection with Fig. 4.5(b). Nevertheless the general point is indicative on a semiquantitative basis.

The molecular chemisorption of carbon monoxide can be considered to involve components of transfer of electron density in opposite directions. Looking first at the gas phase molecule, the arrangement of the electronic orbitals is represented in Fig. 5.4. The order of orbital energies is confirmed by the UPS spectrum shown in Fig. 4.15(c). The effects of molecular chemisorption on iron are indicated in Fig. 4.15(b). The energy of the 5σ orbital is lowered, which suggests coupling of this filled orbital to empty levels in the metal bands, with transfer of electron density towards the metal. The spatial distribution of the 5σ orbital, not unlike that expected for a lone pair of electrons, means that it contributes little to the electron density between the carbon and oxygen atoms and is thus almost non-bonding for the carbon monoxide molecule. Thus transfer of electron density out of this orbital towards the metal exerts only a small influence on the bonding between the carbon and oxygen atoms. However there is a second component of the chemisorptive bonding which depends on the transfer of electron density in the reverse direction (often referred to as back donation) from the populated levels in the vicinity of the Fermi level of the metal into the empty $2\pi^*$ antibonding orbital of carbon monoxide. This transfer weakens the binding between the carbon and oxygen atoms but strengthens the carbon-to-metal bond in increasing the electron density therein. The first of these effects is manifested in the spectral location of the

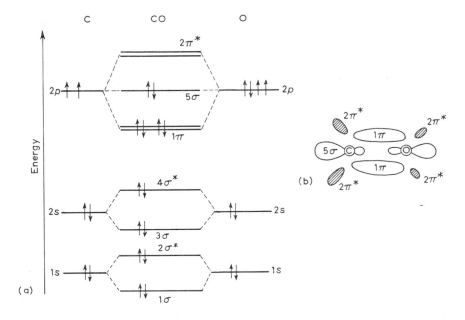

Fig. 5.4 The molecular orbitals of gas phase carbon monoxide. (a) Energy diagram indicating how the molecular orbitals arise from the combination of atomic orbitals of carbon (C) and oxygen (O). Conventional arrows are used to indicate the spin orientations of electrons in the occupied orbitals. Asterisks denote antibonding molecular orbitals. (b) Spatial distributions of key orbitals involved in the chemisorption of carbon monoxide. Barring indicates empty orbitals.

band shown in Fig. 4.21, which corresponds to the stretching frequency of the carbon–oxygen bond in carbon monoxide chemisorbed on platinum. The dissociation energy (D) of a bond is related to its fundamental vibrational frequency (ν_0): on the basis of viewing it as a simple anharmonic oscillator with anharmonicity factor x, an approximate equation expressing the relationship is

$$D(\text{J mol}^{-1}) \approx N_A h \nu_0 / 4x \qquad (5.1)$$

The wavenumber (proportional to the frequency) for the chemisorbed carbon monoxide on platinum is reduced to below $2100\,\text{cm}^{-1}$, compared to that of $2143\,\text{cm}^{-1}$ for the gas phase molecule. This indicates that D is lower for the chemisorbed molecule.

Heats of chemisorption of carbon monoxide on different metals reflect the mode. Molecular chemisorption results in the release of 140–170 kJ mol^{-1} on palladium and 50–60 kJ mol^{-1} on copper surfaces. More heat is released by dissociative chemisorption reflecting the fact that the combined strength of the bonds between the resultant atoms and the surface exceeds considerably the strength of the original carbon monoxide bond. In illustration, dissociative chemisorption on metals such as titanium, manganese and zirconium releases of the order of 400 kJ mol^{-1}.

At this point it is pertinent to consider also the chemisorption of nitrogen, a molecule which is isoelectronic with carbon monoxide. For the homonuclear nitrogen (N_2) molecule the key orbitals for chemisorption are denoted as π (full, bonding) and π^* (empty, antibonding), which have symmetrical spatial distributions. Back donation of electron density from a metal surface into the π^* orbital weakens the nitrogen–nitrogen bond. This has important implications for ammonia synthesis, in which the critical dissociative chemisorption of N_2 on an iron catalyst is believed to be regulated by the passage through a molecularly chemisorbed precursor state.

It is well established that small amounts of an alkali metal (typically potassium) on transition metals promote both the strength of molecular chemisorption and the tendency towards dissociative chemisorption of both carbon monoxide and nitrogen. This phenomenon is referred to as *electronic promotion*. It arises from the donation of electron density initially from the strongly-electropositive potassium (or more often its oxide) to the metal and thence to the chemisorbed molecule. The resultant increase in back donation into the π^* orbitals of the chemisorbed molecules then accounts for the effects. Clear evidence for the stronger chemisorption of carbon monoxide on platinum with potassium present on its surface was revealed in Fig. 4.6. In another exemplifying situation, the heat of adsorption of carbon monoxide on nickel supported on silica rose from around 60 to near 90 kJ mol^{-1} when the surface was promoted with potassium. Figure 5.5 represents the molecular orbital shapes and directions of electron density transfer for nitrogen chemisorbed molecularly on a potassium-promoted iron face. The promotional effect is manifested in the rise in the binding energy of nitrogen molecularly chemisorbed on an iron (111) face from some 37 to around 50 kJ mol^{-1} accompanying the introduction of potassium. It is also interesting to note that when potassium is added as a promoter to the Fe(100) face, the rate of ammonia synthesis thereon may be increased by as much as a factor of 300. This is a direct indication that the rate determining step in ammonia synthesis is the chemisorption of nitrogen.

The strength of molecular chemisorption and the tendency to dissociative adsorption are enhanced at surface defects, such as steps of the types shown in Fig. 4.1. Direct evidence of this may be seen in Fig. 4.21. Accepting that carbon monoxide is chemisorbed at the step sites on this cleaved platinum face at low surface coverages, a wavenumber of

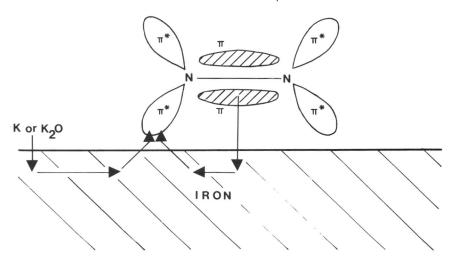

Fig. 5.5 Diagram representing the spatial distribution of the significant molecular orbitals of nitrogen chemisorbed molecularly on iron promoted by potassium (K or K₂O). The arrows indicate the directions of transfer of electron density.

approximately 2066 cm^{-1} is assigned to this form. At higher coverages a peak centred on a wavenumber of 2090 cm^{-1} comes in, which logically may be assigned to carbon monoxide chemisorbed on sites within terraces. On the basis of equation (5.1), the carbon–oxygen bond is thus weaker in the step-adsorbed carbon monoxide. This is consistent with the results of theoretical studies of the electron density distributions at metal surfaces which point up a concentration at defects, particularly of d-band electron density. The resultant enhanced back donation into the $2\pi^*$ antibonding orbital of carbon monoxide weakens the molecular bond, whilst strengthening the attachment between the carbon atom and the metal surface. The latter feature interprets on a simple basis the preferential chemisorption at the step sites. On nickel, a more extreme aspect of this interpretation accounts for the observations in Fig. 4.5(a) and (c) that carbon monoxide is molecularly chemisorbed on nickel crystal faces but is dissociatively chemisorbed on the cleaved nickel surface, presumably at the steps.

Another simple view of the ability of defects on metal surfaces to induce decomposition of adsorbed molecules may be taken in cases such as that of benzene on nickel or platinum. On a perfect crystal face at moderate temperatures, the chemisorbed form shown in Fig. 5.6(a) is expected, with the hydrogen atoms not involved in the attachment. But in the vicinity of a step, as represented in Fig. 5.6(b), one of the hydrogen atoms is encouraged

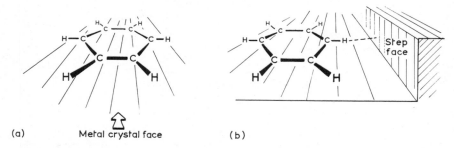

(a)   Metal crystal face   (b)

Fig. 5.6 Representations of the geometrical configurations of a benzene molecule chemisorbed (a) on a perfect crystal face of a metal and (b) on the terrace in the vicinity of a step on a cleaved metal surface.

by the geometrical configuration to interact with metal atoms in the step face. This situation appears to enhance the likelihood of dehydrogenation of the chemisorbed benzene molecule.

Further aspects of the theory of the role of defects on metal surfaces in promoting dissociative processes cannot be developed here. Nevertheless there is already sufficient justification for the point made in Section 4.1, that surface roughness enhances both dissociative chemisorption and catalytic activity in many heterogeneous systems. This circumstance may be regarded as fortunate for the practical operation of industrial-scale processes using metal catalysts.

5.2 Redox oxide surfaces

In this section, attention is directed towards chemisorptive phenomena taking place on the solid surfaces which serve as the main catalysts for oxidation processes. Both reductive (gain of electron density) and oxidative (loss of electron density) actions take place, in concert referred to as redox action.

The simplest view of a metal oxide is that it will have two distinct types of lattice points, a positively charged site associated with the metal cation and a negatively charged site associated with the oxygen anion. However several of the oxides of major importance as redox catalysts have metal (or metalloid) ions with anionic oxygen bound to them through bonds of a coordinative nature. This is the case for elements such as vanadium and molybdenum, which can exist in compounds as complex anions such as are represented by formulae VO_3^- and $Mo_7O_{24}^{6-}$. Correspondingly, vanadia and molybdena surfaces can present bonds represented as $V{=}O$

and Mo=O respectively, which are of crucial significance in many of the reactions which they catalyse.

If an oxide surface is considered to have been produced by cleavage of a piece of the bulk solid, the surface metal centres will have been deprived of some of their oxygen neighbours and will have become coordinatively-unsaturated as a consequence. This provides driving forces for the appearance of double-bonded oxygen on the surface and for the chemisorption of species, both of which relieve the metal centre of coordinative unsaturation. In illustration, one mode of chemisorption of methanol on molybdenum oxide is represented below

$CH_3OH(g)$

A key feature of redox oxide catalysts is the ease with which metal or metalloid centres in the surfaces can change their oxidation state (or formal charge if they are viewed as simple cations). But a solid material must preserve overall electrical charge neutrality and thus a compensatory gain or loss of oxygen from the lattice must occur concurrently. In many instances, oxygen derived from the solid lattice serves as the source of oxygen for catalysed processes achieving selective oxidation. This is readily demonstrated by the fact that selective oxidation can proceed often on a fresh oxide surface in the absence of gas phase oxygen. For example, *n*-butane oxidation on vanadium oxide catalyst can proceed under these conditions to an extent far exceeding that expected if the oxygen used was derived simply from the surface layer alone. Bulk-lattice oxygen is thus released within a gas phase product and when the reaction ceases the solid is composed of several reduced surface layers overlying a core of unreduced material. The initial vanadium oxidation state, V(v), may be reduced to V(iv) as oxygen vacancies are thus created, to the extent preserving the overall electrical neutrality. Upon subsequent contact with gas phase oxygen, the reduced surface chemisorbs the gas and converts it to restore the depleted oxygen sites of the original lattice, with accompanying conversion of V(iv) back to V(v). This is the mode of oxygen chemisorption of most interest generally on redox catalysts, so that it is of immediate interest to consider how the bond rupture occurs in O_2 with electron acquisition to produce formally O^{2-}.

As a gas phase molecule, oxygen (O_2) has three pairs of electrons in bonding outer orbitals and two unpaired electrons in two antibonding π^* orbitals, producing a net double bond. In the process of its chemisorption onto a reduced oxide surface, the O_2 species is initially attached to a reduced metal site (e.g. V(IV)) by coordinative binding. As a result there is transfer of electron density towards O_2 which enters the π^* orbitals and thus weakens the oxygen–oxygen bond. Cooperative action involving more than one reduced site may then effect the overall dissociative conversion, for which the lowest energy pathway is thought to involve a succession of steps represented as

$$O_2 \xrightarrow{\ e^-\ } O_2^- \xrightarrow{\ e^-\ } O_2^{2-} \xrightarrow{\ 2e^-\ } 2O^{2-}$$

with all of these species on the surface. This gives a basic description of the effective chemisorption mechanism of oxygen as involved in many selective oxidation processes. It depends upon the relatively easy release of electrons (e^-) associated with the increase of the oxidation state of the associated metal centre.

The complementary aspect of a hydrocarbon oxidation process is the adsorption and activation of this coreactant on the oxide surface. In the type of process referred to above, in which lattice oxygen is used prior to its replenishment from the gas phase, it could be anticipated that the hydrocarbon must interact initially with the higher oxidation state of the metal concerned. The nature of this process is perhaps best understood for simple alkene molecules and propylene may be used for illustration. There is conclusive evidence that allyl radicals ($CH_2\text{---}CH\text{---}CH_2$) attached to the surface result from contact of propylene with active oxide surfaces. Not only can the presence of this adsorbed intermediate be detected by infrared or electron spin resonance spectroscopic techniques, but allyl radicals are released into the gas phase and have been detected in flowing systems in which propylene was passed over a typical catalyst (a mixed bismuth–molybdenum oxide). Isotopic studies also suggest the formation of the symmetrical allyl radical. When a carbon atom in the propylene was labelled with ^{14}C and the selective oxidation to acrolein occurred, $^{14}CH_3\text{---}CH\text{=}CH_2$ and $CH_3\text{---}CH\text{=}^{14}CH_2$ produced the same mixtures of $^{14}CH_2\text{=}CH\text{---}CHO$ and $CH_2\text{=}CH\text{---}^{14}CHO$. Also the fact that a kinetic isotope effect was observed only when deuterium (^2H) replaced hydrogen in the methyl group of propylene indicates that hydrogen abstraction from this group is a critical part of the mechanism and hence the initial chemisorption step. Theoretical studies of the electronic distributions when allyl radicals are attached to metal centres, such as Mo(VI), Ni(II) or Fe(III), show that the radical donates electron density, consequently acquiring a positive charge and reducing the metal oxidation state (say from M(n) to M($n-1$)). Thus the chemisorption of propylene on a material such as bismuth–molybdenum oxide is dissociative in nature and can be represented as

$$H-CH_2-CH=CH_2(g) \longrightarrow$$

M(n)   H(ads)

$$\overset{\oplus}{\underset{M(n-1)}{\overset{CH}{H_2C}\diagup \hspace{-0.3em}\big|\hspace{-0.3em}\diagdown CH_2}}$$

The chemisorption of alkanes on oxide catalysts which are effective for their oxidation reactions is usually dissociative in nature. For example, ethane on iron(III) oxide or nickel(II) oxide yields chemisorbed ethyl radicals. At the same time the observation of 1,3-butadiene as a common intermediate present during the selective oxidations of *n*-butane or 1-butene on vanadium–phosphorus–oxygen catalysts suggests that the alkane must progressively lose hydrogen atoms to link up with the reaction pathway for the alkene.

Carbon monoxide is chemisorbed molecularly on many oxides of transition metals, donating 5σ electron density (see Fig. 5.4(b)) towards the metal cation. Back-donation of electron density from the positively charged metal ion would be expected to be negligible. In fact the 5σ electrons must be regarded as weakly antibonding with respect to the carbon–oxygen bond. On many oxides, including those of chromium(III) and zinc(II), the observed vibrational frequency of the carbon–oxygen bond is actually increased (by about $70 \, cm^{-1}$ in terms of the corresponding wavenumber) compared to that in the gas phase molecule (see equation (5.1)). At the same time the actual changes in the carbon monoxide electronic structure are relatively small, as reflected by the weak bonding to the surface, amounting to about $50 \, kJ \, mol^{-1}$ in the case of zinc oxide. This chemisorption behaviour indicates that catalytic conversions of carbon monoxide on transition metal oxides will be those which preserve the carbon–oxygen bond. Examples of such processes are the oxidation

$$CO + \tfrac{1}{2}O_2 \rightarrow CO_2$$

and the water-gas shift reaction

$$CO + H_2O \rightarrow CO_2 + H_2$$

In contrast to carbon monoxide, hydrogen and water tend to be dissociatively chemisorbed on most transition metal oxides. This is an obvious requirement in the water-gas shift reaction, for which the typical catalyst is an iron oxide.

5.3 Solid acid surfaces

Silica (SiO_2) and alumina (Al_2O_3) possess only very weak acidity in their pure forms. When however an intimate mixture of these at the microscopic level is created, the resultant material shows pronounced acidity (Section 3.2.2, Fig. 4.20). It is the surface acidity and its role in chemisorption which are the main interests in this section.

The simplest theory of acidity in silica–alumina (or aluminosilicates) is based upon different coordination requirements of aluminium (threefold) and silicon (fourfold) in the polymeric oxide structure. Silica is the excess component in the materials of main interest: this effectively enforces the fourfold coordination of silicon on the aluminium centres. An aluminium atom has valency electron structure of $3s^2\,3p^1$, allowing the formation of bonds to three oxygen atoms (each in turn shared between two aluminium atoms) in the 'natural' arrangement for alumina itself. In the structure imposed by silica, each aluminium atom is obliged to direct its Al—O bonds into three of the orientations corresponding to those of the tetrahedral configuration of Si—O bonds at the silicon atoms. As a result, the vacant tetrahedral direction at the aluminium atom offers a site at which a pair of electrons can be accepted with ease: at the elementary level such a pair of electrons would be regarded as completing the valency shell octet. A site which can accept a pair of electrons from another species is termed a *Lewis acid* site conventionally. The nitrogen atom in ammonia or organic bases such as pyridine has a lone pair of electrons which are available for donation to a Lewis acid site, giving rise to coordinatively bound nitrogenous chemisorbates (see Table 4.5).

There is another way in which the aluminium atom can achieve the fourfold coordination demanded by the silica structure. A Lewis acid site can be converted by interaction with a water molecule (as indicated in Fig. 4.20(b)), represented below in simple terms

$$
\begin{array}{ccc}
\mathrm{H-OH} & {}^{\oplus}\mathrm{H} \quad \mathrm{OH} & \left(\text{c.f. } {}^{O}_{O}{\diagdown}S{\diagup}^{\ominus}_{}O\text{-}\text{-}\text{H}^{\oplus}\right) \\
\mid & \mid \quad \downarrow & \\
-\underset{\mid}{\mathrm{Si}}-\mathrm{O}-\underset{\mid}{\mathrm{Al}}- \longrightarrow & -\underset{\mid}{\mathrm{Si}}-\mathrm{O}-\underset{\mid}{\mathrm{Al}}{}^{\ominus} &
\end{array}
$$

The process has allowed the aluminium atom to form a fourth bond by accepting the pair of electrons on a hydroxide ion (OH^-), which confers a negative charge on to the aluminium atom. At the same time, the complementary proton (H^+) achieves bonding with the neighbouring oxygen atom by accepting electron density associated with one of its lone pairs; this is represented by a broken line, denoting a partial bond. This site offers an easily donatable proton and is termed a *Brønsted acid* site. It is evidently analogous to pure sulphuric acid, shown as the structure in parentheses above. In the case of ammonia, chemisorption at a Brønsted surface site would be regarded simply as represented below

$$
\begin{array}{ccc}
\overset{\mid}{\underset{\mid}{\mathrm{O}}}\text{-}\text{-}\mathrm{H}^{\oplus} & & \overset{\mid}{\underset{\mid}{\mathrm{O}}}\ \mathrm{NH_4^+} \\
-\underset{\mid}{\mathrm{Al}}{}^{\ominus}\!\!-\mathrm{OH} + \mathrm{NH_3(g)} \longrightarrow & & -\underset{\mid}{\mathrm{Al}}{}^{\ominus}\!\!-\mathrm{OH}
\end{array}
$$

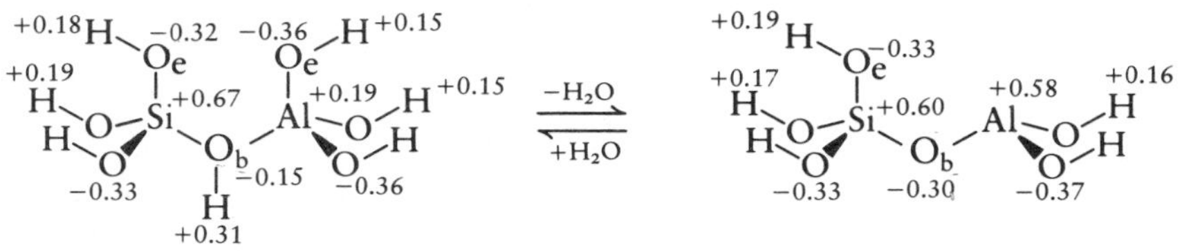

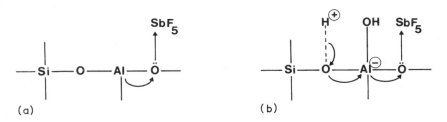

Fig. 5.7 Charge densities calculated for prototype units of Brønsted acid (left structure) and Lewis acid (right structure) forms of silica–alumina. Reproduced with permission of Academic Press Inc. from *Quantum chemical study of acid-base properties of metal oxides. I*, W. Grabowski, M. Misono and Y. Yoneda (1980) *Journal of Catalysis*, **61**, 106.

Spectral effects of the analogous process in the case of pyridine appeared in Table 4.5. Thus the Brønsted site *per se* is associated with the bridging hydroxyl group interposed between a silicon and an aluminium atom.

This simple model of silica–alumina has been developed through theoretical investigations of charge distributions in prototype structures. Figure 5.7 shows some typical results. Key features are the substantial positive charge (i.e. electron deficiency) at the aluminium atom in the Lewis acid form and the relatively large positive charge of the hydrogen atom on the bridging oxygen atom (O_b) in the Brønsted acid form.

The simple model may be pursued to the phenomenon of *superacidity* at solid surfaces. The term superacid is applied generally to substances which show stronger acidity than pure sulphuric acid. Consider what would happen at silica–alumina acidic sites if a species with strong electron-withdrawing ability (such as SbF_5) were introduced. This species would accept the lone pair of electrons on an oxygen atom to achieve bonding to the surface and would as a consequence deplete electron densities of other atoms in the vicinity. Figure 5.8 represents expected significant redistributions of electron densities at the acidic sites on silica–alumina. The extension of electron density withdrawal through to the O--H partial

Fig. 5.8 Electron density redistributions (indicated by arrows) accompanying the development of superacid sites of (a) Lewis acid type and (b) Brønsted acid type on silica–alumina treated with antimony pentafluoride (SbF_5).

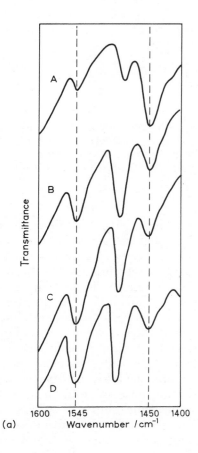

(a)
Transmittance

1600   1545   1450 1400
Wavenumber / cm^{-1}

Fig. 5.9 Features of a silica–alumina (13% w/w Al$_2$O$_3$) treated with antimony pentafluoride to induce superacidity. (a) Infrared absorption spectra after adsorption of pyridine. (b) Profiles indicating the distribution of acidic sites in terms of the heat released (*q*) on adsorption of ammonia gas, as measured by the parameter $\Delta V/\Delta q$, where *V* is the specific amount of ammonia adsorbed.

Identifying label	A and 6	1	B and 2	C and 3	D and 4	5
Sb content/m mol g^{-1}	0	0.69	0.94	1.31	1.72	2.22

Reproduced with permission of the Chemical Society of Japan from *Direct measurement of the interaction energy between solids and gases. VI. Calorimetric studies on acidic properties of solid super acids prepared from silica–alumina,* H. Taniguchi, T. Masuda, K. Tsutsumi and H. Takahashi (1980) *Bulletin of the Chemical Society of Japan,* 53, 2464.

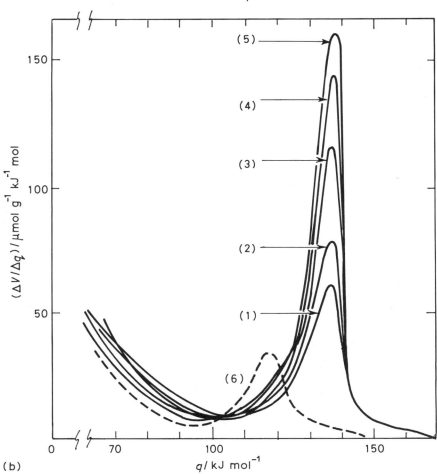

(b)

bond in the Brønsted acid structure (b) results in reinforcement of the positive charge at this nascent proton and hence more powerful Brønsted acid nature. Alternatives to antimony pentafluoride (SbF_5) for the treatment of silica–alumina to produce superacidity include phosphorus pentoxide (P_2O_5), aluminium chloride ($AlCl_3$) and the sulphate ion (SO_4^{2-}).

Figure 5.9 shows the effects on infrared absorption spectra (Section 4.4.6) and differential heats of adsorption (Section 2.3.2) which accompany the generation of superacidity on silica-alumina. As indicated in Table 4.5, the infrared absorption band marked 1545 (wavenumber/ cm^{-1}) in Fig. 5.9(a) arises when pyridine is adsorbed on Brønsted acid sites, whilst that marked 1450 corresponds to pyridine adsorbed on Lewis acid sites. The change of the ratio of the depths of these bands from spectrum A to spectrum D shows that SbF₅ treatment tends to create Brønsted superacid sites. Figure 5.9(b) demonstrates clearly the generation of the superacidic sites, characterized by considerably higher values of q than the predominant, weakly acidic sites of untreated silica–alumina. The number of superacidic sites increases with the amount of SbF₅ present on the surface. It is useful to compare Fig. 5.9(b) with the (integrated) data given in Fig. 2.8 for a similar silica–alumina, to perceive the large number of weakly acidic sites in the latter which are potentially available for conversion to superacidic sites.

Brønsted acidic sites tend to be the most significant for general action of acidic solids as catalysts. Alkenes are typical reactants in this connection; the mechanism of their chemisorption on silica–alumina is the acceptance of a proton from a Brønsted site, with the formation of the corresponding carbenium ion. For ethylene this chemisorption process may be represented

$$C_2H_4(g) + H^+ \text{-- solid} \rightarrow C_2H_5^+ \text{-- solid}$$

With different kinds of acidic solids, the stronger are the Brønsted acid sites, the greater is the ability to adsorb species *via* protonation. Conversely, the more resistant is the gas phase species to protonation, the stronger must be the acidity to effect chemisorption.

A quantitative measure of the strength of acidity is provided by the Hammett acidity function (designated H_0): the values of H_0 for Brønsted acids indicate the ability of sites to donate protons to a neutral base, such as an aniline derivative. For ease of perception, imagine that the overall process occurs through a hypothetical medium within which free protons can exist. Then the acidic solid (H—S) and the base (B) will be involved in equilibria governed by the equilibrium constants K_{HS} and K_a respectively, expressed in terms of activities (a)

$$H\text{—}S \rightleftharpoons H^+ + S^- , K_{HS} = (a_{H^+} a_{S^-})/a_{H\text{—}S}$$
$$BH^+ \rightleftharpoons B + H^+ , K_a = a_B a_{H^+}/a_{BH^+}$$

Invoking the conventional pK format for the K_a equation, one obtains

$$pK_a = -\log_{10} K_a = -\log_{10}(a_{H^+}) + \log_{10}(a_{BH^+}/a_B) \tag{5.2}$$

Activity (a) is defined as the product of the activity coefficient (γ) and the concentration of a species, when equation (5.2) is re-expressed as

$$pK_a = -\log_{10}(a_{H^+}(\gamma_B/\gamma_{BH^+})) + \log_{10}([BH^+]/[B])$$
$$= H_0 + \log_{10}([BH^+]/[B]) \tag{5.3}$$

It is helpful perhaps to note that in the limit of dilute solutions, when activity coefficients are unity, $H_0 = -\log_{10}(a_{H^+}) = pH$; the Hammett acidity function thus coincides with the more familiar definition of acidity under these conditions. It is also worth appreciating that the Hammett acidity function can be expressed as

$$H_0 = -\log_{10}(a_{H^+}(\gamma_B/\gamma_{BH^+})) = -\log_{10}\left(K_{HS}\left(\frac{a_{H-S}}{a_{S^-}}\right)\left(\frac{\gamma_B}{\gamma_{BH^+}}\right)\right) \qquad (5.4)$$

using the above expression for K_{HS} to substitute for a_{H^+}.

Equation (5.3) shows that the equilibrium ratio of concentrations of the forms BH^+ and B in contact with the acidic substance is governed by the difference between H_0 and pK_a. Organic bases (corresponding to B in form) have no strong colour usually but their protonated forms (BH^+) are often highly coloured. Thus when the value of $pK_a - H_0$ is positive (i.e. when $[BH^+]/[B] \gg 1$), strong colour will be observed. Since H_0 depends upon a_{H^+} and K_{H-S} hence (equation (5.4)), whether colour appears or not is governed by the strength of the acid. Values of (γ_B/γ_{BH^+}) do not in fact vary enough from one base to another to obscure this colour test.

Solid acids of catalytic interest offer a wide range of acidic sites in terms of their strengths (see Fig. 2.8 for exemplification). Thus the observation of the appearance of strong colour when an organic base is added to a suspension of the powdered solid in anhydrous benzene, a typical procedure, merely indicates that $pK_a > H_0$, when the value of H_0 concerned reflects the most strongly acidic sites present. Table 5.2 lists values of pK_a for organic bases which may be used in this connection and (minimum) values of H_0 for some acidic materials. None of the other solids in the right hand column of this table have achieved the wide range of usage of silica–alumina, so that discussion of the detailed origins of their acidic natures is not pursued in the present context.

Table 5.2 merely indicates ranges of H_0 values which encompass the most acidic sites present on the solid surfaces. The actual distribution of numbers of sites in terms of their acidic strengths can be determined by a technique which takes into account the established fact that organic bases tend to be adsorbed irreversibly in effect on contact with the acidic materials. The implication is that the base molecule sticks firmly to the site on which it is adsorbed first and does not desorb readily thereafter. Thus at ambient temperatures there is no proper equilibration of the base molecules to reflect the different strengths of acidity at various sites. However if the temperature is raised subsequently, the adsorbed base molecules will desorb from the weakest acidic sites first: ultimately at high temperature only the most strongly acidic sites will retain basic adsorbate species. On bringing the system back to ambient temperature from a particular high temperature (at which evacuation is used to remove desorbed molecules), the material is suspended in anhydrous benzene and contacted with various indicator bases. An indicator will be protonated (and thus will show colour) when it contacts sites from which the organic base (say pyridine) has been desorbed and which produce a positive value

Table 5.2 Values of pK_a for indicators and of H_0 for acidic materials at 300 K

Indicator	pK_a	Acidic material	H_0
2,4-Dinitrofluorobenzene	−14.52	Silica–alumina + SbF₅	>−14.52
2,4-Dinitrotoluene	−13.75	100% Sulphuric acid	−11.9
Diphenylmethanol	−13.30	Silica–alumina ⎫	
m-Nitrochlorobenzene	−13.16	Silica–titania ⎬ { >−12.7	
p-Nitrochlorobenzene	−12.70	Titania–zirconia ⎬ { <−8.2	
Anthraquinone	−8.2	Silica–zirconia ⎭	
Benzalacetophenone	−5.6	Titania–alumina ⎫ { >−8.2,	
Dicinnamylideneacetone	−3.0	Alumina–zirconia ⎭ { <−5.6	
4-Phenylazodiphenylamine	+1.5	SnO₂–MoO₃ ⎫ { >−5.6,	
Aminoazobenzene	+2.8	Alumina–vanadia ⎭ { <−3.0	
p-Dimethylaminoazobenzene	+3.3		
Methyl red	+4.8		

of $pK_a - H_0$. A series of experiments of this type would be conducted, involving progressive raising of the temperature at which the organic base is desorbed. The series of subsequent titrations with a solution of an organic base in anhydrous benzene using the indicator which responds to the most strongly acidic sites from which desorption has taken place then results in a cumulative acidity distribution. The next indicator going upwards in the left hand column of Table 5.2 will not show a colour change on contact with the solid prior to titration. The titration then measures the number of acidic sites on the surface with H_0 values down to (moving to larger negative numbers) but not equal to the pK_a value of this non-responding indicator. A plot representing typical results is shown in Fig. 5.10. Of particular note in this Figure are the large numbers of weakly acidic sites on silica–alumina (as also indicated in Fig. 2.8) and the small number of strongly acidic sites characterized by H_0 values of less than −8.2. In terms of all of the acidic sites having H_0 values below +4.8, this sample of silica–alumina had a surface density of the order of 10^{18} sites m^{-2}. This is a fairly typical value for several mixed insulator oxides, including titania–silica (1 : 1 by weight) for example.

Alumina itself can develop strong acidity when it is treated with various forms of fluorine or chlorine. On a simple view, strong Brønsted acidity induced by treatment with hydrogen chloride can be represented as shown below

$$
\begin{array}{c}
\text{—O—Al—O—} \quad + \quad \text{HCl(g)} \quad \rightarrow \quad \overset{\oplus\text{H}}{\underset{|}{\text{—O—Al}^{\ominus}\text{O—}}} \\
\quad\quad |\quad\quad\quad\quad\quad\quad\quad\quad\quad\quad\quad\quad |\\
\quad\quad \text{O}\quad\quad\quad\quad\quad\quad\quad\quad\quad\quad\quad\quad \text{O}\\
\quad\quad |\quad\quad\quad\quad\quad\quad\quad\quad\quad\quad\quad\quad |
\end{array}
$$

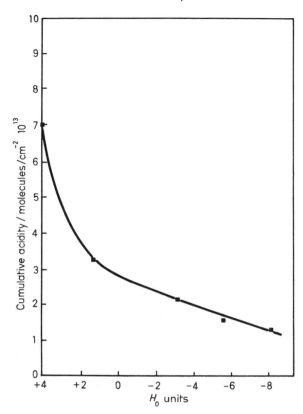

Fig. 5.10 Plot representing the cumulative acidity distribution of a silica–alumina containing 19.2% of Al_2O_3 by weight. A point on the curve indicates the number of acidic sites per unit surface area of the material which are characterized by Hammett acidity function values (H_0) less than or equal to the corresponding value on the horizontal axis. Reproduced from *The measurement of catalyst acidity II: chemisorption studies*, M. Deeba and W. K. Hall, (1985) *Zeitschrift für Physikalische Chemie Neue Folge,* **144,** 97 with the permission of R. Oldenbourg Verlag GmbH.

When fluorine is introduced to alumina, strongly protonic centres are formed, with $H_0 \leqslant -13.3$ as indicated by the strong yellow colour developed in conjunction with diphenylmethanol.

As was discussed in Section 3.1.2, zeolites are composed of silica and alumina building blocks and so will contain acidic centres. The crystalline nature of zeolites creates a rather special microenvironment in comparison with amorphous silica–alumina. Moreover on a geometrical basis,

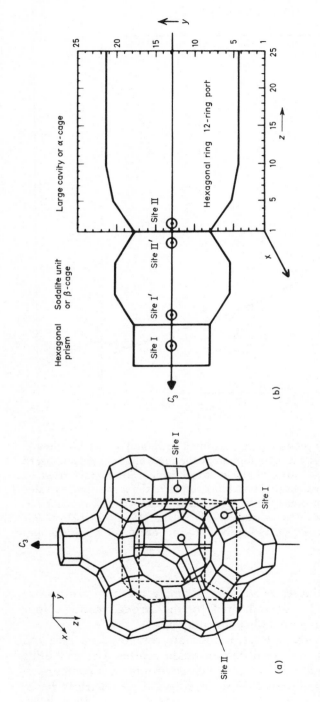

Fig. 5.11 (a) X-type zeolite structure showing axis orientation (x, y, z), three-fold symmetry axis (C_3) and the sites (I and II) occupied by Ca^{2+} cations (see also Fig. 3.3). (b) Section along the C_3 axis of (a) showing length scale along the z axis. The supercage (large cavity or α-cage) is terminated on the right-hand side by a pore aperture incorporating 12 oxygen (and 12 T) atoms. The representation is turned through 90° compared to that in diagram (a). (c) and (d) Three-dimensional plots of the electrostatic potential for a Ca^{2+}-exchanged X-type zeolite with equal numbers of Si and Al atoms. (c) shows the potential in an x–y section through the supercage close to site II $(z = 1)$ and (d) shows that close to the pore aperture $(z = 25)$, when all sites I and II are occupied by Ca^{2+} ions. The lattice points are indicated by the corresponding ions bearing formal charges $(Si^{4+}, Al^{3+}, O^{2-})$. Reprinted with permission from *Model calculations of electrostatic fields and potentials in faujasite type zeolites*, E. Preuss, G. Linden and M. Peuckert (1985) *Journal of Physical Chemistry*, **89**, 2956, 2957. Copyright 1985 American Chemical Society.

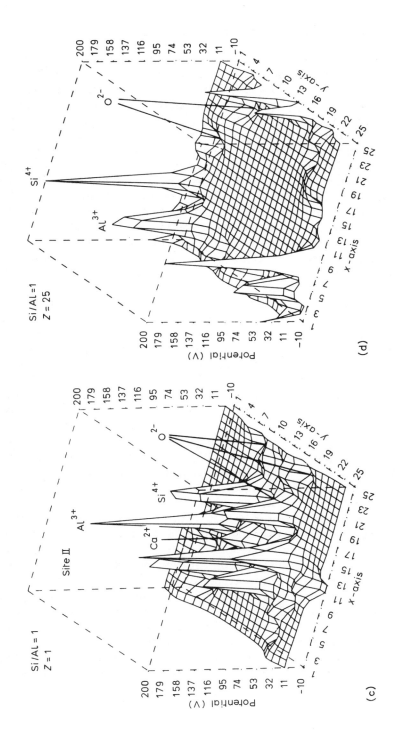

(c)

(d)

molecular sieve action restricts access of molecules above a certain limiting size to the internal surfaces. To exemplify this feature, in the sodium form of A-type zeolite, some of the Na^+ ions occupy positions close to the pore aperture (Fig. 3.4(a)), reducing the effective diameter to approximately 0.40 nm: this is small enough to exclude all hydrocarbons but not carbon dioxide (kinetic diameter = 0.33 nm). Replacement of Na^+ with K^+ inserts a larger cation into the same positions and consequently the pore aperture is restricted to 0.30 nm, small enough to exclude carbon dioxide but not water (kinetic diameter = 0.27 nm). On the other hand, replacement of Na^+ with Ca^{2+} in A-type zeolite results in no cations being located at the pore aperture. Thus unblocked, this pore aperture can be penetrated by linear alkane molecules (kinetic diameters = 0.38 nm (methane, ethane), 0.42 nm (*n*-hexane)) but not by branched alkanes such as isobutane (kinetic diameter = 0.50 nm). These potassium, sodium and calcium forms of A-type zeolite are often referred to as 3A, 4A and 5A molecular sieves respectively.

A feature of zeolites is the existence of localized electrostatic fields within the pore structure. Figure 5.11 illustrates the results obtained by computer modelling for a Ca^{2+}-exchanged X-type zeolite. The Ca^{2+} cations are localized at the two types of site (labelled I and II) indicated. Site I lies in the centre of a hexagonal prism whilst site II is about 0.05 nm removed from the centre of a hexagonal face of a sodalite unit on the wall of the supercage (Fig. 3.3). Figures 5.11(c) and (d) represent an important feature for the much greater catalytic abilities of zeolites as compared to silica–alumina, in showing that very high, localized electrostatic fields exist within the pore structure; this applies to zeolites in general. It is the crystalline structure which creates particular sites at which cations reside, removed spatially from the locations at which the balancing negative charges exist. Molecules entering the regions between such separated charges will be subjected to the influence of high electrostatic fields.

Another important feature is that acidic sites can be produced within X- and Y-type zeolites by exchanging rare earth cations, such as lanthanum (La^{3+}), for Na^+ in the initial sodium form. In this process, some of the sodium ions are not easily available for exchange: they have to be expelled from constricted parts of the structure and a prerequisite is divestment of their hydration shells. Reasonably complete exchange of sodium ions can be achieved by repeated immersions of the zeolite in hot aqueous solutions of the rare earth cation, followed by calcination at temperatures of the order of 600 K, with further immersion thereafter. The calcination results in the emergence of the residual Na^+ ions from constricted sites and their replacement with the rare earth cations already introduced into the zeolite: these Na^+ ions are then easily exchanged in the post-calcination immersion. Regarding La^{3+} as representative, the acidity which results arises from hydrolysis actions

$$La^{3+} + H_2O \rightleftharpoons La(OH)^{2+} + H^+$$
$$La(OH)^{2+} + H_2O \rightleftharpoons La(OH)_2^+ + H^+$$

and the subsequent spatial separation of the charged species at different types of site offered by the zeolite lattice. The equilibria above are also considered to be driven over to the right under the influence of the high electrostatic field gradients within zeolite channels. In fact the $La(OH)_n^{(3-n)+}$ ions occupy sites in the zeolite framework which reinforce its thermal stability, enhancing its usefulness as a hydrocarbon cracking catalyst. The pioneering catalyst was the rare earth exchanged form of X-type zeolite, which was reported on in 1962. Since then the acidic, rare earth-exchanged Y-type zeolites (designated REHY-zeolite) have become dominant in this usage in the oil industry.

The adsorption of alkenes as carbenium ions demands acidic sites of only moderate strengths: the process will occur on all of the solid materials given in the right hand column of Table 5.2. But the ability to adsorb alkanes effectively is restricted to superacidic sites (generally with $H_0 < -12.7$) and the alkane must have secondary or tertiary carbon atoms. Methane cannot be protonated on any known solid acid: in fact liquid trifluoromethanesulphonic acid (CF_3SOOOH) with H_0 decreased to -20 using SbF_5 is required for this process. Two mechanisms for the adsorption of a general alkane (RCH_2R') on a suitable solid acid are possible. A carbenium ion may be formed at a very strong Lewis site by the effective abstraction of a hydride ion (H^-)

$$RCH_2R' + \text{Lewis site} \rightarrow R\overset{\oplus}{C}HR' \text{--} H^{\ominus}\text{---Lewis site}$$

At a very strong Brønsted site, carbonium ions may be formed

$$RCH_2R' + H^+ \text{--Brønsted site} \rightarrow R\overset{\oplus}{C}H_3R' \text{ (Brønsted site)}^{\ominus}$$

The ability of acidic surfaces to chemisorb hydrocarbons is usually deduced from the resultant ability to induce cracking or isomerization reactions. Thus if no reaction of an alkane is induced on contact with a

Table 5.3 Reactivity of alkanes on SbF_5-treated silica–alumina at moderately high temperatures

No reaction induced	Skeletal rearrangement induced
Methane, ethane, 2,2-Dimethylpropane (neopentane)	Propane, *n*-butane, *n*-pentane, *n*-hexane, methylpropane, methylbutanes, cyclohexane, methylcyclohexane

particular acidic surface, even at moderately high temperatures, it may be concluded that adsorption is ineffective. Table 5.3 then reveals the different requirements in terms of the strength of acidity of sites for adsorption of various alkanes on a typical solid superacid. The alkanes which do not undergo reaction are characterized by the primary nature of all of their carbon atoms: these can be considered to demand sites with $H_0 < -14.52$ (Table 5.2) for effective adsorption. Equally it can be deduced that even those alkanes on the right in the Table require acidic sites with $H_0 < -12.7$ for effective adsorption, since superacids are required in order to achieve skeletal isomerization under normal conditions. In effect therefore a material possessing superacidic sites can be identified by its ability to

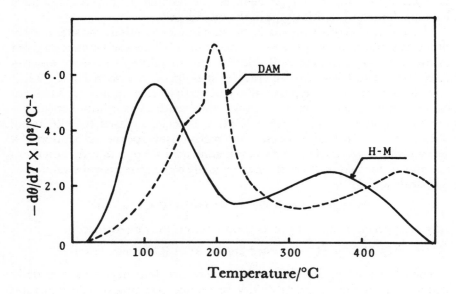

Fig. 5.12 Temperature-programmed desorption profiles for ammonia on acidic (HM) and dealuminated (DAM) mordenite zeolites. The vertical axis parameter $(-d\theta/dT)$ indicates the change in the fraction of the surface coverage by adsorbed ammonia (θ) for a 1 degree rise in temperature at the temperature concerned. The temperature (T) scale can be converted to approximate heat of adsorption values (q) by q (kJ mol^{-1}) = (T(°C) + 273)/3.8 (Section 4.3.1), so that $q = 150$ kJ mol^{-1} corresponds to $T = 300$°C approximately. The molar ratios of SiO_2 to Al_2O_3 in the materials are 14.6 (HM) and 53.0 (DAM). Reproduced from *Hydrogenation of carbon monoxide on Co reducing catalyst and solid acid (III). The effect of pore size and acid properties of zeolite on the product distribution*, H. Saima, K. Fujimoto and H. Tominga (1985), *Bulletin of the Chemical Society of Japan*, **58**, 796 with permission of the Chemical Society of Japan.

initiate skeletal isomerization of alkanes with secondary or tertiary carbon atoms at temperatures below 400 K in general.

The existence of superacidic sites in the acidic forms of some zeolites, such as ZSM-5 (Section 3.2.2), is revealed by their ability to catalyse skeletal rearrangements of alkanes at moderate temperatures. But the presence of these sites cannot be established by indicator colour changes, since they are confined within the porous structure. However, measurements of the differential heats of adsorption of ammonia on acidic zeolites have found considerable extensions of the profiles above 135 kJ mol^{-1}, the regime expected for superacidic sites (see Fig. 5.9(b)). In illustration, Fig. 5.12 shows thermal desorption spectra for ammonia on the acidic form of a zeolite, Mordenite (HM), and on the form which has had some of the aluminium extracted (dealuminated Mordenite (DAM)) by treatment with aqueous hydrochloric acid (8 mol dm^{-3}) for a day. On the basis of the approximate relationship $T_M/K \approx 3.8 E_d/\text{kJ mol}^{-1}$ given in Section 4.3.1 and comparison with Fig. 5.9(b), superacidic sites are responsible for the desorption of ammonia at temperatures exceeding 513 K or 240°C. Not only does Fig. 5.12 reveal the presence of superacidic sites but it also indicates the enhancement of the strengths of acidic sites associated with dealumination. Very strong acidic sites are general features of high-silica zeolites: when the aluminium centres are mutually well separated in a zeolite, there are few acidic sites in total but those present are characterized by much higher acid strength in comparison with a zeolite of higher aluminium content. It appears that when aluminium centres are in close proximity, they interact to decrease the strength of the associated acidity. It is also worth pointing out another important feature of high-silica zeolites at this stage. The solid is hydrophobic when the silicon/aluminium ratio exceeds 10, whereas zeolites with lower silicon/aluminium ratios are in fact hydrophilic.

5.4 Concluding remarks

This chapter has established the main features which govern chemisorption processes on the major classes of catalytic solids. The process of attachment to the surface involves different types of interaction for each broad class. This may be illustrated by bringing together the various ways in which propylene is chemisorbed. On a typical transition metal at temperatures of interest from the viewpoint of catalytic conversion, the chemisorption of propylene is dissociative in nature, resulting in atomic hydrogen and the propylidyne ($\equiv C-CH_2CH_3$) radical appearing on the surface and reflecting the tendency towards dehydrogenation on this type of surface. On a redox oxide, propylene may be expected to be dissociatively chemisorbed also, but in the form of an allyl radical ($CH_2{=}{=}{=}CH{=}{=}{=}CH_2$) bearing some positive charge. On acidic oxides, in contrast again, propylene is taken on to the surface in the form of the corresponding carbenium ion ($CH_3{-}\overset{\oplus}{CH}{-}CH_3$) which interacts electrostatically with a negatively charged centre on the surface. Such variations in the nature of the initial chemisorption acts with the type of adsorbent clearly signpost the routes to different types of products in the subsequent conversion processes which are central to catalytic reactions. The mechanisms of reactions catalysed by solid surfaces form the subject of the next chapter.

6

Catalytic actions on
solid surfaces

In this chapter the aim is to examine the factors which operate at the microscopic level to determine the rates and particularly the mechanisms of heterogeneous catalytic reactions. As has been emphasized in Chapter 5, the ability of a particular solid surface to chemisorb a reactant molecule in a specific form is a prerequisite for an individual reaction pathway to be followed. To exemplify in the case of carbon monoxide, non-dissociative chemisorption is essential for the synthesis of methanol whilst dissociative chemisorption must occur if hydrocarbons are to be synthesized from mixtures of carbon monoxide and hydrogen. In the large majority of surface catalysed reactions it is the set of microscopic actions on the surface after chemisorption of the reactants which controls the rate of reaction and the distribution of the products. It is to these cases that this chapter is addressed principally.

6.1 Reactions catalysed by transition metals

6.1.1 *Rate variations across the transition series*

The first points of interest are the general factors which result in variations of the rate of the same reaction under the same conditions, when the catalysts are in turn the progression of the metals along a transition series. Figure 6.1 represents an idealized summary of results in this respect, often termed a 'volcano' plot in obvious analogy of shape. Table 6.1 shows some representative data for the three reactions.

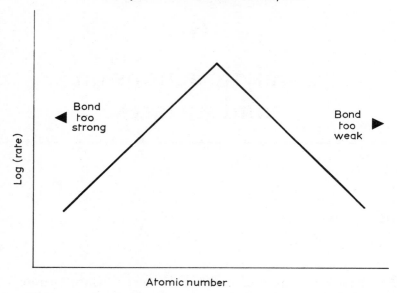

Fig. 6.1 Idealized 'volcano' plot of the variation of the rate of a specified catalytic reaction under the same conditions along a transition metal series.

1. Hydrogenation of ethylene with hydrogen on metals of the first transition series.
2. Hydrodesulphurization of dibenzothiophene on sulphides of metals of the second transition series.
3. Hydrogenolysis of methylamine (rate of formation of methane therein) on metals of the third transition series.

The general feature in this table is a maximum in the rate for the metals which have 6 to 8 *d* electrons in their atoms and this extends to a wide range of reactions catalysed by transition metals and also their oxides and sulphides. Reaction 2 above and the corresponding rows in the table exemplify this for a series of metal sulphide catalysts.

A simple understanding of the volcano phenomenon comes from consideration of the basic acts which must be parts of the catalytic reaction. Reactants must be chemisorbed on to the surface initially: to produce high adsorbate concentrations the chemisorption bond(s) concerned must be strong. But later each bond must be broken: the stronger is the chemisorption bond then the smaller will be the rate at which the species concerned can be transferred from the surface (to a coreactant for instance). A compromise is evidently needed. The chemisorption bond must be strong enough to produce reasonably high surface coverage by

Table 6.1 Variations of rates of catalysed reactions along transition series

			Cr		Fe	Co	Ni	Cu
1.	{ Metal		Cr		Fe	Co	Ni	Cu
	{ Rate		0.95		15	100	36	1.2
2.	{ Metal	Nb	Mo	Tc	Ru	Rh	Pd	
	{ Rate	0.5	2	13	100	26	3	
3.	{ Metal			Re	Os	Ir	Pt	Au
	{ Rate			0.008	0.9	100	11	0.5

Rate values are expressed in arbitrary units, the same along each row. The reactions (1), (2) and (3) are identified in the text.

the surface reactant species (and hence reasonably high rate on the basis of mass action), but not too strong to result in inhibition of the rate at the later stage. Following the trends evident in Fig. 5.3, chemisorption bond strengths are expected to decrease along transition series. Thus, as indicated within Fig. 6.1, at the start of the transition series the chemisorption bonds are too strong to be broken easily in the later stage, whilst late in the transition series the chemisorption bonds are too weak to produce surface coverage at the level required to lead to a high rate.

6.1.2 *Mechanisms*

It is the mechanism of the reaction on the surface and the relative rates of any competing steps which govern the selectivity achieved. Three general types of reaction, hydrogenation, hydrogenolysis and oxidation, are catalysed commonly by transition metal surfaces. Representative examples of these were given in Table 2.1. From the discussion of the chemisorption of hydrogen and oxygen in Section 5.1, it is evident that the corresponding chemisorbed atoms are intermediates in all of these reactions.

6.1.2.1 *Hydrogenation / dehydrogenation*

Unsaturated organic molecules can be chemisorbed on transition metal surfaces through π-bonding, involving donation of π-electron density from the adsorbate towards the metal surface. The *Horiuti–Polanyi* mechanism then pursues the logical course through stepwise addition of chemisorbed hydrogen atoms, breaking the bonding to the metal surface and creating new C—H bonds in turn. A chemisorbed radical, created by the addition of one hydrogen atom and attached to the surface through a single bond, is thus the likely intermediate. This mechanism may be illustrated by an example of hydrogenation of an unsaturated alcohol, as represented

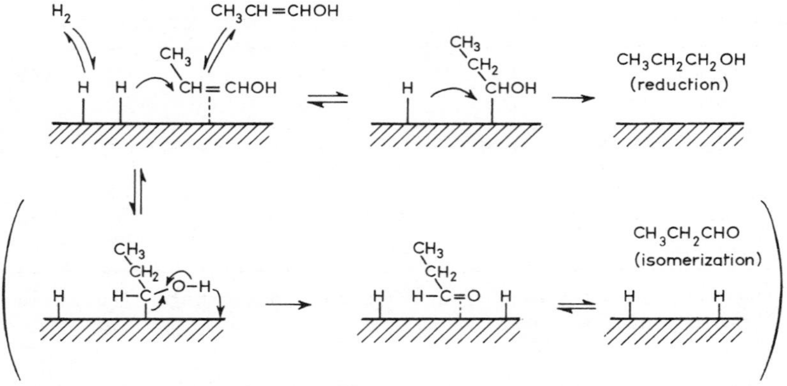

Fig. 6.2 Representation of the Horiuti–Polanyi mechanism for the hydrogenation of 2-propen-1-ol ($CH_3CH{=}CHOH$) to *n*-propanol (propane-1-ol, CH_3CH_2-CH_2OH), labelled as reduction, and the competing mechanism of isomerization, as conducted in methanol solution under hydrogen gas at temperatures in the range 293–323 K using a catalyst consisting of 1% (w/w) rhodium on an aluminium phosphate support. After J. A. Cabello, J. M. Campelo, A. Garcia, D. Luna and J. M. Marinas (1984) *Bulletin Société Chimique Belges*, **93**, 859.

in Fig. 6.2. In this instance the hydrogenation is accompanied by an isomerization process, resulting from competing dehydrogenation of the intermediate chemisorbed radical. The equilibria represented in this diagram bear out the fundamental point that catalysts which are active for hydrogenation will also be active for the reverse dehydrogenation under other conditions. The industrially important process of the hydrogenation of vegetable oils will be discussed in Section 8.1.

The ability of transition metal surfaces to effect the dehydrogenation of saturated hydrocarbons is of high importance, particularly in the oil industry. The Horiuti–Polanyi mechanism in reverse points to an initial act of dissociative chemisorption of an alkane to yield adsorbed alkyl radicals and hydrogen atoms. A further dehydrogenation step would then convert the alkyl radical to an alkene. But in the case of a larger alkane such as *n*-hexane, various dehydrogenation/rehydrogenation equilibria involving reorganization of carbon–carbon bonds can result in the first three processes shown in Fig. 6.3. Aromatization, cyclization and isomerization are valuable processes in the production of gasoline (see Fig. 6.10).

Ethylene becomes dehydrogenated in stages when it is adsorbed on transition metal surfaces and the temperature is raised steadily. Temperature-programmed reaction spectra (Section 4.3.1) show distinct peaks for hydrogen evolution. For example, on a platinum (111) face, the

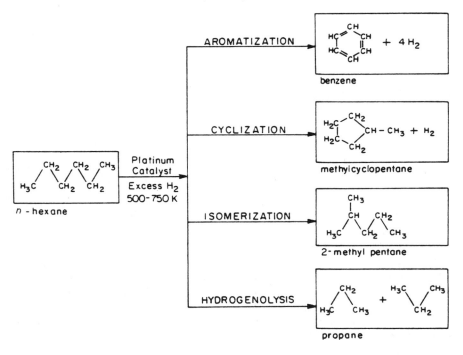

Fig. 6.3 Skeletal rearrangement reactions of *n*-hexane on platinum. Reproduced with permission of the Royal Society of Chemistry from *Molecular ingredients of heterogeneous catalysis*, G. A. Somorjai (1984) *Chemical Society Reviews*, **13**, 328.

stages are represented below with the temperatures at which the processes occur indicated.

$$C_2H_4(ads) \xrightarrow{250\,K} C\text{---}CH_3(ads) \xrightarrow{440\,K} CH_x(ads) \xrightarrow{>600\,K} C(ads)$$

The final product is a graphitic layer of carbon. This general scheme applies for other metal surfaces, although the temperature regimes for the stabilities of intermediates will vary. For instance on an iron (111) face at 200 K, the adsorbed ethylene undergoes partial decomposition whilst at 370 K the conversion to surface carbon is complete.

Hydrocarbons can be generated by the hydrogenation of forms of surface carbon. Experimental evidence is shown in Fig. 4.14(b): the AES carbon peaks reflect the creation of CH_x species arising from the contact of carbon monoxide and hydrogen with an iron surface. The ultimate results of the hydrogenation of these forms of carbon (deriving initially from the dissociative chemisorption of carbon monoxide) are processes such as methanation, represented as

$$CO + 3H_2 \rightarrow CH_4 + H_2O$$

and Fischer–Tropsch synthesis of longer hydrocarbon chains (Section 8.4). Steam-reforming of hydrocarbons is used industrially to generate hydrogen for various processes. In its extreme form, this results in the conversion of methane according to

$$CH_4 + H_2O \rightarrow CO + 3H_2$$

It is evident that this is the reverse of methanation (see equation above) and therefore the same catalysts, usually forms of metallic nickel, are used in both processes. The fact that the typical temperature used for steam-reforming of methane (1100 K) is much higher than that (600 K) used for catalytic methanation reflects the overall endothermicity ($206\, kJ\, mol^{-1}$ under standard conditions) involved in moving towards the carbon monoxide/hydrogen side of the corresponding equilibrium. All of these processes are expected to have carbon atoms and partially hydrogenated forms of surface carbon (see also Fig. 4.7) as essential intermediates; thus they work in one direction or the other through common elements of mechanism consequently. Further discussion of this is reserved to Section 8.4.

6.1.2.2 Hydrogenolysis

This process, as illustrated in the lowest part of Fig. 6.3, depends upon a much more complex set of factors than does hydrogenation. Subtle features of mechanism operate to determine whether one or more carbon–carbon bonds are cleaved and whether these bonds are terminal or medial in the original hydrocarbon. Platinum (as illustrated in Fig. 6.3) and palladium lie at one extreme, catalysing the scission of one carbon–carbon bond in the primary act, whereas iron tends towards the other extreme in catalysing multiple hydrogenolysis of higher alkanes to yield methane as the main product. Molybdenum induces single and multiple hydrogenolysis concurrently. With regard to the location of carbon–carbon bonds cleaved in higher alkanes, palladium and nickel favour terminal action, iridium favours medial bond cleavage and molybdenum and rhodium induce less selective actions but with some bias towards terminal cleavages. Faced with this plethora of reflections of mechanisms, only the most general points can be made. It appears that the carbon chain must be attached to the surface in the form of a bridge across several of the metal atoms, when electron densities in one or more of the carbon–carbon bonds are depleted by withdrawal towards the metal. Thereafter these weakened bonds break and the resultant fragments are hydrogenated to produce the smaller alkanes which are released to the gas phase.

Hydrogenolysis, in contrast to hydrogenation, appears to require sites consisting of an ensemble of metal atoms at the surface. Dilution of an active metal with an inactive metal would therefore be expected to reduce dramatically the number of locations on the surface at which the required ensembles exist. Accordingly the rate of hydrogenolysis falls sharply with increasing dilution of the catalyst metal. A dramatic exemplification is found in the combination of tin (inactive) with platinum (active), when an ordered solid solution results. Thus even with moderate tin contents, substantial ensembles composed of only platinum atoms do not exist. As a consequence, tin (25% atomic)–platinum surfaces offer almost no hydrogenolysis activity for *n*-hexane at temperatures up to 720 K (c.f. Fig. 6.3). On a similar basis, strong suppression of hydrogenolysis activity on nickel surfaces is observed when as little as 5% of copper (inactive) is alloyed in.

The ensemble requirement of hydrogenolysis would also be expected to be reflected in variations of the activity with the degree of dispersion of an active metal on a support. At high degrees of dispersion, many of the metal particles on the surface would be anticipated to become too small to create the required ensemble. An effect which may be explained in this way has been found in the hydrogenolysis of methylcyclopentane on rhodium supported on alumina. At a temperature of 493 K, the measured turnover frequency on a catalyst with 75% dispersion of rhodium (Section 3.1.1) was over an order of magnitude lower than that on the catalyst with 25% dispersion. In contrast, the turnover frequency for the hydrogenation of benzene (a process not subject to an ensemble requirement) was independent of the mean particle size of the metal down to 1.5 nm.

The general origins of the ensemble requirement can be perceived in two major features of general mechanism. Surface intermediates (including bridging forms) in hydrogenolysis demand multiple bonding to groups of adjacent metal atoms. Also the alkane is dissociatively chemisorbed and further adjacent metal atoms must presumably be required as adsorption sites for the hydrogen atoms so released.

6.1.2.3 Oxidation

Relatively few of the transition metals can be used as oxidation catalysts, since in contact with oxygen under the conditions concerned they produce stable oxides. Only the noble metals can be regarded as generally active catalysts in this respect. Chemisorbed atomic oxygen would be expected to be the effective reactant when molecular oxygen is used in conjunction with these metal surfaces. Evidence in connection with the oxidation of carbon

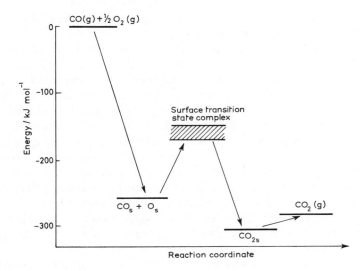

Fig. 6.4 Energy diagram representing the course of the oxidation of carbon monoxide proceeding catalytically on the platinum (111) crystal face.

monoxide on iridium was given in Section 4.4.4 and similar considerations would be expected to pertain for other transition metal surfaces. Oxygen is known to be dissociatively chemisorbed on platinum surfaces at temperatures above 150 K, whilst carbon monoxide is molecularly chemisorbed on platinum at all normal temperatures (Section 5.1). Figure 6.4 represents the energetic course of the oxidation of carbon monoxide on a platinum (111) crystal face. Discussion of some industrially important oxidation processes catalysed by transition metals will appear later in Sections 8.2 (ammonia oxidation) and 8.4 (ethylene partial oxidation).

In conclusion to this section, it can be stated that transition metals are effective as catalysts largely because they chemisorb hydrogen and oxygen dissociatively even at low temperatures. The chemisorbed atoms retain considerable reaction potentials; their disengagements from the surface in conjunction with the formation of new bonds (say to other chemisorbed species) are highly feasible in both kinetic and energetic terms.

6.2 Oxidation reactions on redox catalysts

A redox catalyst may be defined as a material with the ability to induce consecutive microscopic acts of oxidation and reduction at its surface, resulting in net chemical conversion of reactants derived from the gas phase. Two general mechanisms can be envisaged for the oxidation of a molecule X at these oxide surfaces.

$$\left. \begin{array}{c} \frac{1}{2}O_2(g) \rightarrow O(ads) \\ X(ads) + O(ads) \rightarrow Products \end{array} \right\} \text{(A)}$$

$$\left. \begin{array}{c} X(ads) + O(lattice) \rightarrow Products + lattice\ vacancy \\ \frac{1}{2}O_2(g) + lattice\ vacancy \rightarrow O(lattice) \end{array} \right\} \text{(B)}$$

These mechanisms are distinguished by the nature of the oxygen with which the adsorbed X reacts. In A the oxygen is adsorbed more rapidly than X and X(ads) reacts to remove this 'excess' oxygen. In B, X(ads) reacts with oxygen from the oxide lattice and the resultant vacancy is replenished afterwards using gas phase oxygen.

When X is an organic molecule, experience indicates that mechanisms of type A result in 'deep' oxidation, when the products are carbon oxides and water. This is of relatively little industrial significance. On the other hand, mechanisms of type B often result in selective oxidation, generating partially oxidized organic molecules such as carbonyl or unsaturated species. Almost one-quarter of the total production volume of the top 20 chemicals worldwide depends upon selective oxidation catalysed by solid oxides; many of these processes provide valuable feedstocks for the chemical industry. The general action represented by (B) is referred to as the Mars–van Krevelen mechanism and several key features of this have been discussed already in Section 5.2. The purpose here is to develop the microscopic chemical aspects of the reaction steps which occur on the oxide surface in this type of action.

The most selective catalysts used for selective oxidation processes formally contain a cation with an empty or full outermost d-orbital, typically Mo^{6+} ($4d^0$) or V^{5+} ($3d^0$) and Sb^{5+} or Sn^{4+} (both $4d^{10}$): the corresponding representations in terms of oxidation states are Mo(VI), V(V), Sb(V) and Sn(IV) respectively, the highest normally possible for these elements. The oxides of such elements have the ability to release associated lattice oxygen (formally O^{2-}) for incorporation into organic adsorbates, with compensating reduction of the oxidation state of the metal centres to preserve formal electrical neutrality. As stated in Section 5.2, the detailed structures of these oxides are not lattices composed of separate metal cations and oxide anions but involve coordinative bonds between oxygen and metal, not unlike those in the grafted structures shown in Fig. 3.5. Active vanadia and molybdena surfaces show infrared absorption bands corresponding to the presence of V=O and Mo=O bonds respectively. In exemplification, Fig. 6.5(a) displays the infrared absorption spectra for a vanadia catalyst working at various partial pressures of oxygen, revealing features at wavenumbers of 825 and 1021 cm^{-1} which mark the presence

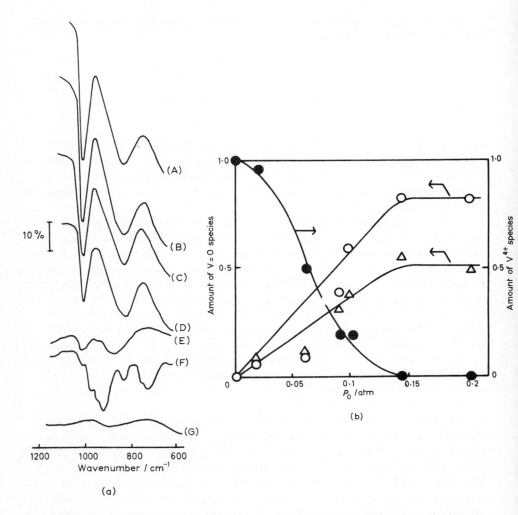

Fig. 6.5 (a) Infrared absorption spectra of vanadia catalysing the oxidation of benzene (partial pressure = 14.5 kPa) at a temperature of 662 K with partial pressures of oxygen (A) 206, (B) 145, (C) 101, (D) 92, (E) 61, (F) 21 and (G) 0 kPa. (b) Infrared absorbances (○ at 1021 cm^{-1}, △ at 825 cm^{-1} wavenumbers) corresponding to absorption by V=O groups and electron spin resonance signals (●) corresponding to V^{4+} (V(IV)) species as functions of the partial pressure of oxygen (p_O) (multiply by 101.3 to convert to kPa units) for the conditions specified in (a). Reproduced with permission of the Royal Society of Chemistry from *Activity and selectivity in the oxidation of benzene on supported vanadium oxide catalysts*, K. Mori, M. Inomata, A. Miyamoto and Y. Murakami (1984) *Journal of the Chemical Society, Faraday Transactions I*, 80, 2660, 2661.

of V=O groups. The variation of the rate of oxidation of benzene on this catalyst as a function of the oxygen partial pressure proved to be similar to the variation of these absorbances as shown in Fig. 6.5(b). At the same time the selectivities to the products (50% for maleic anhydride, 6% for benzoquinone and 44% for carbon oxides) did not vary. Similar relationships of the rate of oxidation to the number of V=O groups present on the surfaces of vanadia catalysts have been found in the catalysed oxidations of hydrogen, carbon monoxide, ethylene, butenes, butadienes and xylenes. Further evidence of the direct involvement of V=O groups in oxidation is that, when the supply of gaseous oxygen was terminated, oxidation continued until V=O groups had been eliminated from the surface, as marked by the disappearance of the corresponding absorption bands.

The V=O group has vanadium in the V(v) oxidation state. Vanadium in the lower oxidation state V(ɪv) can be detected in working vanadia catalysts by electron spin resonance techniques. The variation of the V^{4+} (V(ɪv)) signal shown in Fig. 6.5(b) shows an inverse relationship to the reaction rate. The vanadia surface can be regarded as responding to oxygen through the structures represented below

$$
\begin{array}{cc}
\overset{O}{\underset{|}{\overset{\|}{V}}}(v)-O-\overset{O}{\underset{|}{\overset{\|}{V}}}(v)- & \xrightleftharpoons[\tfrac{1}{2}O_2(g)]{\text{O to reactant}} \quad -\overset{O}{\underset{|}{V}}(ɪv)-O-\overset{}{\underset{|}{V}}(ɪv)-
\end{array}
$$

The corresponding Mars–van Krevelen mechanism then proceeds through oxidation of the chemisorbed organic species using oxygen derived from V=O groups, resulting in the reduction of pairs of V(v) centres to V(ɪv). Oxygen from the gas phase subsequently reoxidizes V(ɪv) centres to V(v), recreating V=O groups. The bond strength of V=O is approximately $300 \, kJ \, mol^{-1}$, which allows the oxygen atom to be reasonably labile. Confirmation of the Mars–van Krevelen mechanisms has been obtained in experiments with oxygen isotopes. In the oxidation of butane over vanadia ($V_2^{16}O_5$) using $^{18}O_2(g)$, only ^{16}O appeared in the products initially. This shows that it is oxygen in the surface of vanadia and not oxygen chemisorbed from the gas phase which induces the oxidation process.

Vanadia catalysts can be promoted by addition of a potassium salt. For example, in the oxidation of methanol to formaldehyde the selectivity of 85% on pure vanadia can be raised to 97% on the addition of 10 to 20% by weight of potassium sulphate. There is also an increase of the rate at a specified temperature. One interpretation is that potassium species on the surface donate electron density into the oxide; this reduces the strength of the coordinative bond V=O, which depends upon the extent of electron density transfer in the direction from O to V. This feature bears out the

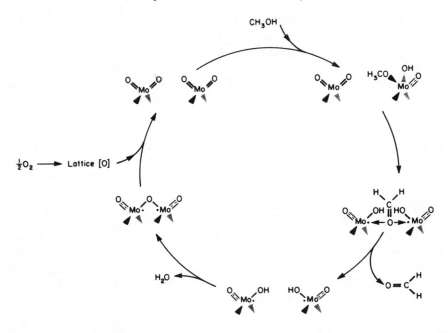

Fig. 6.6 Sequence of steps and intermediate species proposed for the conversion of methanol to formaldehyde on a molybdena surface. Reproduced with permission of Academic Press Inc. from *Oxidative dehydrogenation of methanol to formaldehyde,* J. N. Allison and W. A. Goddard III (1985) *Journal of Catalysis,* **92,** 132.

fundamental point that the performance of selective oxidation catalysts is strongly related to their ability to release lattice oxygen.

Equally in the case of molybdena catalysts, Mo=O bonds have been identified as the sites of selective oxidation. Figure 6.6 shows the sequence of steps which is believed to be involved when methanol is selectively oxidized to formaldehyde on a molybdena catalyst. Reference back to Fig. 3.5 will then make clear the origin of the selective oxidation ability of grafted molybdena catalysts, such as the structure (5) in that diagram.

Many of the most selective oxidation catalysts are chemical mixtures of oxides of metals or metalloids. The basic component is a transition metal oxide of groups V, VI or VII in the periodic table, because these oxides have the ability to make the nucleophilic addition of their lattice oxygen. Most commonly the oxides of vanadium or molybdenum are used in this role, whilst antimony pentoxide is also used sometimes. The other component is the oxide of an element with a lower oxidation state number, such as iron(II), bismuth(III) or uranium(IV); these lower valent centres act as the

Table 6.2 Examples of selective oxidation processes catalysed by chemically mixed oxides in the presence of molecular oxygen

Reactant	Major product	Catalyst components	Typical temperature /K
Propylene	Acrolein	$\left\{ \begin{array}{l} Bi_2O_3, MoO_3 \\ UO_2, Sb_2O_5 \end{array} \right\}$	650
Isobutene (+water)	Acetone	$\left\{ \begin{array}{l} UO_2, MoO_3 \\ SnO_2, MoO_3 \end{array} \right\}$	600
Methanol	Formaldehyde	Fe_2O_3, MoO_3	653
Acrolein	Acrylic acid	V_2O_5, MoO_3	673
1-Butene	Butadiene	CdO, MoO_3 (2% TeO_2)	683
1-Butene	Maleic anhydride	CoO, MoO_3	753

active sites concerned in the dissociative chemisorption of the organic reactant. Table 6.2 gives some examples of the catalysts and products. On these mixed oxides there is cooperative action between different structural units, which is perhaps best understood for the selective oxidation of propylene to acrolein on the mixed oxides of bismuth and molybdenum. Table 6.3 indicates the microscopic action considered to be associated with various parts of the structure. The vital role of the molybdenum centre is indicated further by the fact that when propylene/oxygen mixtures are contacted with bismuth oxide (Bi_2O_3) itself, 1,5-hexadiene, the product of the dimerization of allyl radicals, is the main product.

$$2CH_2{=}CH{=}CH_2 \rightarrow CH_2{=}CH{-}CH_2{-}CH_2{-}CH{=}CH_2$$

Thus bismuth oxide alone only induces the 'front end' of the selective oxidation process (i.e. the formation of chemisorbed allyl radicals) achieved on the mixed oxide.

Table 6.3 Action of structural units of chemically mixed oxides of bismuth and molybdenum in the selective oxidation of propylene

Unit	Action
Bi–O–Mo	Dissociative chemisorption of propylene to form the allylic radical by abstraction of the α-hydrogen atom
Bi centre	Chemisorption of the allylic radical
Mo centre	Supply of lattice oxygen for insertion into the allylic radical
Bi–O–Bi	Chemisorption of oxygen from the gas phase to replenish lattice oxygen at the molybdenum centre, achieved through solid state diffusion of oxide ions

Table 6.4 Selective (partial oxidation) range, activity (all products) and values of the heat of adsorption (Q) for 1-butene on chemically mixed oxide catalysts

Solid components	$\left\{ \begin{array}{c} Fe_2O_3 \\ P_2O_5 \end{array} \right.$	$\begin{array}{c} Fe_2O_3 \\ As_2O_5 \end{array}$	$\begin{array}{c} Fe_2O_3 \\ Sb_2O_5 \end{array}$	$\begin{array}{c} Bi_2O_3 \\ MoO_3 \end{array}$	$\begin{array}{c} Sb_2O_4 \\ SnO_2 \end{array}$	$\begin{array}{c} UO_2 \\ Sb_3O_8 \end{array}$	$\left. \begin{array}{c} Fe_2O_3 \\ Bi_2O_3 \end{array} \right\}$	Fe_3O_4
Selective range	$\mid \longleftarrow$					$\longrightarrow$	$\mid$	
Activity (rate)		Low			Medium			High
$Q/kJ/mol^{-1}$	25	43	49	50	59	67	73	86

The process shown in Table 6.2 for the oxidation of methanol to formaldehyde is of major industrial importance. The Fe_2O_3–MoO_3 catalysts (Mo/Fe = 2.0 to 3.6) achieve selectivities of 88 to 91% at temperatures in the range 570–670 K.

Table 6.4 indicates progressions of the values of the heat of adsorption of an alkene on oxide surfaces and the activity and selectivity achieved in the corresponding oxidation process. These data suggest a simple interpretation of the trends. When Q is relatively small, the chemisorption bonding is weak and consequently the surface coverage (θ) by the organic species is low, resulting in a low rate (activity). Conversely a high value of Q is expected to result in high coverage and high activity. Oxidation of the adsorbed organic species can be expected to proceed in stages: the first steps result in partial oxidation whilst the full set of steps yields deep oxidation. When the organic species reside on the surface for a shorter time on average (corresponding to lower Q), only the early steps can occur and selective oxidation is achieved. But when the adsorbate–surface bond is very difficult to break (corresponding to high Q) organic species are held on the surface for sufficient time that all steps have time to occur and deep oxidation is the result. Although the values of Q listed are for the alkene, intermediate species (such as doubly unsaturated molecules) have sufficiently similar chemisorption characteristics that it is not unreasonable to regard Q as providing a semi-quantitative measure for these also.

6.3 Hydrocarbon conversions on solid acid surfaces

In section 5.3 it was indicated that hydrocarbon molecules are chemisorbed on to acidic sites as positively charged species. Here the discussion is extended to the fates of these species with particular reference to the catalysed processes of isomerization, cracking and polymerization which are of major importance for the oil industry.

A simplifying assumption of general validity in this connection is that kinetic factors are often not limiting in the conversion processes. This implies that the majority of straightforward reaction steps are very rapid on the timescales concerned, so that thermodynamic factors have a considerable bearing on the resulting product distributions.

In cases where the hydrocarbon is an alkene, the adsorbed form is a carbenium ion. The thermodynamic stabilities of isolated carbenium ions may be considered first. Specific information with regard to chemisorbed carbenium ions is not available but relative stability trends observed for fluid phase carbenium ions appear to offer useful interpretations. Tertiary carbenium ions are the most stable, are the easiest to generate and tend to be the most prevalent of the isomeric forms. Denoting the directions favoured in the equilibria by longer arrows, the relative stability trend of the C_4 carbenium ions may be represented as

$$(CH_3)_3C^\oplus \xleftrightarrow{} CH_3CH_2\overset{\oplus}{C}HCH_3 \xleftrightarrow{} CH_3CH_2CH_2\overset{\oplus}{C}H_2$$

(tertiary)   (secondary)   (primary)

In keeping with extending this view to species on surfaces, theoretical chemical calculations have produced supportive results. For example, specific results have suggested that on the acidic zeolite HZSM-5 the 2-propyl carbenium ion ($CH_3\overset{\oplus}{C}HCH_3$) is some $87\,kJ\,mol^{-1}$ more stable than the 1-propyl carbenium ion ($CH_3CH_2\overset{\oplus}{C}H_2$) and that the tertiary butyl carbenium ion ($(CH_3)_3\overset{\oplus}{C}$) is about $133\,kJ\,mol^{-1}$ more stable than the 1-butyl ion ($CH_3CH_2CH_2\overset{\oplus}{C}H_2$). On a similar basis, the formation of the adsorbed ethyl carbenium ion (primary) from ethylene is a slightly endothermic process whereas formation of adsorbed 2-propyl carbenium ion (secondary) from propylene is exothermic. This accords with the general observation that propylene undergoes much faster oligomerization (see Fig. 6.8) than does ethylene on acidic materials at relatively low temperatures.

The necessary kinetic routes for interconversion of chemisorbed carbenium ions, including steps in which methyl (CH_3) groups migrate, are readily accessible, as may be inferred from product distributions. For example, the favoured product resulting from the interaction of 1-butene with an acidic surface would be expected to be isobutene, by way of the scheme represented in Fig. 6.7. This is a process of apparent kinetic control reflecting the thermodynamic stabilities of the surface carbenium ions rather than full chemical equilibrium between the gas phase species.

Other conversions of alkenes *via* carbenium ions on acidic surfaces are governed by the temperatures concerned. Two general types of processes

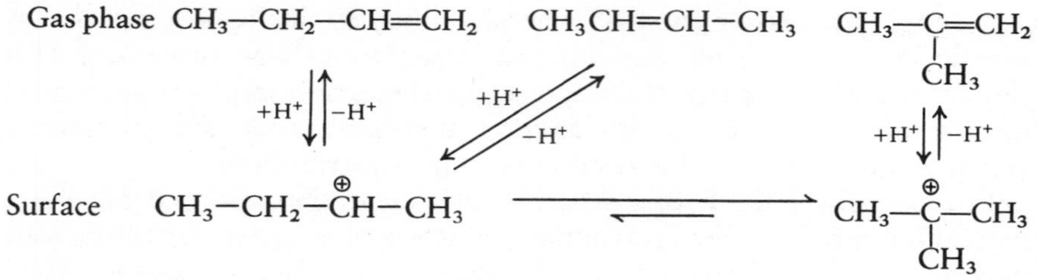

Gas phase $CH_3-CH_2-CH=CH_2$ $CH_3CH=CH-CH_3$ $CH_3-\overset{\displaystyle |}{\underset{\displaystyle CH_3}{C}}=CH_2$

$+H^+ \updownarrow -H^+$ $+H^+ \nearrow$ $-H^+ \swarrow$ $+H^+ \updownarrow -H^+$

Surface $CH_3-CH_2-\overset{\oplus}{CH}-CH_3$ $\xrightleftharpoons{\hspace{4cm}}$ $CH_3-\overset{\displaystyle |}{\underset{\displaystyle CH_3}{\overset{\oplus}{C}}}-CH_3$

Fig. 6.7 Scheme representing the mechanism of isomerization of 1-butene catalysed by Brønsted sites on an acidic surface.

may occur. *Cracking* occurs when longer chains fragment through the breaking of carbon–carbon linkages within the backbone. *Polymerization* occurs when new carbon–carbon bonds are created *via* the incorporation of an alkene molecule from the gas phase into a chemisorbed carbenium ion. The changes in enthalpy (ΔH) and entropy (ΔS) associated with these processes can be expected to be almost independent of the total number of carbon atoms involved and to differ mainly in terms of the sign for the two types of process. For cracking, ΔH will be positive (energy input required to break the C—C bond) and ΔS will also be positive (one chain generates two smaller chains). For the chain growth of polymerization on the other hand, ΔH and ΔS will both be negative. The value of the corresponding equilibrium constant and the net direction of reaction induced at a particular temperature (T) will be governed by the resultant sign of the Gibbs (free energy) function change (ΔG)

$$\Delta G = \Delta H - T\Delta S$$

ΔG is negative for a spontaneous process. When T is low, chain growth is favoured by the negative ΔH; although $-T\Delta S$ is positive, it is relatively small. On the other hand when T is high, cracking is favoured by a large and negative value of $-T\Delta S$.

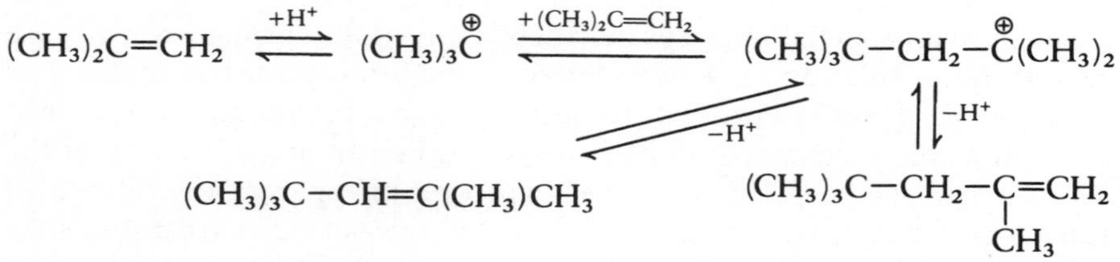

$(CH_3)_2C=CH_2 \xrightleftharpoons{+H^+} (CH_3)_3\overset{\oplus}{C} \xrightleftharpoons[-H^+]{+(CH_3)_2C=CH_2} (CH_3)_3C-CH_2-\overset{\oplus}{C}(CH_3)_2$

$\Big\updownarrow -H^+$

$(CH_3)_3C-CH=C(CH_3)CH_3$ $(CH_3)_3C-CH_2-\overset{\displaystyle |}{\underset{\displaystyle CH_3}{C}}=CH_2$

Fig. 6.8 Scheme representing the first stages of the oligomerization of isobutene on an acidic surface.

The process known as *oligomerization* of alkenes, in which dimers, trimers etc. are formed, provides an illustration of polymerization. A typical instance is the oligomerization of isobutene at 373 K temperature and 20 bars pressure in the presence of the acidic surface offered by sulphonated styrene–divinylbenzene copolymers. These solids are moderately acidic, the sulphonic acid groups having H_0 values in the range -5.6 to -2.4 (Section 5.3). The carbenium ion mechanism through which this oligomerization proceeds is represented in Fig. 6.8. Further similar acts form trimers, tetramers etc. The value of this process industrially is that it provides a means of converting alkenes into higher alkenes without

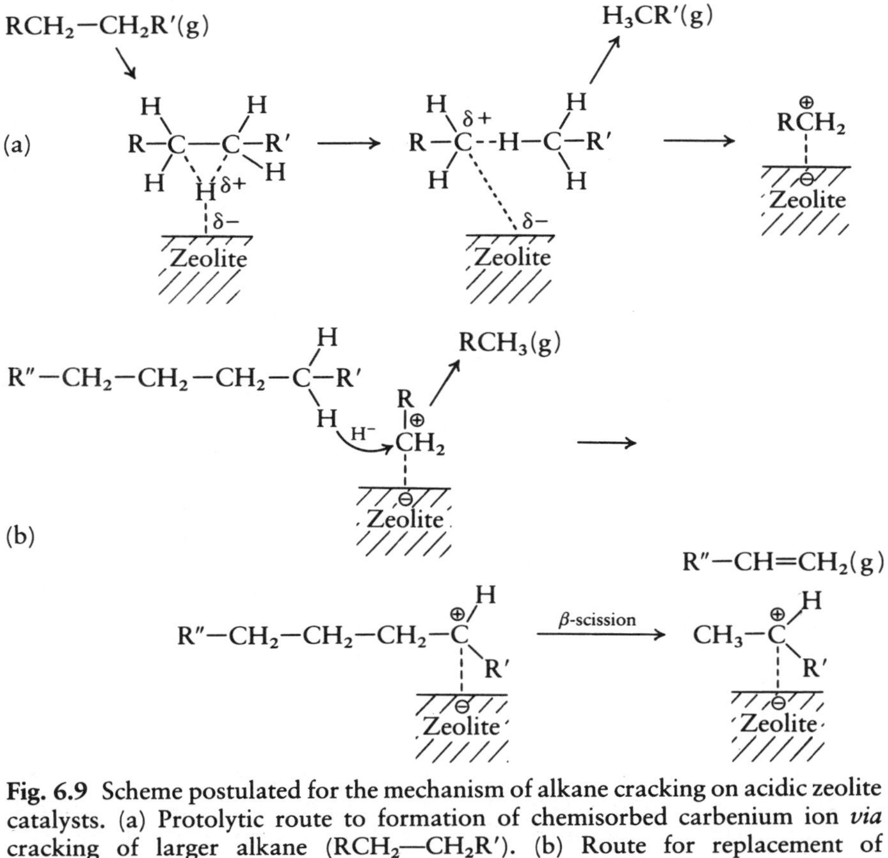

Fig. 6.9 Scheme postulated for the mechanism of alkane cracking on acidic zeolite catalysts. (a) Protolytic route to formation of chemisorbed carbenium ion *via* cracking of larger alkane (RCH_2—CH_2R'). (b) Route for replacement of carbenium ion *via* hydride transfer from a gas phase alkane (R''—CH_2—CH_2—CH_2—CH_2—R'), showing the β-scission process leading to the release of an alkene (R''—CH=CH_2) to the gas phase. After a scheme given by A. Corma, J. Planelles, J. Sáuchez-Marín and F. Tomás (1985) *Journal of Catalysis*, **93**, 30–37.

opening up pathways leading to aromatic hydrocarbons. Thus propylene may be used to produce 4-methylpent-1-ene, the latter serving as an important monomeric feedstock for the production of various polymers.

Cracking takes place usually at temperatures of 800 K or higher. Aspects of this are discussed in Section 8.8.

Alkanes (paraffins) are not chemisorbed effectively on moderately acidic solids (Section 5.3). Only superacids have the ability in general to donate protons to alkane molecules at moderate temperatures. Some of the acidic sites of zeolites are strong enough to qualify as having superacidity and can therefore create positively charged, chemisorbed species from alkanes. The process may involve hydride (H^-) transfer at a Lewis site. At Brønsted superacidic sites, it is believed that a process of protolytic cracking by way of an intermediate carbonium ion may occur, as represented in Fig. 6.9(a). Figure 6.9(b) illustrates a mechanism whereby a subsequent process of hydride transfer can occur to result in the chemisorption of another large alkane molecule on to the surface. The latter process establishes a general chain cycle, during the course of which the surface remains covered with carbonium ions but no molecular hydrogen is released to the gas phase, as has been observed in practice.

6.4 Reforming catalysts

A substantial proportion of the product which emerges from the cracking of crude oil (Section 8.8) is composed of linear alkane chains. In the gasoline range (C_5–C_{11}), linear alkanes are inferior fuels for a spark ignition engine, as reflected in their low octane numbers. The scale of octane numbers is based upon the allocation of a value of zero to *n*-heptane and a value of 100 to isooctane. The higher is the octane number, the more acceptable is the fuel for conventional automobile engines. Figure 6.10 represents how octane numbers vary with the structural characteristics of the molecules of hydrocarbons. This makes it clear that the upgrading of the output of an oil cracking plant must involve the induction of chain branching and aromatization, but in the absence of further cracking action.

The common acidic catalysts, such as silica–alumina and acidified alumina, interact with alkenes, but not with alkanes, to promote chain branching. In Section 6.1 the abilities of transition metals to catalyse dehydrogenation of alkanes to alkenes were pointed out. Consider then the result of an alliance between say platinum and silica–alumina effected by way of dispersion of the metal on the latter (Section 3.2.3). Figure 6.11 represents the general action to be expected, with alkenes diffusing through the gas phase from metal to acidic sites and *vice versa*. It is easy to prove

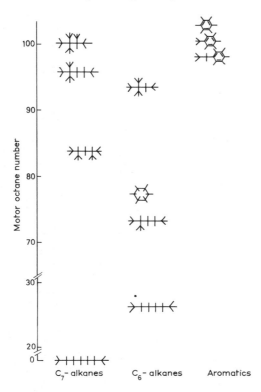

Fig. 6.10 Diagram showing the (motor) octane numbers found for various hydrocarbon structures and types.

that migration between the two types of sites occurs through the gas phase. A mechanical mixture of particles of platinum dispersed on silica (no acidic functionality) and silica–alumina (no metal functionality) can also catalyse this reforming of alkanes. Here the two types of site are isolated spatially and diffusion of the alkenes through the gas phase from one to the other provides the only conceivable mechanism for linking their actions.

In conjunction with the ability (Fig. 6.3) of platinum to induce cyclization and aromatization of alkanes with six or more carbon atoms, the dual function, reforming catalyst can yield branched and ring structures without the induction of significant cracking. In practice the reforming process is conducted at temperatures of around 750 K in the presence of added hydrogen to suppress both coking and excessive degrees of aromatization. Hydrogen/hydrocarbon molar ratios in the range 5–8 are fed to the catalytic reformer unit, which contains pressures of 35–50 bars.

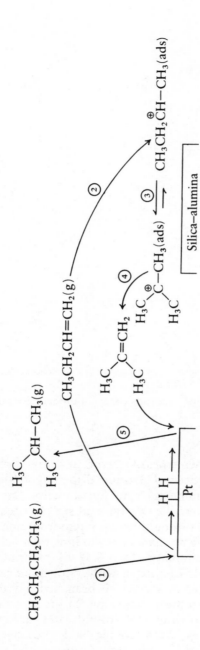

Fig. 6.11 Representation of the mechanism of reforming of *n*-butane on a platinum/silica–alumina dual function catalyst. The stages are (1) chemisorption of *n*-butane on platinum with dehydrogenation to release 1-butene (say), (2) and (4) diffusion of butenes through the gas phase, (3) carbenium ion interconversion and (5) the release of the reformed butane (isobutane) resulting from hydrogenation of the reformed butene (isobutene).

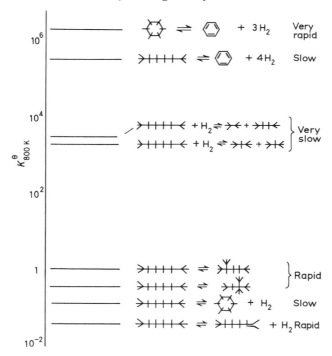

Fig. 6.12 Magnitudes of values of standard equilibrium constants at a temperature of 800 K ($K^{\ominus}_{800\,K}$) for various structural conversions of *n*-hexane and cyclohexane, with commentary on the rates of the forward reactions on a typical reforming catalyst on the right. Data based upon tabulated data given in *The Chemical Thermodynamics of Organic Compounds*, D. R. Stull, E. F. Westrum, Jr. and G. C. Sinke (1969) John Wiley & Sons Inc, New York.

A platinum–rhenium alloy supported on acidic alumina provides the superior reforming catalyst, when significant amounts of sulphur have been used to poison the metal surface partially. The combined action of rhenium and sulphur suppresses coking. The sulphur atoms are bound preferentially to rhenium atoms, reflecting the stronger bonding to $Re(5d^5)$ than to $Pt(5d^8)$ on the basis of the trends shown in Fig. 5.3. It is believed that the sulphur atoms act to impede the reorganization of hydrocarbon fragments adsorbed on platinum atoms into large pseudo-graphitic structures which are the precursors of coke. In fact it is essential to block the rhenium atoms with chemisorbed sulphur since otherwise the rhenium–carbon bonds which would form would tend to be too strong to permit easy desorption of hydrocarbon species. As a transition metal catalyst itself, rhenium would lie well down the branch marked as 'bond too strong' in the corresponding volcano plot of the form shown in Fig. 6.1.

Figure 6.12 indicates thermodynamic and kinetic features of significance for catalytic reforming. This diagram suggests the scale of contact times used in catalytic reforming. Linear alkanes will form branched chains rapidly: in the case of C_{6+} alkanes the number of isomers is large, so that for example an *n*-octane feedstock will be converted largely into branched chain octanes. Cycloalkanes (often known as naphthenes) are converted rapidly and almost completely to aromatics. However it is advantageous to restrict contact times in order to limit the extent of hydrocracking (achieving the same effect as hydrogenolysis (Section 6.1.2.2)) and excessive aromatization of *n*-alkanes, represented as being very slow, and slow processes respectively in the upper part of Fig. 6.12.

6.5 Concluding remarks

This chapter has examined the microscopic action involved in catalytic reactions on different types of solid surfaces. Those factors, particularly of an electronic nature, which operate to associate particular catalytic conversions with surfaces of each of the broad classes of solids have been explained at a basic level. Reasons should now be apparent for the application of transition metal surfaces to hydrogenation/dehydrogenation processes, of oxides of transition metals and metalloids to selective oxidation of organic species and of acidic surfaces to skeletal rearrangements of hydrocarbons. The discussion of specific industrial processes exemplifying the principles will be taken up in Chapter 8.

7

Catalytic action by enzymes

The main interests in this chapter are the microscopic aspects of catalytic actions by enzymes and the applications of enzymes in large scale processes. The discussion follows on from introductions given in Sections 2.2 and 2.4.3.

7.1 Origin of reactivity at the active site

Enzymes are self-contained entities at the molecular level. Unlike a solid catalytic material, the active site of an enzyme cannot be regarded as having been produced as a result of the cleavage of a larger bulk. Rather, catalysis by enzymes depends upon the ability of the active site (Fig. 2.1) to subject at least part of a substrate molecule to the special conditions of the microenvironment within its cleft structure. The interior of the globular form adopted by the enzyme molecule tends to be hydrophobic in nature and thus might be regarded as having the characteristics of a non-polar organic phase. In other cases, the active site may present metal atoms in particular oxidation states (Table 2.3) which are available for interaction with substrates.

The large majority of enzymes of commercial significance are hydrolases (Tables 2.5, 2.6). Lysozyme may be considered as a representative example of this class: it catalyses the splitting of polysaccharide chains with incorporation of a water molecule to 'patch' the broken ends. Lysozyme is one of the relatively few enzymes for which full details of the molecular structure are known. It is composed of 129 amino acid residues joined through peptide linkages. Each amino acid residue along the chain from the end with the uncondensed amino (NH_2) group is allocated a number in sequence from 1 to 129, this last residue having an uncondensed carboxylic acid group (COOH). Those units in the coiled chain which are crucial to the catalytic ability can be identified by measurements of residual activity when controlled excisions/replacements of particular parts of the polypeptide chain have been performed. Often these key units have widely differing sequence numbers. In lysozyme a glutamic acid residue at position 35 (Glu 35) and an aspartic acid residue at position 52 (Asp 52) are vital to the activity. It is the folding and coiling of the chain in achieving the overall globular shape of the enzyme molecule which bring these two units into contiguity across the active site. The carboxy groups of these units may be regarded as 'the cutting edges of the chemical scissors'.

Saccharides (sugars) can be cleaved hydrolytically in aqueous solution, but strong mineral acids (e.g. sulphuric) are required to achieve significant rates. Weakly acidic carboxylic groups (e.g. acetic acid) do not induce significant rates in aqueous solution, but these are spectacularly effective at the enzyme active site. The fundamental reason for the ineffectiveness of hydrolytic action by organic acids in aqueous solution is the solvation of charged entities therein by dipolar water molecules. This results in electrostatic shielding of substrate molecules from the polarity associated with the acid and thus suppression of hydrolytic cleavage. In the absence of such screening of charges, as would be expected in an organic solvent of low dielectric constant (i.e. low polarity), even weak acids in conventional terms can induce reactivity in substrate molecules by transmitting their polar nature more effectively. This latter condition corresponds with the general nature of the microenvironment presented within the active site (cleft) of the enzyme, reflecting the 'organic solvent' properties of the interior. Within the cleft there is an effective interface between 'organic' and aqueous phases.

Figure 7.1 represents a view of the action of the 'chemical scissors' in the hydrolysis of a polysaccharide chain effected by lysozyme. A water molecule derived from the aqueous phase is used to repair the severed ends of the cleaved substrate chain, with OH groups. In this representation, electron density redistribution in the carbon–oxygen bond which links the rings of the polysaccharide is considered to be induced by the polarity of the carboxylate (COO^-) group of Asp 52. The resultant partial negative charge on the oxygen atom in the substrate chain induces in turn a proton (H^+) transfer from the carboxylic acid group of Glu 35. The water molecule incorporated may be envisaged to dissociate into ions, the H^+ replacing that lost by Glu 35, the OH^- attaching to the positively charged carbon at the base of the ring of the substrate. The carbon–oxygen bond of the substrate cleaved and electron redistribution having taken place, hydroxylic (OH) groups are the terminal groups of the polysaccharide

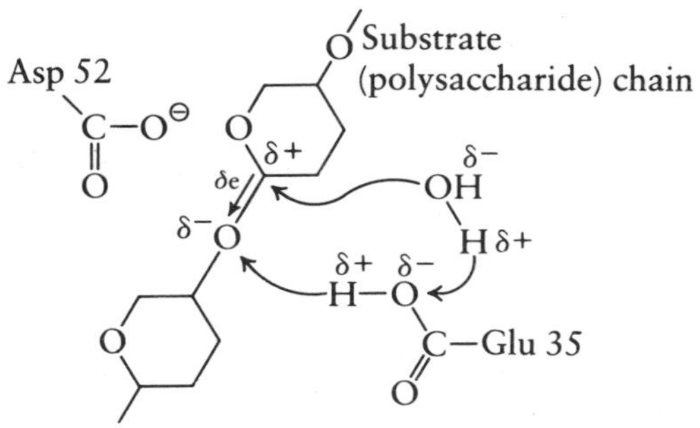

Fig. 7.1 Representation of the critical action at the active site of the enzyme lysozyme resulting in the cleavage of a polysaccharide chain. Symbols $\delta +$ and $\delta -$ indicate partial charges and curved arrows directions of eventual movement of atoms.

fragments generated as products. With these released, the active site of the enzyme is made available for further hydrolysis action.

Serine proteases, such as chymotrypsin, possess a so-called 'catalytic triad' of three amino acid residues critical for activity, designated aspartate 102, histidine 57 and serine 195. Figure 7.2 represents the disposition of these groups for the hydrolytic action which is catalysed. An alcohol group on serine (Ser 195), an imidazole ring on histidine (His 57) and a carboxylate group on aspartate (Asp 102) in line are indicated as the key groups of these residues. In the case illustrated in Fig. 7.2, the substrate is represented simply as $>\!C\!\!=\!\!O$, the critical part of the peptide or ester linkage being hydrolysed. This triad constitutes a sort of charge relay system. It is believed that the oxygen atom of the Ser 195 side chain interacts through a lone pair of electrons with the carbon atom of the substrate, leading to the formation of an acyl–enzyme intermediate complex. At the same time, the hydroxylic hydrogen atom of the Ser 195

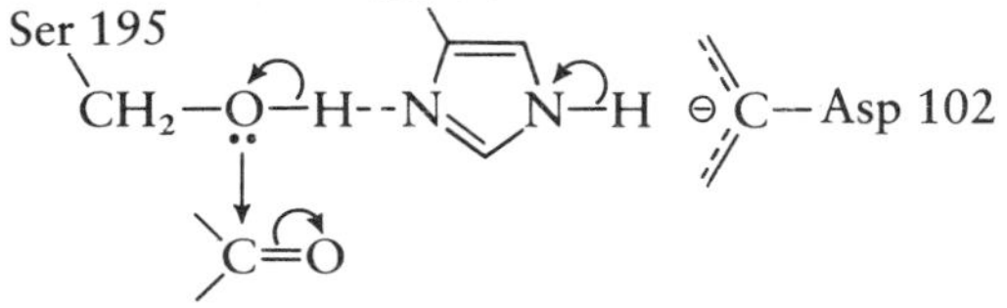

Fig. 7.2 Basic representation of the action of the 'catalytic triad' of serine proteases (key groups of the enzyme in the top row) on a peptide or ester substrate (only carboxyl $C\!\!=\!\!O$ shown). Electronic charge density movements are indicated by arrows.

side chain is transferred as a proton (H^+) to the imidazole side chain of His 57. The consequence is that an intermediate state with a negative–positive–negative charge distribution is created along the triad. This alternating polarity is believed to induce a complementary charge redistribution in the substrate, destabilizing the linkage which breaks eventually. A water molecule is incorporated to provide the new end groups of the resulting chain fragments.

The specificity of the action of an enzyme originates from the need for the substrate molecule to fit in the appropriate manner into the configuration created by the cleft constituting the active site. In the simplest terms, this could be regarded as a 'lock–key' analogy, which could be developed into requirements of configurational and electronic complementarity between the active site and the suitable substrate. In other words, the substrate must be able to adopt both a shape and electron-density distribution compatible with crucial units within the cleft. The substrate molecule generally will be subjected to several spatially distributed forms of interaction at the active site. For example, the substrate tyrosyl adenylate is known to be attached to the enzyme tyrosyl-*t*-RNA-synthetase through at least eight hydrogen bonds. As a general consequence of its multiple points of attachment, the substrate molecule might be envisaged as being geometrically distorted from its normal configuration as it resides within the active site of the enzyme. In conjunction with redistributions of electron densities within bonds under the influence of charges, as indicated in the examples given above, this could be considered to render the substrate molecule into a reactive condition. In fact some enzymes induce remarkable activities, manifested by turnover numbers which may extend above 10^5 s^{-1}: it is spectacular indeed when a single active site can convert such huge numbers of substrate molecules in a single second.

7.2 The pH-sensitivity of enzyme catalysis

In many enzyme catalysed reactions, the rate is a strong function of the pH of the aqueous medium and achieves a maximum value at the optimum pH value. Figure 7.3 shows the form of a plot representing the variation of rate against pH for lysozyme-catalysed hydrolysis of a substrate, under conditions when the substrate concentration is very much greater than the value of the Michaelis constant, K_m, for the system (equation 2.21). The effect can be interpreted in this case by considering the effect of pH variation on the key groups at the active site of the enzyme shown in Figure 7.1. When the pH is progressively decreased, the carboxylate (COO^-) group of Asp 52 will eventually become a carboxylic acid group (COOH). In view of the critical electron density redistribution in the substrate

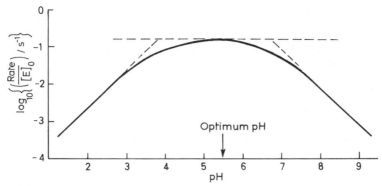

Fig. 7.3 Idealized plot representing the pH dependence of the rate of the lysozyme-catalysed hydrolysis of the $\beta(1 \rightarrow 4)$-linked hexamer of N-acetyl-D-glucosamine. $[E]_0$ is the added concentration of enzyme. Constructed from data given by S. K. Banerjee, I. Kregar, V. Turk and J. A. Rupley (1973) *Journal of Biological Chemistry*, **248**, 4786–4792.

induced by the negative charge of this carboxylate group, it is logical that its conversion to an uncharged carboxylic acid group will destroy the enzyme activity. Equally with progressively increasing pH, the carboxylic acid group of Glu 35, vitally concerned in proton donation to the substrate, will be expected to become a carboxylate group, again destroying the activity of the enzyme. Thus if the form of the enzyme represented in Fig. 7.1 is denoted as EH, the optimum pH phenomenon can be regarded as originating in a series of proton exchange equilibria as expressed in the simplified scheme shown in Fig. 7.4. Only EHS of the enzyme–substrate

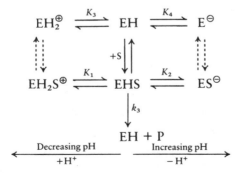

Fig. 7.4 Representation of the protonation/deprotonation equilibria of an enzyme (EH) and enzyme–substrate complex (EHS) imposed on the Michaelis–Menten mechanism. Dashed lines indicate possible additional processes to the main scheme.

complexes has the key groups in the forms required to induce the conversion of the substrate S to the product P. It is evident that there will be some intermediate pH value when the fraction of total enzyme in the active forms EH and EHS will achieve a maximum value: this corresponds to the optimum pH condition.

Quantitative analysis of the variation of enzyme activity of this type with pH can be made in terms of the pK values of the critical groups. On the basis of their assignation in Fig. 7.4, pK_1 and pK_2 correspond to equilibrium constants expressed in concentrations as

$$K_1 = \frac{[EHS][H^+]}{[EH_2S^+]}, \quad K_2 = \frac{[ES^-][H^+]}{[EHS]} \tag{7.1}$$

Analysis of the reaction scheme on the basis of the Michaelis–Menten mechanism (as used to produce equation (2.21)) under the condition that $[S] \gg K_m$ yields the rate equation (7.3) through application of equation (7.2). Under these conditions, the overwhelming fraction of the enzyme present in total exists in the enzyme–substrate complex forms, so that the effective expression for the added enzyme concentration, $[E]_0$, is

$$[E]_0 = [EHS] + [EH_2S^+] + [ES^-] = [EHS]\left\{ 1 + \frac{[H^+]}{K_1} + \frac{K_2}{[H^+]} \right\} \tag{7.2}$$

$$\text{Rate } (R) = k_3[EHS] = \frac{V_{max}}{(1 + [H^+]/K_1 + K_2/[H^+])} \tag{7.3}$$

This analysis makes the reasonable assumption that the proton exchange reactions are always in equilibrium. At low pH, the second denominator term in equation (7.3) will be dominant, whilst at high pH, the third term will be dominant. The derived forms of equation (7.3) expressed on a decadic logarithmic basis are then as follows

$$\log R = \log V_{max} + pH - pK_1 \text{ (low pH)} \tag{7.4a}$$
$$\log R = \log V_{max} - pH + pK_2 \text{ (high pH)} \tag{7.4b}$$
$$(pH = -\log[H^+], pK = -\log K)$$

These equations predict linear plots of log R *versus* pH (as seen in the wings of Fig. 7.3): the dashed extrapolated lines intersect at the condition log R = log V_{max} i.e. when pH = pK_1 on the left and pH = pK_2 on the right when the assumption is made that the second and third denominator terms in equation (7.3) are very much less than unity at the optimum pH. In Fig. 7.3 it is thus indicated that pK_1 = 3.8 for the protonation of the Asp 52 carboxylate group and that pK_2 = 6.7 for the deprotonation of the Glu 35 carboxylic acid group, both being in the enzyme–substrate complex.

In usual practice, investigations of the pH variation of enzyme activity must be conducted under conditions in which [S] and K_m are of similar orders of magnitude (equation 2.21). One route to the extraction of separate variations of the parameters V_{max} and K_m from the experimental data is the generation of a series of Lineweaver–Burk plots (equation 2.22), each plot obtained at a particular pH value. The series of the reciprocals of the intercepts on the R^{-1} axis gives the variation of V_{max} with pH, which corresponds to the right hand side of equation (7.3). The series of gradients of the plots reflects the variation of K_m/V_{max} with pH: this actually reflects the variation of rate which would have been observed under the condition $[S] \ll K_m$, when the overwhelming proportion of the added enzyme is present in the uncomplexed (free) forms represented by EH_2^+, EH and E^- in Fig. 7.4. A corresponding plot to that given in Fig. 7.3 for this condition yielded extrapolated intersections indicating $pK_3 = 4.2$ and $pK_4 = 6.1$, as defined in Fig. 7.4. The differences between pK_1 and pK_3 (both referring to protonation) and pK_2 and pK_4 (deprotonation) may be considered to reflect the interactions set up by the presence of the substrate lodged at the active site of the enzyme. As indicated in Fig. 7.1, electron redistribution in the substrate will have the effect of stabilizing the Asp 52 carboxylate and the Glu 35 carboxylic acid groups, making them more resistant to protonation and deprotonation respectively. These expectations are supported by the observations that pK_1 is less than pK_3 and that pK_2 is

Table 7.1 Optimum pH values for enzyme–substrate systems in aqueous solution at ambient temperatures

Enzyme	Substrate	Optimum pH
Ribonuclease	2′,3′-cyclic phospho-diester	6.0
Horse-liver alcohol dehydrogenase	Acetaldehyde (reduction)	6.7
Lactate dehydrogenase	Pyruvate	7.0
Malic enzyme	L-malate	7.4
Glucose isomerases from { B. coagulans / S. flavogriseus / S. flavovirens / S. phaeochromogenes }	Glucose	{ 7.0 / 7.5 / 8.5 / 9.4 }
α-Chymotrypsin	ATEE†	8.5
Alkaline protease	Casein	10.5
HB-Horse-liver alcohol dehydrogenase*	Ethanol (oxidation)	11.8

* HB = hydrobutyrimidylated, † N-Acetyl-L-tyrosine ethyl ester.

greater than pK_4. The first shows that higher $[H^+]$ is required to lead to a given degree of protonation for the species corresponding to EHS as compared to EH, for example.

Optimum pH values can vary between 5 and 12 and Table 7.1 lists some illustrative examples.

7.3 Roles of metal centres in enzymes

As was indicated in Table 2.3, many enzymes incorporate metallic elements within their generally organic structures. These metallic centres are often involved in the action at the active site. That in the glucose isomerase derived from *B. coagulans* can be exchanged for a different metal. With cobalt present as Co(II), the enzyme is active for the isomerization of glucose and ribose, but the presence of manganese as Mn(II) at the active site is required for the enzyme to have activity for the isomerization of xylose.

Zinc as Zn(II) is present at the active sites of many enzymes: its presence is essential since the activity disappears if the zinc is removed, say by using chelating agents. Liver alcohol dehydrogenase (LADH) contains two Zn(II) centres. One, essential for activity, is attached to one histidine and two cysteine residues. The other, displaced from the first by a distance of about 2 nm and attached to four cysteine residues, is not essential for catalytic activity but serves to stabilize the enzyme structure. In the reduction of acetaldehyde catalysed by LADH, the critical features of the mechanism are believed to be represented as shown in Fig. 7.5. The zinc shown is the essential one and S and N represent the sulphur atom in cysteine and the nitrogen atom in histidine respectively to which this is attached. The key aspect appears to be that Zn(II) forms a coordination bond to the oxygen atom of the acetaldehyde substrate by accepting a lone pair of electrons; in

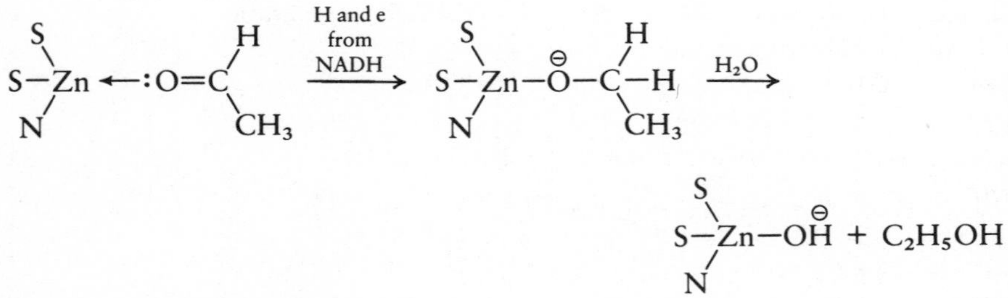

Fig. 7.5 Representation of part of the mechanism of the reduction of acetaldehyde catalysed by liver alcohol dehydrogenase. S represents the sulphur of a cysteine residue and N the nitrogen of a histidine residue.

this respect Zn(II) acts like a Lewis acid site at an aluminium centre in silica–alumina (Section 5.3). The donation of electrons towards Zn(II) induces a slight positive charge on the carbonyl carbon, which then accepts a hydrogen atom and an electron from the co-enzyme, reduced nicotinamide adenine dinucleotide (NADH), as this is converted to the oxidized form NAD$^+$. The resultant ethanolate (middle structure in Fig. 7.5) is hydrolysed to release ethanol, leaving a coordinated hydroxide (OH$^-$) at the zinc centre. Ultimately this must acquire a proton (H$^+$) to produce a coordinatively-bound water molecule; subsequent displacement of the water molecule by an acetaldehyde molecule then allows the cycle to recommence.

Zinc in enzymes remains in the Zn(II) oxidation state throughout the action and does not work by redox action of the type to be discussed in connection with nitrogenase below. Effectively Lewis acidity and variable coordination to ligands, some of which are quite labile, are the major features of the metal centres during catalysis by the more than 200 enzymes incorporating Zn(II).

Oxidoreductase enzymes often make use of easily variable oxidation states of metal centres, in this respect resembling the action on solid redox catalysts (Sections 5.2, 6.2). Molybdenum is an important element in both connections, even if the number of known molybdenum-containing enzymes is less than 20. These enzymes are vital to life however: not only do most living organisms demand the availability of trace amounts of molybdenum, but common nitrogenase, the enzyme essential to plant life through its ability to fix nitrogen from the air, is one of this number.

Only partial structural information is available for nitrogenase. It is known that it incorporates a complex pairing of two proteins, one of which (termed the Fe–Mo protein) contains iron, molybdenum and sulphur at the active site, whilst the other (the Fe-protein) is limited to iron and sulphur. EXAFS techniques (Section 4.4.5) have been applied to reveal that in the Fe–Mo protein, the molybdenum centres are surrounded by four sulphur atoms and are furthermore within interaction range of two or three iron centres. Additionally the fact that degradation of this protein can release the anionic species MoS$_4^-$ suggests that four sulphur atoms are directly linked to the molybdenum centres in the protein structure.

In the course of the catalytic action of nitrogenase, the Fe-protein is believed to supply electrons to the Fe–Mo protein, the latter having the active site for nitrogen fixation. The impetus for the breaking of the nitrogen–nitrogen triple bond is likely to come from the formation of multiple metal–nitrogen bonds. The hydrogen of the ammonia (ammonium) product is considered to be gained in the initial form of protons (H$^+$). Representing the active site of the enzyme simply as A, the process might proceed along general lines summarized in Fig. 7.6. Along

$$A-N\equiv N \xrightarrow{H^+,\,e} A=N=NH \xrightarrow{H^+,\,e} A\equiv N\!\cdots\!NH_2$$

$$\Big\downarrow H^+,\,e$$

$$A + NH_4^+ \xleftarrow{4H^+,\,3e} A\equiv N + NH_4^+ \xleftarrow{H^+} A\equiv N-NH_3$$

Fig. 7.6 Representation of the general features of a possible mechanism by which nitrogen is fixed at the active site (A) of nitrogenase. Protons (H^+) are derived from the surrounding medium and electrons (e) originate from the Fe-protein.

the top row of this diagram, two electrons, which have originated from the Fe-protein and have reduced the molybdenum centre, are donated to nitrogen, weakening the bonding therein (see Fig. 5.5) and allowing it to accept protons. A major function of the molybdenum is thus revealed: it holds electronic density initially by decreasing its oxidation state, before regaining the higher oxidation state by donating electron density into antibonding π^* orbitals of the nitrogen.

There is also a further aspect of the choice by nature of molybdenum as the essential metal in this connection, in preference to other metals of Group VI of the periodic table, tungsten and chromium, which also have the ability to exist in a range of high oxidation states. It turns out to be relatively easy for the energy carrying compounds of nature (such as adenosine triphosphate (ATP)) to effect the conversion of molybdenum between the states Mo(IV) and Mo(VI), but they find it very difficult to oxidize Cr(III) or to reduce W(VI) for example. Furthermore in its appearances within some oxidases, molybdenum binds oxygen as terminal Mo=O bonds: this indicates oxidation activity by analogy with the catalytic abilities associated with Mo=O centres on solid surfaces (see Figs. 3.5 and 6.6). This analogy must not be pursued too far however, since the capability of transition metal oxides for catalytic action is much more diverse but far less specific than the action of corresponding metal centres within enzymes.

Molybdenum is in fact the only element in the second transition series which is biologically essential, through its unique action within molybdoenzymes. It is worth pointing out that there are fewer exclusions in the first transition series; iron, nickel, cobalt and copper are biologically essential metals in reflection of their presence within many enzymes (Table 2.3). Furthermore vanadium has been found to be functional at the active sites in some rarer types of nitrogenase enzymes recently.

It is interesting to compare the ability of nitrogenase enzymes to fix nitrogen at ambient temperature with that of the iron catalysts used in the industrial process in which temperatures of the order of 700 K are required. The outstanding point of difference in the respective mechanisms is that nitrogen must be dissociated initially to atoms on the iron surface, whereas the action of nitrogenase delays the cleavage of the nitrogen–nitrogen bond until it has been severely weakened by acts of electron transfer and bonding to hydrogen. It becomes clear that nature has exploited a kinetic route of a less demanding nature than that used in the industrial synthesis of ammonia. The complexities of these mechanisms and their energy demands in individual steps are disguised in the overall reaction process, which is actually strongly exothermic.

$$N_2 + 3H_2 \rightarrow 2NH_3 \, , \Delta H^{\ominus}_{298 \text{ K}} = -92 \text{ kJ mol}^{-1}.$$

7.4 Examples of enzymes in industrial use

Free enzymes are generally inapplicable in industrial scale processes and all of the examples in this section are of the use of immobilized enzymes to yield commercial products.

7.4.1 *The corn syrup process*

Sucrose, the sugar used commonly for sweetening, has the disadvantage that its production is based on two types of growing plant, sugarcane and sugarbeet. There are much larger supplies of another sugar, glucose, which can be made available through the hydrolysis of starch obtained from widely-grown crops such as maize (corn). But glucose is not sweet to the taste. In this it contrasts with its isomer fructose, which has been rated as two to four times as sweet as sucrose on an equal weight basis, according to taste no doubt! Glucose isomerase enzymes, in catalysing the conversion of glucose to fructose, provide the final stage of a process going from corn to a high quality sweetening agent, the so-called corn syrup process. In the USA alone, annual production of corn syrup is now some two million tonnes (dried weight). Many soft drinks and confectionery items are now sweetened with corn syrup, to the evident benefit of those people concerned with limiting their intake of 'calories'!

Glucose isomerases are extracted from a variety of living cells and are liberated when the cell walls are disintegrated. This may be achieved by processes of autolysis with cationic detergents (such as dimethylbenzyl-alkylammonium chloride), of the action of organic liquids (such as toluene or 2-propanol) or of digestion using lysozyme. Almost all glucose isomerases in natural modes exist as intracellular enzymes and it is possible to immobilize either the whole cells or the extracted enzyme. The straightforward method of achieving immobilization in either case is by adsorption on DEAE-celluloses (Section 3.2.4). Many other procedures, involving variants of adsorption, polymer lattice entrapment and linkage by chemical bonding using a wide range of carrier materials have been demonstrated. Several immobilized forms of glucose isomerases are available commercially.

'Standard' corn syrups supplied commercially contain 42% of fructose and these are approximately of equivalent sweetness to the corresponding weight of sucrose syrup. Other corn syrups can contain up to 90% of fructose.

7.4.2 *The cocoa butter process*

Cocoa butter, as a natural product, is a relatively expensive fat used in the food industry. The major constituents are triglycerides which are mixed esters of palmitic acid ($C_{15}H_{31}COOH$), oleic acid ($C_{17}H_{33}COOH$) and stearic acid ($C_{17}H_{35}COOH$). Representing palmitoyl, oleoyl and stearoyl units as P, Ol and S respectively, the two main triglycerides of cocoa butter have the structures I and II below

$$
\begin{array}{ccc}
\text{CH}_2\!-\!\text{O}\!-\!\text{P} & \text{CH}_2\!-\!\text{O}\!-\!\text{S} & \text{CH}_2\!-\!\text{O}\!-\!\text{P} \\
\mid & \mid & \mid \\
\text{CH}\!-\!\text{O}\!-\!\text{Ol} & \text{CH}\!-\!\text{O}\!-\!\text{Ol} & \text{CH}\!-\!\text{O}\!-\!\text{Ol} \\
\mid & \mid & \mid \\
\text{CH}_2\!-\!\text{O}\!-\!\text{S} & \text{CH}_2\!-\!\text{O}\!-\!\text{S} & \text{CH}_2\!-\!\text{O}\!-\!\text{P} \\
\text{I} & \text{II} & \text{III}
\end{array}
$$

Structure III is the major triglyceride of palm oil, which is widely available and of comparatively low commercial value. It is evident that substitution of the palmitoyl units in III by stearoyl units would be a process of considerable value.

The basic nature of the required conversion is interesterification, selectively working on the terminal glyceride linkages (positions 1 and 3 of the glycerol backbone). The enzyme applied to this task is described as a 1,3 specific lipase (or glycerol ester hydrolase) and is a member of primary division 3 (Table 2.4). As used in one variant of the process, this lipase was immobilized by adsorption on kieselguhr (a siliceous solid) and worked in suspension in a solution of triglycerides and excess stearic acid in water-saturated *n*-hexane held at a temperature of 313 K for a few hours. The overall action may be considered to be achieved by consecutive processes of hydrolysis and re-esterification at the 1 and 3 positions, effectively exchanging palmitoyl groups for stearoyl. Only minimal amounts of water should be present in order to inhibit the appearance of hydrolysis products themselves. To this end, an organic solvent is used.

Lipases can work in hydrocarbon solvents because they bind essential water tightly and with a hydrocarbon solvent there is little tendency for the essential water molecules to escape from their attachment to the enzyme molecule. These water molecules are essential to the functioning of the enzyme because they take part in most of the non-covalent interactions which are responsible for maintaining the catalytically active conformation at the active site.

Similarly other common plant oils, such as olive oil, can be converted to the more valuable products.

7.4.3 *ICI polyphenylene process*

Oxidoreductase enzymes are more difficult to use in their isolated forms than are hydrolases, because they require continuous supplies of appropriate amounts of cofactors such as NADH. This need has inhibited the wide usage of these enzymes as such. However when oxidoreductases within whole living cells are used, the cell metabolism will attend to the supply of cofactors given a suitable feed.

Polyphenylene is a polymer of considerable potential usefulness. Its structure is made up by an array of benzene rings interlinked through *ortho* positions. The basic planar nature of this structure makes the material very amenable to fabrication into sheets, whilst it is also readily soluble in organic solvents.

The obvious starting point for synthesis of polyphenylene is benzene with an initial bifunctionalization at *ortho* positions. This selectivity requirement immediately commends an enzymic process for production of this monomeric precursor. But at the outset of the development no organism was known which could convert benzene into the target intermediate species, benzene *cis*-glycol (BCG). Once BCG could be obtained, subsequent treatment *via* esterification and thermal conversion of the resultant diester would lead to polyphenylene, as represented in the lower part of Fig. 7.7.

A microorganism containing an oxidase enzyme which would convert benzene into BCG using gas phase oxygen was required for the front end of the process. Equally this microorganism would also have to be tolerant of aromatic liquids. These requirements induced an interesting process of lateral thinking by the team developing the scheme, which went along the following lines. Nature is very versatile in throwing up microorganisms suited to particular environments, even those which might be regarded in normal terms as thoroughly hostile. Thus the locations in which to seek a microorganism with the ability to convert benzene to BCG would be those in which aromatic liquids have been exposed to the natural elements over

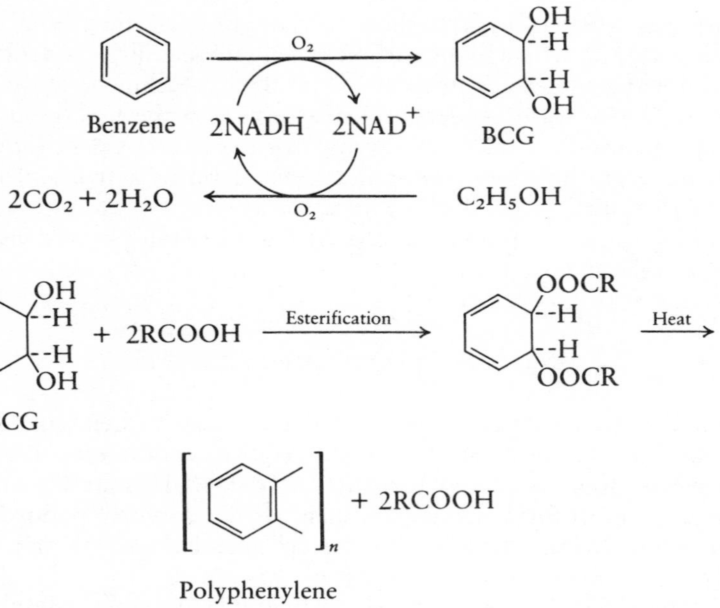

Fig. 7.7 Representation of the conversions involved in the polyphenylene production process developed by ICI p.l.c. The upper part shows the primary action accomplished by the *Pseudomonas putida* bacteria when it is supplied with benzene and ethanol in the presence of oxygen. The lower part indicates the subsequent steps for the production of the polymer.

long periods of time. It was realized that dump pools used to dispose of waste organic solvents would offer just these conditions. Following extensive microbiological investigations of these pools, a strain of the bacteria *Pseudomonas putida* was found which possessed the desired enzyme, benzene dioxygenase. Furthermore these bacteria could use ethanol to provide for their metabolism, in particular that part associated with the generation of NADH from its oxidized form, NAD^+. Ultimately these bacteria have been harnessed to induce the action represented in the top part of Fig. 7.7.

7.4.4 6-Aminopenicillanic acid (6-APA) production

The previous three examples may be considered as directed at large scale production of useful materials. There are also many instances of the usage of enzymes as catalysts for smaller scale processes aimed at yielding fine or speciality products. The instance discussed here is the functionalization of raw penicillin (Pen G) to 6-APA: the latter contains the basic structure which serves as the primary precursor for the synthesis of newer forms of penicillins, such as amoxicillin or carbenicillins. What is required in the process is the enzymic hydrolysis of Pen G: this is the product (as a secondary metabolite) of the fermentation process when a nutrient (such as molasses) and phenylacetic acid in aqueous solution are acted upon by the microorganism *Penicillium chrysogenum* over a period of typically 10 days. The fermenting vessels used for this can have volumes of up to about $4 \times 10^5 \, \mathrm{dm}^3$. The subsequent production of 6-APA is conducted with the immobilized enzyme penicillum acylase, which effects the hydrolytic cleavage of a side-chain from the Pen G molecule. The enzyme may be immobilized by covalent linkage to functionalized glass beads (Section 3.2.4). The solution of Pen G is flowed continuously through the reactor with addition of potassium hydroxide solution to maintain a neutral pH. The conversion of Pen G to 6-APA involves a six hour residence time in the reactor typically and achieves some 85% efficiency.

7.4.5 L-*Aspartic acid production*

The enzyme aspartase is a lyase (Table 2.4, primary division 4) which can be used to create a carbon–nitrogen bond by addition of ammonia across a carbon–carbon double bond. It is used to synthesize L-aspartic acid from ammonia and fumaric acid, as represented below

$$
\begin{array}{ccc}
\mathrm{H-\underset{\parallel}{C}-COOH} & + \;\; \mathrm{H} & \longrightarrow \\
\mathrm{HOOC-\underset{}{C}-H} & \;\;\; \mathrm{NH_2} &
\end{array}
\qquad
\begin{array}{c}
\mathrm{H} \\
\mathrm{H-\underset{}{C}-COOH} \\
\mathrm{HOOC-\underset{}{C}-H} \\
\mathrm{NH_2}
\end{array}
$$

Whole microbial cells of strains of *E. coli* possessing high aspartase activity have been immobilized by entrapment in κ-carrageenan gel, with the retention in subsequent usage being enhanced by cross-linking treatment with glutaraldehyde and hexamethylenediamine. A column of these immobilized cells in continuous operation at a temperature of 310 K can retain activity for more than a year.

L-Aspartic acid is used extensively in the food and pharmaceutical industries. In recent years its usage has been boosted by the rising demand for the protein *Aspartame®*, an artificial sweetener, for which L-aspartic acid is a component in the synthesis.

7.5 Concluding remarks

The specificity of enzyme catalysis can be viewed as originating from a 'lock–key' interaction between the enzyme and substrate molecules in broad analogy. The cleft nature of the enzyme active site provides a special interfacial region within which a substrate is subjected to interactions which reflect non-polar characteristics in the cases of many hydrolase enzymes or coordinative bonding to metal centres in the cases of metalloenzymes. Resultant redistributions of electron densities have been indicated through several examples to lead to the catalytic action.

Five instances of commercial processes based on catalytic action by immobilized enzymes or living cells have been given above. These operate at close to ambient temperature, in contrast to the much higher temperatures used in most processes employing conventional solid catalysts. This general feature offers the prospect of better energy efficiency in biotechnological competitors to existing heterogeneous catalytic processes. Furthermore the high specificity of enzyme catalysed reactions in general ensures that competitive generation of unwanted by-products will usually be minimal. In contrast, processes catalysed by bulk solid surfaces often involve more than one reaction pathway.

In offering highly selective action induced at modest temperatures, enzymes as catalysts give comparable general achievements to those of homogeneous catalysts of several types, including organometallic species. In fact, when such homogeneous catalysts are anchored to supporting solid materials (Sections 3.1.4, 3.1.5), the resultant surface has a general

Table 7.2 Enzyme (cell) induced conversions of potential industrial value

Reactants	Enzyme or Microorganism	Product(s) (Yield)
Methane, oxygen	Methane monooxygenase	Methanol
Propylene, oxygen	*Mycobacterium* sp. (Strain E3)	Propylene oxide
Ethanol, oxygen	Yeast alcohol dehydrogenase	Acetaldehyde
Methanol, hydrogen peroxide	Catalase	Formaldehyde
Formaldehyde, water	Formaldehyde dismutase	Methanol, formic acid
Glucose, oxygen	*Klebsiella oxytoca*	Butan-2,3-diol (50%)
	Clostridium acetobutylicum	Butanol (20%)
	Clostridium thermoacetium	Acetic acid (50%)
	Clostridium beijerinckii	Butanol, acetone, isopropanol
Hydrogen, carbon dioxide	*Alcaligenes eutrophus*	Formic acid (30%)

resemblance to that concerned with immobilized enzymes. In both cases the general picture is of an inactive continuous surface dotted with uniform microscopic centres of catalytic activity.

Table 7.2 lists some enzyme catalysed reactions which may become important in the bulk chemical industry in the future. It must be acknowledged that there are other products of the present chemical industry which are so inimical to enzyme molecules that it seems improbable that the conventional processes will be challenged from the biotechnological direction. Sulphuric and nitric acids are instances in this connection.

8

Industrial processes based on solid catalysts

This chapter completes the book by collecting together a series of the heterogeneous catalytic processes which are of significance on an industrial scale. It must be acknowledged at the outset that the content cannot be all-embracing and that only a judicious selection is presented. Fundamental aspects of the catalytic actions are highlighted when these amplify the principles introduced in previous chapters. The order in which the processes are introduced is roughly parallel to that followed in Chapters 5 and 6, with progression through metallic, transition-metal oxidic and acidic catalytic surfaces.

8.1 Hydrogenation of vegetable oils

The hardening of vegetable oils, through hydrogenation of double bonds therein, is a major activity in the food industry. The process not only results in a physical change from a liquid oil to a solid (e.g. margarine) at ambient temperature but it extends the range of usage and gives the product stability against oxidation to rancid smelling derivatives with exposure to air.

The traditional catalyst used in this connection is nickel supported on silica. The Horiuti–Polanyi mechanism for the hydrogenation of double bonds has been discussed (Section 6.1.2.1). The main objectives in the commercial process are to eliminate linolenic acid residues (Table 8.1) as far as possible and to reduce the content of linoleic acid residues to a substantial extent. In the product it is desired to maximize the amount of oleic acid residues without going too far towards producing the fully saturated stearic acid chains, since these are not easily digested as foodstuffs. At the same time, it must be recognized that oleic acid is a *cis*-isomer: the corresponding *trans*-isomer (elaidic acid) is undesirable in its glyceride forms in margarine at levels exceeding one-third of those of oleic acid glycerides. Table 8.1 shows the typical compositions of soyabean oil (a starting material) and the resultant margarine. The stepwise set of hydrogenations occurs readily in the presence of a pressure of 0.3 MPa of hydrogen above the liquid phase containing suspended particulate catalyst when the typical working temperature is 470–480 K. The process is most frequently conducted in the batch mode for a variety of technical reasons. Termination of reaction is effected by cutting off the hydrogen supply and subsequently dropping the temperature to around 370 K.

One fortunate circumstance for the desired degree of hydrogenation of the side chains of the glycerides is that the strength of adsorption is determined by these acid residues and decreases in the order moving down Table 8.1. This means that the more unsaturated chains will be hydrogenated preferentially: this phenomenon accounts for the small increase seen in stearic acid residues in the Table, even when linolenic acid chains have disappeared and linoleic acid chains have been depleted substantially. Usually the rate of hydrogenation shows a zero order dependence on the oil concentration but is first order in the hydrogen pressure. This indicates (Section 2.4.1) that the nickel surface is almost completely covered by adsorbed unsaturated molecules (R—CH=CH—R′) whilst hydrogen is weakly adsorbed. The mechanism takes the form

$$H_2(g) \; \underset{\longleftarrow}{\overset{\longrightarrow}{}} \; 2H\,(ads)$$

$$R-CH=CH-R'\,(l) \; \underset{\longleftarrow}{\overset{\longrightarrow}{}} \; R-CH=CH-R'\,(ads)$$

$$H(ads) + R-CH=CH-R'\,(ads) \; \underset{\longleftarrow}{\overset{\longrightarrow}{}} \; R-CH_2-CH-R'\,(ads)$$

$$H(ads) + R-CH_2-CH-R'\,(ads) \; \longrightarrow \; R-CH_2-CH_2-R'\,(l)$$

The last step is rate determining.

There is an interesting exemplification in this connection of the lesser power of copper as compared to nickel as a hydrogenation catalyst. Using copper, the stepwise hydrogenation of unsaturated triglycerides does not proceed beyond oleic acid chains, which thus constitutes a selective hydrogenation of linolenic to oleic acid residues. However the use of copper as the catalyst for the commercial process is excluded due to the unavoidable persistency of traces of this metal in the margarine. This is not a problem with nickel.

On a wider basis, palm, rapeseed and sunflower oils can be used as feedstocks. There is usually a certain amount of pretreatment of the oils.

Table 8.1 Triglyceride residue compositions of soyabean oil and derived margarine

Residue chain structure	Parent acid	% Compositions	
		Soyabean oil	Margarine
$CH_3-CH_2-\left(CH_2 \atop CH=CH\right)_3 -(CH_2)_6COO-$	Linolenic	7	0
$CH_3(CH_2)_3-CH_2-\left(CH_2 \atop CH=CH\right)_2 -(CH_2)_6COO-$	Linoleic	53	12
$CH_3(CH_2)_6-CH_2 \quad CH_2-(CH_2)_6COO- \atop \qquad CH=CH$	Oleic	28	57
$CH_3(CH_2)_6-CH_2 \atop \qquad CH=CH \qquad CH_2-(CH_2)_6COO-$	Elaidic	0	16
$CH_3(CH_2)_{16}COO-$	Stearic	4	7
$CH_3(CH_2)_{14}COO-$	Palmitic	8	8

Palm oil, for example, is deodorized using live steam at a temperature of 520 K.

A representative hardening plant will hydrogenate the oil in a 15 tonne capacity reaction vessel and will produce 90 tonnes of hardened fats each day. The catalyst is removed by filtration after the batch process has been terminated.

8.2 Ammonia and nitric acid productions

Ammonia is oxidized catalytically to produce nitric acid, so that it is appropriate to consider the two production processes in turn within one section, particularly as both use transition metals as catalysts.

Typical conditions under which ammonia is synthesized from nitrogen and hydrogen gases on an iron catalyst are temperatures of around 720 K and pressures in the range of 13 to 35 MPa. High total pressures are necessary to push the equilibrium concerned to the right as written below

$$N_2 + 3H_2 \rightleftharpoons 2NH_3$$

Even if the pressure were as high as 100 MPa, the ammonia content of the equilibrium mixture would only be some 16%. In fact the elevated temperature is unhelpful to the equilibrium yield of ammonia (the process is exothermic to the right), but is required to induce practicable rates of synthesis.

It is important to realize that as the above equilibrium is approached, the rates of both forward and reverse reactions become significant. Accordingly ammonia synthesis plants use catalytic loop systems within which the level of ammonia produced per pass corresponds to about 75% at most of that which would represent equilibrium composition. Ammonia is removed from the exit stream of gases by condensation, usually involving chilling by refrigeration, and the residual gases are recycled. *Space velocity* in a reactor containing solid catalyst is defined by the quotient of volumetric flowrate of gases reduced to standard conditions divided by the volume occupied by the catalyst. Typical space velocity values used in industrial ammonia synthesis plants are in the range of 8000 to 60000 h^{-1}. The iron based catalyst (see Table 4.4) is usually derived from the oxide magnetite and commonly it is present in the form of particles 5 to 10 mm across and offering surface areas of the order of $10 \, m^2 \, g^{-1}$. The main source (75 to 80% worldwide) of hydrogen for ammonia synthesis is the steam-reforming of hydrocarbons (Section 6.1.2.1), mainly natural gas (60–65%). The entering mixture of the nitrogen and hydrogen is usually made up to the stoichiometric ratio for ammonia synthesis.

The course of microscopic events on the iron surface during ammonia synthesis has been discussed in earlier chapters. The chemisorption of nitrogen, the step which determines the overall rate, has been dealt with in connection with Fig. 5.5. Both reactant gases are dissociatively chemisorbed; stepwise additions of the resultant atomic hydrogen on the surface to the adsorbed nitrogen atoms build up the ammonia molecules. It is interesting to note that the energy change involved in moving along the reaction coordinate from $N(ads) + 3H(ads)$ to $NH_3(g)$ may be surprisingly small, possibly only $+90\,kJ\,mol^{-1}$.

Nitric acid manufacture is usually based upon the combustion of ammonia in air over a platinum–rhodium(10%) gauze, the overall process being expressed by the equation

$$NH_3(g) + 2O_2 \rightarrow HNO_3(aq) + H_2O\,(l),\ \Delta H = -437\,kJ\,mol^{-1}.$$

Preheated mixtures of about 10% of ammonia in air, compressed to pressures of 0.8 to 1.0 MPa, pass through a stack of some 30 layers of the catalytic gauze, achieving an exit temperature of around 1210 K. The need for the catalyst to resist bulk oxidation at these high temperatures restricts it to noble metals. Ammonia and oxygen are dissociatively chemisorbed and the mechanism on the surface must involve reactions of atomic oxygen with fragments of ammonia, NH_2, NH and N atoms. Conversion to nitric oxide is achieved with a typical efficiency of 95% *via* an overall reaction

$$4NH_3 + 5O_2 \rightarrow 4NO + 6H_2O$$

Temperature and composition control in the industrial process are crucial. The gas mixture must enter the reactor at temperatures exceeding 480 K, so that the first layer of gauze encountered is able to induce significant reaction rates. Equally the exit temperature must not exceed that at which material loss from the upper layers of gauze becomes severe. The initial ammonia content cannot exceed 10% significantly for two reasons. At 10% content, the adiabatic temperature rise corresponding to the above reaction amounts to 710 K, which is close to the maximum tolerable temperature difference from end to end of the gauze column. Also mixtures in air of ammonia above about 12% create an explosion hazard. Under usual working conditions, 1 kg of catalyst will be required for a yearly production capacity of the order of 3000 kg of nitric acid, taking into account an expected catalyst renewal period of around 2 months.

Downstream of the reactor producing nitric oxide, the secondary stages leading to nitric acid are the non-catalytic processes represented by the equations

$$NO(g) + NO(g) + O_2(g) \rightarrow 2NO_2(g)$$
$$3NO_2(g) + H_2O(l) \rightarrow 2HNO_3(aq) + NO(g)$$

The regeneration of nitric oxide in the second process means that recycling is required.

8.3 Methanol synthesis

Methanol is synthesized by contacting mixtures of carbon monoxide, carbon dioxide and hydrogen with a copper/zinc oxide catalyst in the modern processes. This type of catalyst (often referred to as the ICI methanol catalyst) allows the synthesis to be conducted at relatively low pressures (down to 4 MPa) and temperatures (500–560 K), in comparison with those demanded by earlier types of catalyst based on zinc and chromium oxides. Selectivities very close to 100% are achieved with the modern catalysts.

As in ammonia synthesis, the yield of product and modes of operation are restricted by thermodynamic considerations of the equilibrium, which in this case is represented as

$$CO + 2H_2 \rightleftharpoons CH_3OH$$

The variation of the corresponding standard equilibrium constant ($K^\ominus$) as a function of temperature (T) is closely approximated by the linear equation

$$\ln K^\ominus = 1.124 \times 10^4/(T/K) - 27.84 \qquad (8.1)$$

Taking $T = 573$ K, the equilibrium yield of methanol in terms of its mole fraction (α) as a function of total pressure is shown in Fig. 8.1. This diagram and equation (8.1) indicate that high pressure and low temperature favour the equilibrium yield. But offsetting these considerations in the practical synthesis are the needs to achieve reasonable rates of reaction (demanding relatively high temperature) and to avoid the unfavourable economic and safety implications of plant designed to contain pressures much above 10 MPa. Thus although the typical operating temperature of 550 K represents a compromise between kinetic and thermodynamic considerations when the typical operating pressure of say 5 MPa locates a point which is on the slope in Fig. 8.1, these constitute working conditions for the industrial synthesis.

The synthesis of methanol, under conditions when even the equilibrium yields would be low, presents a broadly similar situation to that involved in ammonia synthesis (Section 8.2). Correspondingly methanol synthesis reactors also operate in a recycling mode. At the exit from a typical reactor, the gas stream will contain some 3 to 6% of methanol on a molar basis, representing perhaps half of the theoretical equilibrium yield. As implied by equation (8.1), the methanol synthesis process is strongly exothermic. Copper/zinc oxide catalysts undergo irreversible deactivation when they

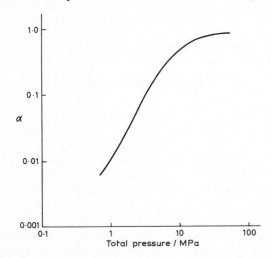

Fig. 8.1 Plot of the number of moles (α) of methanol produced at equilibrium at a temperature of 573 K from an initial mixture of 2 moles of hydrogen and 1 mole of carbon monoxide as a function of the total pressure.

are subjected to temperatures above about 570 K. The consequent need to avoid hot spots developing within a packed bed of catalyst is made more demanding by the kinetic requirement to operate the reactor at bulk temperatures within a few tens of degrees of the deactivation limit in order to induce sufficient rates of conversion. Accordingly in the common reactor design, using the quenched bed mode, the catalyst is held in a series of vertically stacked, separate beds, each of which receives an input of cold synthesis gas from a set of inlet ports.

An advanced type of reactor has been developed by Lurgi, with the basic design represented in Fig. 8.2. The large heat capacity of the boiling water in efficient thermal contact with the catalyst tubes works strongly against the development of hot spots. Points of obvious note in the diagram are the relatively high yield of methanol per pass and the high selectivity implied by the low level of ethanol, the only detectable impurity.

The copper/zinc oxide catalyst may be generated as follows. The starting point is an aqueous solution of nitrates of copper and zinc, together with the nitrate of aluminium; this element improves the structural properties of the final material. The solution is warmed and the metals are coprecipitated by addition to a solution of sodium bicarbonate at about 340 K. The solid is separated by filtration, washed thoroughly, dried at around 360 K over 12 h and then calcined at 623 K for a day. The material is thereafter reduced in flowing nitrogen/hydrogen mixtures, increasing the hydrogen

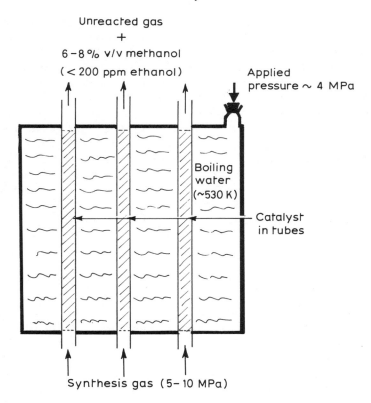

Unreacted gas
+
6 – 8 % v/v methanol
(< 200 ppm ethanol)

Applied
pressure ~ 4 MPa

Boiling
water
(~530 K)

Catalyst
in tubes

Synthesis gas (5 – 10 MPa)

Fig. 8.2 Features of the Lurgi design of a methanol synthesis reactor, in which the temperature is controlled by regulation of the valve above the water boiling under pressure. Based upon description by E. Supp (1981) *Hydrocarbon Processing*, **March**, 71.

partial pressure progressively (typically from 10^{-2} to 1.5 MPa) as the temperature is raised from 373 to 523 K. This process of reduction generates both Cu(I) and metallic copper. An X-ray diffraction pattern will reveal features corresponding to CuO and metallic copper. A representative active catalyst with atomic ratios of Cu:Zn:Al :: 60:30:10, after contact with synthesis gas (H_2:CO:CO_2 :: 65:32:3 v/v), has 50% of its copper content present in the form of the metal, 35% as CuO and 15% as Cu(I) dissolved in the zinc oxide phase. The copper crystallite dimension at the surface is of the order of 10 nm, which is also typical of the catalysts used in the industrial synthesis.

Until recently it was considered that Cu(I) centres within the ZnO phase were the active sites for methanol synthesis under industrial conditions. On this basis it was also thought that the presence of carbon dioxide, which is essential for maintaining the activity of the catalyst in the continuous process, acted to preserve the $Cu(I)$ centres against reduction. But there is now conclusive evidence that it is metallic copper in the form of small crystallites which is the active catalyst and that carbon dioxide serves as a primary reactant in the industrial process.

Experiments on the synthesis of methanol with $CO/CO_2/H_2$ mixtures in which only one of the carbon oxides incorporated ^{14}C tracer have shown that it is carbon monoxide which provides the overwhelming initial source of carbon for the methanol, even in mixtures with large excess of carbon dioxide. The activity of a copper/zinc oxide catalyst in methanol synthesis in the presence of CO_2 is proportional to the surface area of the copper metal phase. This has also been observed when copper crystallites are supported on other oxides, such as MgO, MnO and silica, so that zinc oxide has no special role in the industrial catalysts. The key feature of an active catalyst is that the copper must be highly dispersed to present a large specific surface area.

The mechanism of methanol synthesis under industrial conditions is indicated by several observed phenomena. Hydrogen is known to be dissociatively chemisorbed on copper surfaces (Fig. 5.3) whereas carbon monoxide will exist in a chemisorbed molecular form on the surface (Section 5.1). Figure 4.4 indicates that adsorbed formate (HCOO) is a stable species on copper surfaces at temperatures close to those concerned in methanol synthesis, under vacuum conditions. Application of the principle of microscopic reversibility to the decomposition mode specified in connection with the CO_2 and H_2 desorption peaks in Fig. 4.4 then implies that formate can be generated in the reverse direction using CO_2 derived from the gas phase. Figure 4.12 likewise suggests that methoxy (CH_3O) is a fairly stable species on copper surfaces under vacuum conditions. It is reasonable to suggest that both formate and methoxy are likely to be more stable still under high pressure conditions.

These observations provide pointers to the mechanism set out below, which is supported further by a considerable body of experimental evidence. All steps take place on copper surfaces.

$$H_2(g) \rightarrow 2H(ads)$$
$$H(ads) + CO_2 \rightarrow HCOO(ads)$$
$$HCOO(ads) + 2H(ads) \rightarrow CH_3O(ads) + O(ads)$$
$$CH_3O(ads) + H(ads) \rightarrow CH_3OH(g)$$
$$CO(ads) + O(ads) \rightarrow CO_2(g)$$

Some of these equations are likely to describe the overall effect of several, consecutive elementary steps. The critical action seems to be likely to be that represented by the middle equation; the hydrogenolysis of formate has in fact been shown to occur on copper surfaces. The role of carbon monoxide is indicated to be the stripping of atomic oxygen from the surface, which maintains the carbon dioxide content of the gas phase. It is this last feature of the synthesis mechanism which masks the true role of carbon dioxide as a primary reactant: carbon monoxide becomes this primary reactant after it has gained an oxygen atom from the surface.

8.4 Synthesis gas conversion processes

Mixtures of carbon monoxide and hydrogen are often referred to as synthesis gas, on account of the wide range of products which can result from their catalytic conversion. Major products can range from methane, through longer chain alkanes and alkenes, to oxygen-containing species such as alcohols and aldehydes. Which products are produced depends upon the nature of the catalyst and the reaction conditions employed.

The first point to make is that many conversion processes are feasible on a thermodynamic basis under typical conditions. This is illustrated in Table 8.2, in which standard Gibbs (free energy) function changes for a number of conversion processes are listed. Also given in this Table are solid catalysts which achieve a substantial degree of selectivity towards the products indicated. The fact that different metals as catalysts lead to the preponderance of different types of products points up the prime

Table 8.2 Standard Gibbs function changes $(\Delta G^{\ominus})$ at a temperature of 500 K for synthesis gas conversion processes and examples of catalysts

Process	$\Delta G^{\ominus}/\text{kJ mol}^{-1}$	Typical catalyst (Total pressure used)
$CO + 3H_2 \rightarrow CH_4 + H_2O$	-96.3	Ni/Al_2O_3 (0.1–30 MPa)
$2CO + 5H_2 \rightarrow C_2H_6 + 2H_2O$	-122.2	
$3CO + 7H_2 \rightarrow C_3H_8 + 3H_2O$	-156.1	
$4CO + 9H_2 \rightarrow n\text{-}C_4H_{10} + 4H_2O$	-193.1	Fe/SiO_2 (1 MPa)
$2CO + 4H_2 \rightarrow C_2H_4 + 2H_2O$	-46.5	
$6CO + 12H_2 \rightarrow 1\text{-}C_6H_{12} + 6H_2O$	-201.5	
$CO + 2H_2 \rightarrow CH_3OH$	$+21.3$	$\begin{cases} Cu/ZnO \text{ (5 MPa)} \\ Pd/La_2O_3 \text{ (0.1 MPa)} \end{cases}$
$2CO + 4H_2 \rightarrow C_2H_5OH + H_2O$	-28.4	
$2CO + 2H_2 \rightarrow CH_3COOH$	-24.2	Rh/SiO_2 (7 MPa)
$2CO + 3H_2 \rightarrow CH_3CHO + H_2O$	-16.9	

importance of the mechanisms of the surface reactions. Those which induce the apparently least-favourable synthesis of methanol to the exclusion of all other pathways illustrate this most emphatically.

The mode of chemisorption of carbon monoxide is of prime importance. Hydrocarbons can only be produced if the carbon–oxygen bond is broken, whereas this linkage must be preserved in the formation of oxygenates. It is obvious that catalysts inducing the formation of hydrocarbons must chemisorb carbon monoxide dissociatively whilst those inducing the formation of oxygenates must be able to chemisorb carbon monoxide molecularly. In fact the metals which are active catalysts for hydrocarbon synthesis are not too far removed from the borderline in the transition series in the periodic table separating tendencies for dissociative and molecular chemisorption of carbon monoxide (Section 5.1). This may be interpreted in terms that surface carbon must be formed but must not be held too firmly to inhibit subsequent hydrogenation acts leading to eventual release of the hydrocarbon products. Experimental evidence for the presence of forms of carbon on iron surfaces has been presented in Fig. 4.15(a) (XPS spectrum) and 4.14(b) (AES spectrum). AES techniques have also been used to reveal the presence of a reactive carbonaceous phase covering about 10% of a nickel surface which has contacted synthesis gas at temperatures which result in significant rates of methanation (the first entry in Table 8.2). Such carbon is commonly termed carbidic: it can be formed by heating a nickel surface in the presence of carbon monoxide alone and thereafter, with introduction of hydrogen, it can be removed in the formation of methane. Carbidic carbon is to be distinguished from the more tenacious form of graphitic carbon.

The basic mechanism concerned in the synthesis of hydrocarbons on metal surfaces can be represented in outline as

$$CO(g) \longrightarrow C(ads) \longrightarrow \text{carbidic surface carbon} \xrightarrow{H_2} \text{hydrocarbons}$$

The circumstances which will be expected to encourage the generation of longer hydrocarbon chains can be specified. The higher is the degree of surface coverage by carbonaceous species, the lower will be the coverage achieved by chemisorbed atomic hydrogen. This must increase the probability of the formation of carbon–carbon bonds prior to the eventual hydrogenation which leads to the release of hydrocarbon products to the gas phase. A typical commercial nickel catalyst can yield 96% selectivity for methane in the conversion of synthesis gas (the process being termed catalytic methanation accordingly) at a temperature of 500 K. This predominant formation of methane is consistent with the relatively low coverage by carbonaceous phase on nickel mentioned above; this allows substantial coverage by atomic hydrogen which promotes the formation of C—H bonds rather than C—C bonds. Ruthenium and rhenium are also good catalysts for methanation, which may be expected on the basis that these elements, like nickel, roughly mark the borderline in the periodic table concerned with dissociative and molecular chemisorption of carbon monoxide.

On nickel surfaces, various experiments have thrown light on the nature of the carbonaceous species. Figure 4.7 for example shows direct evidence from SSIMS experiments for the presence of CH_3, CH_2, CH and carbon on a nickel surface which has contacted synthesis gas. In another experiment, when synthesis gas of composition $H_2:CO::3:1$ was flowed over a catalyst consisting of 9% (w/w) nickel on alumina at a temperature of 533 K and the supply of carbon monoxide was cut off suddenly, methane formation continued for a significant time thereafter. This contrasted with the rapid termination of water formation. Also in another experiment in which a flow of $^{12}CO + H_2$ was suddenly replaced with a flow of $^{13}CO + H_2$, production of $^{12}CH_4$ continued for over a minute. These experiments reveal the reservoir of carbidic species held on the nickel surfaces under steady methanation conditions. The most abundant carbon-containing species on nickel surfaces during methanation has been identified as $\equiv$C—H: this is indicated to be the most strongly bound of the CH_x species by the evidence discussed in connection with Fig. 4.7. Moreover infrared reflectance–absorption spectra (Section 4.4.6) of nickel surfaces in contact with synthesis gas under methanation conditions show a prominent band centred on a wavenumber of 3250 cm^{-1}. This has been assigned to the chemisorbed $\equiv$C—H species on the basis that an identical band appeared when acetylene was adsorbed on nickel. The evidence available then suggests the general mechanism for methanation represented in Fig. 8.3.

Auger electron spectroscopy (Section 4.4.3) has been used to follow the rate of formation of carbidic carbon on nickel surfaces. Under steady state conditions this matches the rate of methane formation. Thus the pathway represented in Fig. 8.3 can account quantitatively for the methanation rate, so that there is no intervention of any pathway involving the hydrogenation of carbon monoxide prior to the cleavage of the carbon–oxygen bond in dissociative chemisorption. All of the evidence points to the maintenance during catalytic methanation of a rather delicate balance between rates of formation and hydrogenation of carbon species on nickel surfaces. Under these circumstances, none of the individual steps concerned can be designated as the unique rate determining one in the conventional sense.

It is interesting to attempt to predict the effects of the promotion of nickel surfaces by say potassium. In accordance with the discussion in Section 5.1 of the electronic consequences for the chemisorption of carbon monoxide when an electropositive element is present on the surface, dissociative chemisorption should be enhanced. This is manifested directly in the

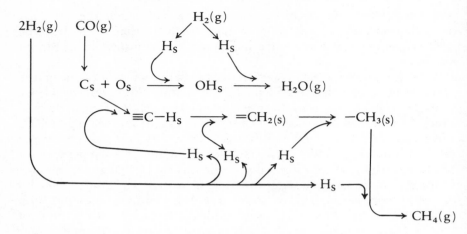

Fig. 8.3 Representation of mechanism of methanation of carbon monoxide on nickel surfaces. Subscript s denotes surface species and open bonds are to the surface.

increased coverage (typically 30%) by carbidic carbon which has been detected on potassium-promoted as compared to unpromoted nickel surfaces. From this it would be predicted that the promoted nickel should catalyse the formation of hydrocarbons larger than methane, and indeed this has been observed experimentally. Promotion in this way makes the nickel surface tend towards the unpromoted iron surface in its synthesis action. Higher coverage by carbonaceous species would be expected on iron as opposed to nickel surfaces in reflection of the stronger chemisorption bonds thereon (Fig. 5.3 shows the trend) and the enhancement of dissociative chemisorption of carbon monoxide.

Fischer–Tropsch synthesis is the general nomenclature for catalysed conversions of synthesis gas which lead to a range of organic products. On an unpromoted iron surface in contact with synthesis gas under reaction conditions, coverage by carbidic carbon is extensive. Promotion using potassium would be expected to lead to still higher carbon coverage. Methane formation is thus expected to be inhibited: the higher ratio of carbon to hydrogen on the promoted iron surface also enhances the formation of longer chain and unsaturated products, both features consistent with reduced availability of chemisorbed hydrogen. These tendencies are illustrated in Fig. 8.4. The simpler catalyst surface (designated as CFe) is that which arises when iron is exposed to synthesis gas and is conventionally termed 'carbided'. The promoted catalyst was prepared by co-impregnation of potassium carbonate and ferric nitrate

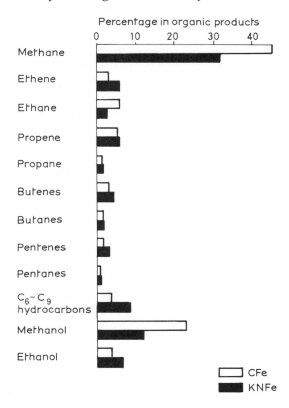

Fig. 8.4 Product distributions obtained when synthesis gas $(CO : H_2 :: 1 : 3 \text{ v/v})$ undergoes small extents of conversion (3–4%) on catalysts consisting basically of 9.9% w/w of iron metal dispersed on silica at a total pressure of 0.79 MPa at 523 K temperature. See the text for the detailed nature of the surfaces. Derived from data given by E. B. Yeh, L. H. Schwartz and J. B. Butt (1985) *Journal of Catalysis*, **91**, 241–253.

into silica gel: it also had some nitrogen on the surface, resulting from pre-exposure of the calcined/reduced solid to ammonia at a temperature of around 770 K for 12 h. This nitrogen on the surface is believed to reinforce the promotion action of potassium. The doubly promoted nature of this catalyst is indicated by its designation as KNFe and Fig. 8.4 shows that it produces the expected shift towards unsaturated and longer chain products compared to CFe.

Rhodium is known for its ability as a catalyst for the conversion of synthesis gas to induce high selectivities towards C_2-oxygenated products under particular conditions. With rhodium supported on silica as the catalyst used for conversion of synthesis gas at atmospheric pressure and temperatures of around 470 K, the major products are in fact hydrocarbons. But when zirconia is used as the support, the major selectivities on a carbon basis are 42% for ethanol, 32% for methane and 12% for methanol. Then when zinc oxide is the support, the synthesis is directed overwhelmingly towards methanol (94%). XPS techniques (Section 4.4.4) have been used to investigate the state of the rhodium (deposited by impregnation *via* rhodium carbonyls (Section 3.2.3)) on the various supports. On silica, the rhodium showed an XPS peak at a binding energy of 307.0 eV, which corresponded with that shown by rhodium metal. But when the rhodium was supported by zinc oxide, the XPS peak appeared at a higher binding energy (308.4 eV), which matched that produced using Rh(I) compounds. When zirconia provided the support, the XPS peak appeared between these two extremes, indicating the presence of both Rh(0) and Rh(I) on the surface. It may be considered that Rh(I), viewed as Rh^+, is unlikely to act as a centre for the dissociative chemisorption of carbon monoxide, as is indicated directly by EXAFS results (Fig. 4.19). The positive charge on Rh^+ makes it much less likely to back donate electron density into the $2\pi^*$ antibonding orbital of carbon monoxide (Fig. 5.4 and last paragraph of Section 5.2). Thus rhodium, present apparently as Rh^+ on zinc oxide and also on lanthanum oxide (La_2O_3), catalyses methanol synthesis mainly on these supports, which is consistent with only molecular chemisorption of carbon monoxide. Rhodium metal on the other hand, as it is when silica is the support, dissociatively chemisorbs carbon monoxide, as is implied by the appearance of hydrocarbon products only. It might then be attractive to interpret the product spectrum when rhodium is supported on zirconia (as coexisting Rh(0) and Rh(I) centres on the basis of the XPS evidence) as follows. Rh(0) centres dissociatively chemisorb carbon monoxide and induce hydrogenation to yield chemisorbed CH_x species as a result. A neighbouring Rh(I) site will chemisorb carbon monoxide molecularly. If some form of interaction between the two types of chemisorbed species can occur, it is conceivable that the result might be a chemisorbed carbonyl species, CH_xCO. Subsequent hydrogenations of CH_x and CH_xCO species could then yield the major products, methane and ethanol respectively. The apparent straightforwardness of this scheme must however be tempered by recent controversy as to whether or not the most active catalysts for the formation of C_2-oxygenates do contain unreduced rhodium centres. The mechanism concerned may be considerably more complex than that advanced above. Nevertheless these rhodium catalysts provide an interesting instance of how XPS may be applied in the investigation of surface processes.

The principal industrial usage of catalytic methanation is for the removal of carbon monoxide from hydrogen feedstocks, as used in ammonia synthesis for example. Fischer–Tropsch synthesis on iron catalysts is at the centre of the liquid fuel production enterprises in South Africa. There the Sasol plants produce of the order of 10^{10} kg year^{-1}, with coal used as the primary feedstock for the generation of the synthesis gas.

8.5 Ethylene oxide production

Selective oxidation of ethylene can proceed by the addition of an oxygen atom across the double bond to yield ethylene oxide

$$CH_2{=}CH_2 + \tfrac{1}{2}O_2 \longrightarrow \underset{\displaystyle O}{CH_2{-}CH_2}$$

Silver provides the unique catalyst of high selectivity for this, when other pathways of selective oxidation (producing formaldehyde and acetaldehyde) are insignificant. There is however a competitive deep-oxidation pathway corresponding to

$$C_2H_4 + 3O_2 \rightarrow 2CO_2 + 2H_2O$$

Commercial processes use recycling modes through packed bed, multitubular reactors. The annual production of ethylene oxide from a single reactor can extend up to 8×10^7 kg. Typical operating conditions are temperatures in the range 470 to 600 K with total pressures of 1 to 3 MPa. Both reactions expressed by the equations above are exothermic: the selective oxidation releases 3.8 MJ and deep oxidation 50.7 MJ, both per kg of ethylene at 600 K. Accordingly reactor tubes are narrow (20–50 mm internal diameter and 6–12 m length are typical dimensions), with heat removed by oil circulation externally. These tubes are filled with a supported silver catalyst, preferred supports being low surface area (<1 m^2 g^{-1}) materials such as α-alumina. The silver may be deposited on to the support *via* impregnation (Section 3.2.3) in association with an essential promoter, commonly rubidium or caesium. A representative catalyst will have about 8% w/w of silver (existing as metal particles of diameter 50–200 nm) on α-alumina particles of about 8 mm diameter, incorporating about 10% of caesium. Silver metal itself cannot be used because its physical structure degrades badly under reactor conditions. Selectivities to ethylene oxide of 60 to 80% are achieved industrially. Chlorine compounds, such as ethylene dichloride or vinyl chloride, are added because the resultant presence of chlorine on the silver surfaces within the reactor exerts a useful retardation of deep oxidation. Two major types of plant are in use; one uses air as the oxidant whilst the other uses nearly pure oxygen. In air-using plants, the conversion of ethylene per pass through the reactor is restricted to 20 to 50%, giving an exit gas containing 1 to 2% on a molar basis of ethylene oxide. Higher conversion rates are penalized by lower selectivities. The exit gas is cooled to around 310 K prior to entry to an absorber unit within which water is used to dissolve the ethylene oxide. Subsequently the aqueous solution passes to a desorber unit, within which the product is taken off by steam-stripping under reduced pressure. Ethylene oxide is an important bulk chemical with major usage in productions of antifreeze agents (ethylene glycol), polyesters and surfactants.

That silver is the effective catalyst for this selective oxidation can be understood on the basis of the general action required. Ethylene must be chemisorbed molecularly at fairly high temperatures. This requirement excludes transition metals with unfilled d orbitals: the rearrangements of the structure of chemisorbed ethylene on nickel for example were discussed in Section 5.1. On silver ($4d^{10}$), EELS spectra (Section 4.4.2) have indicated that ethylene is chemisorbed in a π-bonded form. In fact it has been shown that ethylene is significantly more strongly bound on a silver (110) surface which has been precovered with atomic oxygen than it is on the corresponding clean surface. The promoting actions in this respect of both atomic oxygen and chlorine are then interpreted in terms of their electronegative natures. In its π-bonding, ethylene is chemisorbed on silver with transfer of electron density towards the metal, which is promoted when an electron-withdrawing species is also present on the surface.

Recently strong evidence has been obtained that chemisorbed atomic oxygen is the coreactant species, rather than a form of dioxygen as had been accepted previously. The most conclusive parts of such evidence are as follows. Ethylene oxide is formed when a conditioned silver surface is exposed to ethylene/nitrous oxide (N_2O) mixtures at a temperature of 580 K. Nitrous oxide is expected to decompose to form chemisorbed atomic oxygen under these conditions, but molecular oxygen formation has been shown to be insignificant. Also in temperature programmed reaction studies (Section 4.3.1), when a silver (111) surface was dosed with oxygen at ambient temperature, the peaks corresponding to desorption of molecular oxygen and atomic oxygen appeared at temperatures of 380 and 570 K approximately respectively. When the oxygen-predosed surface was taken up to 450 K (thus desorbing all of the adsorbed dioxygen), cooled to ambient temperature and dosed with ethylene before a temperature-programmed reaction spectrum was obtained, ethylene oxide appeared corresponding to a peak at about 370 K. Under these circumstances only atomic oxygen is available as the coreactant.

Atomic oxygen on the surface is also considered to be effective in inducing the competing deep oxidation pathway. The factors which control these competing pathways are not yet resolved fully. Electronic effects are certainly involved in this, since the presence of chlorine on the surface greatly promotes the selectivity to ethylene oxide. However secondary chemistry, including the isomerization of ethylene oxide to acetaldehyde, is also likely to be important. There is some evidence that caesium on the surface of the selective catalysts acts to suppress this isomerization and hence the further oxidation to carbon oxides to which acetaldehyde seems to be more susceptible than ethylene oxide.

Finally in this section, it is worth pointing out that ethylene is the only alkene for which heterogeneous catalysis provides a viable means of industrial production of the corresponding epoxide. Although propylene is converted to propylene oxide to some extent on silver surfaces, the selectivity achieved (about 5% at most) is too low to be of practical significance. It is believed that acrolein is the major intermediate in this case but that this is induced to polymerize: the resultant larger species remain on the silver surface for too long to avoid being deeply oxidized to carbon dioxide and water.

8.6 Sulphuric acid production

The oxidation of sulphur dioxide results in sulphur trioxide, the anhydride of sulphuric acid

$$SO_2 + \frac{1}{2}O_2 \rightarrow SO_3 \ (+ H_2O \rightarrow H_2SO_4)$$

Thermodynamic parameters are favourable for the conversion in air, but the process must be conducted in a well controlled manner. Figure 8.5(a) shows the conversion of sulphur dioxide achieved at chemical equilibrium as a function of temperature and indicates 700 K as an upper limit for reasonably complete conversion. But the rate at which the conversion proceeds increases sharply with rising temperature: suitable rates to allow a close approach to equilibrium conversion with practicable contact times are only achieved at temperatures above 820 K under normal circumstances. The design of the reactor for the Contact Process, as it is known, is a set of catalyst beds separated by cooled zones. The mixture of sulphur dioxide and air, preheated to a temperature of around 710 K, enters at the top of the reactor column. The exothermicity of the reaction (91 kJ $(\text{mol SO}_2)^{-1}$ at 800 K) raises the temperature of the uppermost bed to about 870 K, resulting in favourable rates but only about 75% conversion of the sulphur dioxide. The cooling coils between each bed reduce the temperature of the gas. The temperatures at which successive beds operate are progressively lower but so also are the kinetic demands for approach to the corresponding equilibrium composition. Figure 8.5(b) represents

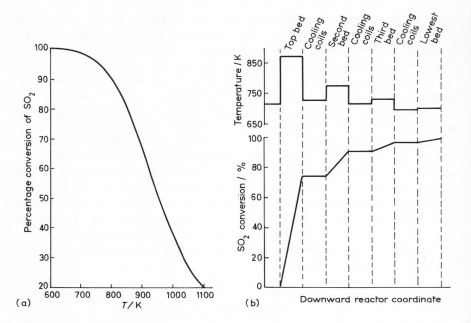

Fig. 8.5 (a) Percentage conversion of sulphur dioxide achieved at equilibrium for a feedgas of representative initial composition of 8% SO_2, 12% O_2 and 80% N_2 and other inert gases (often produced by roasting sulphide ores in air) at atmospheric pressure as a function of temperature. (b) Typical temperature and conversion profiles through a contact process reactor with four catalyst beds.

typical profiles of conversions and temperatures moving downwards in the reactor. The interstage cooling systems can be applied to generate steam for other space- and water-heating requirements.

Nowadays vanadia-based catalysts are used almost exclusively in the Contact Process (rather than platinum as in earlier reactors), in reflection of their low costs. The vanadia catalyst is promoted by incorporating potassium sulphate and exists under reaction conditions as a liquid phase supported on porous solids such as kieselguhr (Section 3.1.3). Optimized industrial reactors offer useful working lifetimes of the order of five years for the catalyst in the beds achieving higher temperatures (about 870 K) and about one year for that in the beds working at lower temperatures (about 700 K). Representative rates of conversion of sulphur dioxide per day can be about 5000 kg m^{-3}, expressed with respect to the volume of the catalytic material.

In recent years there has been considerable progress in understanding the nature of the active catalyst and its mechanism of operation. A major role of the potassium sulphate promoter is to create a molten layer at temperatures well below the normal melting point of pure vanadium pentoxide (963 K). The optimum amount of vanadia on the support appears to be that which allows the entire solid surface to be covered with a thin layer of the active liquid phase. Further increase in the loading of vanadia depresses the activity for sulphur dioxide oxidation: this may reflect simply the filling of the pores of the support by the liquid layer, with consequent decrease of the area of the active surface presented to the gas phase.

Characteristic infrared absorption bands of sulphate (SO_4^{2-}) and pyro-sulphate ($S_2O_7^{2-}$) have been detected in this molten liquid phase. Also a substantial body of evidence exists to indicate that the vanadium in the working catalyst exists in the cationic forms VO^{3+} (V(v)) and VO^{2+} (V(IV)), bonded to two or three sulphate or pyrosulphate anions. Complexes of this sort may associate further to create polymeric chains, within which each vanadium centre is surrounded by several oxygens. Redox action within the liquid phase appears to be the essential feature of the mechanism: in this general respect the catalytic oxidation of sulphur dioxide appears to be very similar to the other catalysed oxidations on solid vanadia discussed in Section 6.2. The basic mechanism can be considered to be of the Mars–van Krevelen type when it is represented simply by the two equations

$$SO_2 + 2V(v) + O^{2-} \rightarrow SO_3 + 2V(IV) + \text{oxygen vacancy}$$
$$\tfrac{1}{2}O_2 + 2V(IV) + \text{oxygen vacancy} \rightarrow 2V(v) + O^{2-}$$

using O^{2-} to represent lattice oxygen. The most straightforward evidence in support is the detection of electron spin resonance signals corresponding to V(IV) in the catalyst (initially containing only V(v)) when it was working in oxidizing sulphur dioxide at temperatures in the range 690–770 K. There is also considerable evidence that the overall rate of the catalysed reaction is governed by the effective concentration of V(IV) present. This satisfies the requirement of the Mars–van Krevelen type of mechanism that it is the reoxidation of the metal centres which acts as the rate determining step for the overall process. But there is also evidence which suggests that the first of the two steps above can limit the overall rate if the ratio of concentrations of V(v) to V(IV) becomes too small. This implies that there is an optimum value of this concentration ratio. In the case of catalysts with molar ratios of K_2O/V_2O_5 of approximately one, the optimum rates of sulphur dioxide oxidation are achieved with ratios of V(v) to V(IV) in the range 1.2–1.6 at usual operating temperatures. By analogy with other oxidation reactions (Section 6.2) in which (solid) vanadia serves as an effective catalyst, it might be expected that V=O groups supply the oxygen for the initial conversion of sulphur dioxide to sulphur trioxide. This and other details of what is a highly complex catalytic system remain to be investigated further in the future.

8.7 Linear polyethylene production

Oxidized forms of the transition metals, chromium and titanium, on various supports have valuable activity as catalysts for the polymerization of ethylene into linear chains. The corresponding processes have the virtues of operating with relatively low pressures of ethylene and temperatures, in the range 350–500 K. Earlier processes produced polyethylene of lower density on account of the high degrees of chain branching incorporated into the material. The modern processes are referred to as the Phillips process (based on chromium) and the Ziegler–Natta process (based on titanium). The discussion here will concentrate on the former, since the general nature of the polymerization processes are similar.

A Phillips catalyst is prepared usually by impregnation of a Cr(VI) salt into amorphous silica gel (or alumina or silica–alumina) to create a metal loading of about 1%. The resultant dried material is calcined at temperatures of 800–1300 K and, after cooling, is stored in a dry environment. It is believed that the important feature of this activation process is the removal of surface silanol (Si—OH) groups which can interact with the chromium sites. At this stage the chromium is present as a hexavalent oxide, monodispersed on the silica surface probably as a surface chromate or a dichromate ester

Chromate   Dichromate

The active site for polymerization is believed to be a highly coordinatively unsatisfied chromium centre, with chromium in oxidation state II or III, produced by reduction with ethylene, as exemplified below for the chromate site

$+$ 2HCHO (detected product)

In fact, catalysts have been prepared by special procedures through which Cr(III) or Cr(II) centres have been put directly on to the surface. The relative performances of these catalysts show that Cr(III) centres have much higher activities for polymerization, but that Cr(II) centres do have some activity, particularly at temperatures exceeding 370 K. Further it has been demonstrated clearly that only isolated chromium centres, and not those aggregated together, act as active centres for polymerization. This feature is likely to account for observations that only a small fraction of the normal loading of chromium is in fact active. But abnormally low loadings (30–100 parts per million) induce maximum effectiveness per unit amount of chromium. Under these circumstances most chromium centres are likely to be isolated from others.

The high degree of coordinative unsaturation at the transition metal centres is the key feature of both Phillips and Ziegler–Natta catalysts. There is then a resultant ability to bind both the growing chain and the monomer molecule at the same time. There is no redox action here since the transition metal centre does not change its oxidation state during the polymerization process but rather varies its linkages to ligands. The apparently critical demand is for the availability of more than one vacant $3d$ orbital in what may be regarded as partially-coordinated transition metal ions for simplicity. Figure 8.6 represents one view of the microscopic action which explains the linearity of the resultant polymer. The implied mechanism of chain growth is the insertion of two CH_2 units between the metal centre (M) and the original alkyl chain $(R-(CH_2)_n-CH_2-)$, so that there is no possibility for the incorporation of chain branches into the growing polymer. The product is known generally as a linear polyethylene and it offers a range of properties suited to numerous applications. Useful extensions of these properties can result from the deliberate introduction of branches which are themselves fairly short chains. This objective may be accomplished if ethylene is copolymerized with a 1-alkene $(CH_2=CHR)$: $CH_2=CH_2$ and $CH_2=CHR$ compete to be incorporated

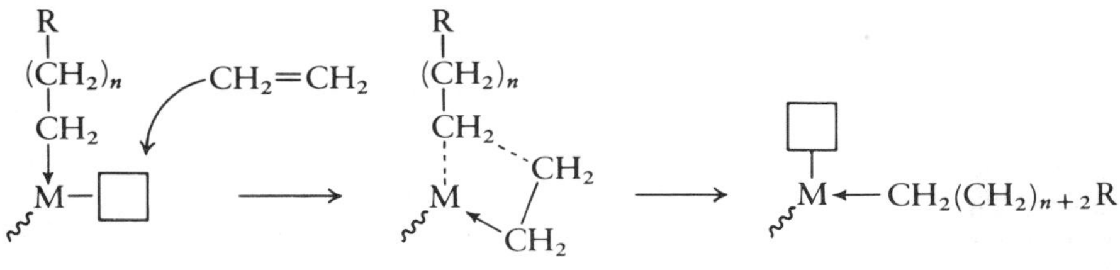

Fig. 8.6 Representation of a polymerization step at a metal (M) centre of a Phillips or Ziegler–Natta catalyst, where □ represents a coordination vacancy and dashed lines indicate partial bonds. The wavy line indicates the attachment to the support.

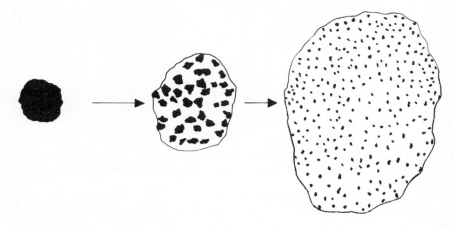

Fig. 8.7 Representation of the growth of polymer (enclosed white area) bulk on a Phillips catalyst supported by a porous material (black), indicating the shattering of the original catalytic particle.

into the chain *via* the mechanism indicated in Fig. 8.6. When $CH_2{=\!=}CHR$ is taken into the growing chain, a pendant R group (alkyl chain) appears on the polymer backbone; the positioning of these R groups is random.

In addition to their ability to provide a mechanism for linear growth of polymer chains, chromium and titanium are successful also in imposing the required kinetic factors. Appropriate relative values of rate constants for propagation steps and termination steps lead to chain growth to desirable extents in the final polymers. These factors will originate in subtle features of the various interactions concerned and account for the successful usage of chromium and titanium rather than other metallic elements.

The initial particles of a Phillips catalyst are fragmented severely during the polymerization process. In the presence of ethylene the active sites may be viewed as 'seeds' from which polymer chains grow outwards. When the support is porous, polymer accumulation within the pores generates forces of expansion which ultimately shatter larger particles. For example, catalysts with initial particle diameters ranging up to 250 μm may finish with individual particle dimensions reduced to less than 10 μm. Figure 8.7 represents a typical history of the growth of a polymer particle, showing the shattering phenomenon for the catalyst particle upon which the process starts. The main industrial processes of ethylene polymerization use the monomer in solution in a volatile saturated hydrocarbon as feedstock. Within the reactor, the grown polymer chains detach from the catalyst by passing into solution under these circumstances. In modern systems in which the rate of production is high, the polymeric product precipitates out

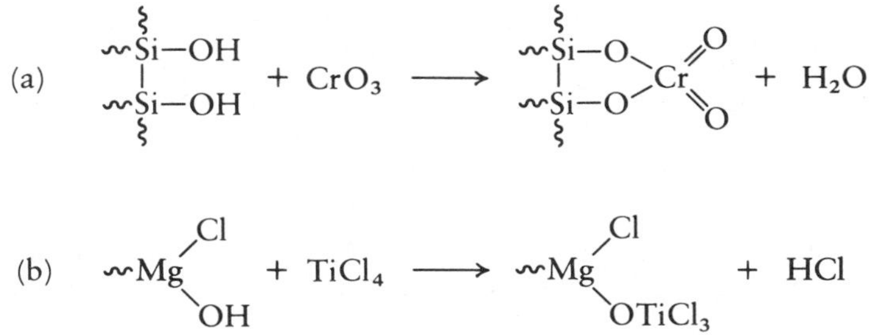

Fig. 8.8 Processes involved in creating precursor forms of (a) Phillips and (b) Ziegler–Natta catalysts.

of solution ultimately, thus separated from the catalyst particles. Using the Phillips catalyst, the length of the polymer chains is controlled by the temperature at which the catalyst was pretreated in its calcination: this governs the extent of dehydroxylation of the support and in turn the number of isolated chromium centres which are active as a consequence of their coordinative unsaturation.

Finally it is worth mentioning that the Phillips catalyst and some forms of Ziegler–Natta catalysts are in fact grafted catalysts (Section 3.1.5). This is indicated in Fig. 8.8, which shows typical processes involved in the creation of the precursor forms of the catalysts.

8.8 Catalytic cracking

The basis of the process of catalytic cracking of hydrocarbons on acidic solid surfaces was discussed in Section 6.3. The origin of the acidity of the rare earth forms of zeolites which are the typical catalysts used was discussed in Section 5.3.

Modern, fluid catalytic cracking was developed commercially after 1940. The catalysts are present as small particles (40–150 μm diameter) and act to fragment the larger molecular chains in crude oil to the small hydrocarbons more suitable as fuels. In their common forms, commercial cracking catalysts contain a rare earth acidic zeolite (REHY), composing 5% to 40% of particles containing also a silica–alumina binder and clay. In the conventional mode of the cracking process, a feedstock, preheated to around 570 K, is sprayed into the base of the column where it mixes with hot catalyst particles to produce a process temperature of some 820 K. As cracking commences, the generated gases in association with added steam move the reacting components and the catalyst particles upwards. At the top of the column and after they have been separated from the exit stream of gaseous products, the catalyst particles are fed into the regenerator. Here air is blown through the descending hot catalyst to burn off the around 1% of deposited carbon: the exothermicity of this combustion process heats the catalyst particles prior to their return to the cracking column. In practice, this type of reactor/regenerator combination can be operated almost in heat balance. The typical weight ratio of catalyst to oil in the cracker column will be around 5. Each catalyst particle can go round the cycle more than 10 000 times on average before its useful working life is over.

Heavy crude oils can contain up to 25% by volume of residual oil (the fraction with boiling point above 823 K) and around 30% of heavy gas oil (the fraction distilled off in the temperature range 613–823 K). The latter provides the usual feedstock for fluid catalytic cracking. Using modern types of catalytic cracking catalysts and technology, most of the heavy gas oil can be converted into hydrocarbons containing less than 20 carbon atoms in the molecules. Even with a residual oil feedstock, about three-quarters of the volume can be cracked to yield a liquid product of which 60–65% by volume is in the gasoline (C_5–C_{11}) range and 15–17% is in the diesel fuel (C_{12}–C_{20}) range. Thereafter gasoline fuels of high octane numbers are made by catalytic reforming as described in Section 6.4.

8.9 Synthetic gasoline production

Gasoline (petrol) is a complex mixture of a large number of individual hydrocarbons containing 5 to 11 carbon atoms generally. A chemist, with access to conventional organic synthesis methods only, would be realistic in regarding a requirement to produce gasoline from synthesis gas or from a simple alcohol as practically impossible. The fact that catalysts have been found to effect these transformations in single stage processes (in principle) is then almost incredible. Perhaps even more impressive is the pace of technological development: within less than 20 years this has taken the situation from the initial laboratory synthesis of the outstanding catalyst in this respect (the zeolite ZSM-5) through to a production process for gasoline which is able to satisfy about one-third of a nation's transportation fuel needs. This large scale production, in New Zealand, amounts on an annual basis to over half a billion (0.5×10^9) litres of M-gasoline, as the synthesized fuel is known. The M- prefix denotes the Mobil Oil Corporation, the originators of both the catalyst (Section 3.2.2) and the reactor technology.

Fischer–Tropsch synthesis also provides a route to generate liquid fuels (Section 8.4). In South Africa this process, commencing with synthesis gas which has been generated from coal, has been developed to total

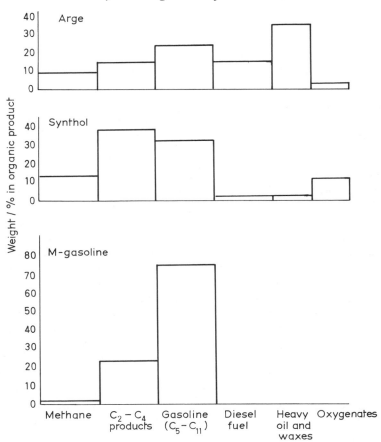

Fig. 8.9 Typical general product distributions achieved by two different types of Fischer–Tropsch plants (Arge and Synthol) and an M-gasoline plant which uses a recycling loop for C_1–C_4 products.

production of liquid fuels which exceeds presently that of M-gasoline in New Zealand by over an order of magnitude. Figure 8.9 compares the typical general distributions of products from such processes. The outstanding point of contrast is evident. The Fischer–Tropsch processes yield a wide spectrum of products, extending to the long chains of heavy oil and waxes. The M-gasoline process does not produce hydrocarbons beyond the gasoline range. As discussed in Section 8.4, the Fischer–Tropsch synthesis products are created by the growth of carbon chains on an iron-based surface and there is no restriction on a size selectivity basis on

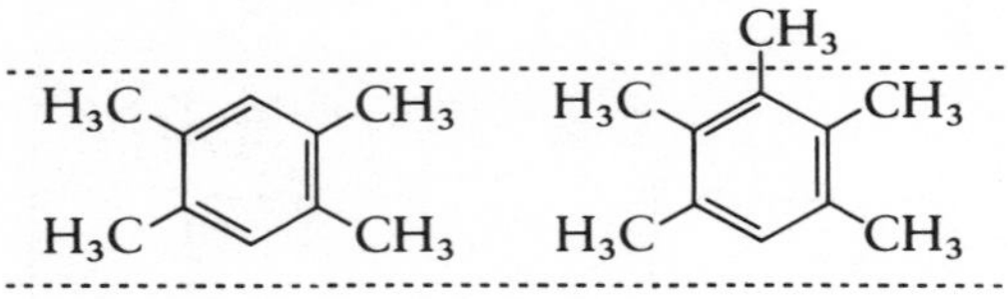

Fig. 8.10 Simple representation of the origin of the different, effective molecular dimensions (in the vertical direction) of 1,2,4,5-tetramethylbenzene (a C_{10} species also known as durene) and 1,2,3,4,5-pentamethylbenzene (C_{11}).

the length to which these chains may grow. But it is very clear that an outstanding property of the zeolite catalyst used in the M-gasoline process is its ability to inhibit the formation of molecules with more than about 10 carbon atoms. It is appropriate at this stage to recognize that the larger molecules in M-gasoline are mainly methyl substituted benzene rings. This provides an immediate pointer to a geometrical selectivity imposed by the internal structure of the zeolite catalyst, since a significant difference is expected between the effective diameters of four- and five-substituted benzene rings, as is illustrated in Fig. 8.10 in a simple manner. The preparational procedure for the zeolite concerned, ZSM-5, was discussed in Section 3.2.2. The detailed microstructure of this aluminosilicate material is based on pentagonal units of the type shown in Fig. 8.11(a), where the intersections of lines define the positions of the T atoms (T = Si or Al). This is the origin of the general designation of 'pentasil' often applied to zeolites of a high silica nature with structures based upon this type of unit. Figures 8.11(b), (c) and (d) show how the microstructure of ZSM-5 is built up to create pore apertures incorporating 10 T atoms with 10 intervening oxygen atoms. The structure of the three-dimensional channel system as defined by the pore apertures is shown in Fig. 8.11(e). The pore aperture of the linear channels (which appear in cross-section in Fig. 8.11(d)) is slightly elliptical with principal axial dimensions of 0.56 and 0.54 nm. The sinusoidal channel system has pore aperture dimensions of 0.55 and 0.51 nm; this pore aperture appears in cross-section in Fig. 8.11(c). The effective channel system in the third dimension is created by components of the other two systems and may be described as tortuous in nature. The supercages which separate the pore apertures along the channels have diameters of the order of 0.9 nm; these are not represented in Fig. 8.11(e).

In Section 3.2.2 evidence was presented to justify the statement that the area of the internal surfaces of a zeolite far exceeds that at the external surfaces of the crystallite. This factor, in alliance with the strong, localized electrostatic fields which exist within the pore system (Fig. 5.11) and induce high reactivity in molecules therein, implies that the products from

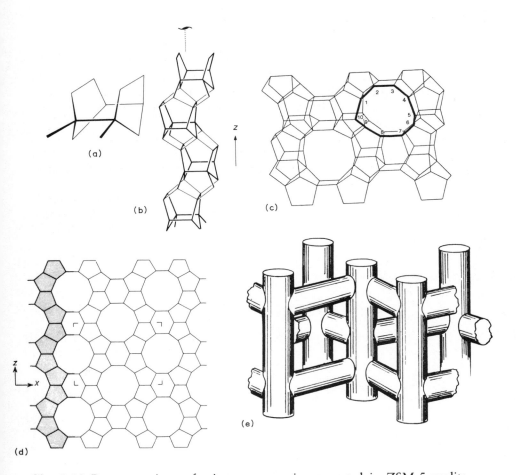

Fig. 8.11 Representations of microstructures incorporated in ZSM-5 zeolite. (a) Basic pentagonal building block represented following the same principles as used in Fig. 3.3 (T atoms at line intersections). (b) Extension of the structure in the vertical direction, by joining together units of (a). (c) Representation of the creation of pore apertures containing 10 T atoms (numbered) by extension of the structure shown in (b). The leading edges of the pore aperture are thickened. (d) Simplified representation of the uniform pore structure in a main axes cross-section. (e) Representation of the directional characteristics of the channel structure of ZSM-5, as indicated by cylinders of identical cross-sections to the pore apertures directed through them. In the actual zeolite structure the intersections of the cyclinders would correspond to supercages. Figures 8.11(a), (b) and (d) reprinted by permission from *Crystal structure and structure-related properties of ZSM-5*, D. H. Olson, G. T. Kokotailo, S. L. Lawton and W. M. Meier (1981) *Journal of Physical Chemistry,* **85**, 2241. Copright 1981 American Chemical Society. Figure 8.11(e) reprinted by permission from *Nature* (1978), **272** (5652), 437. Copyright © 1978 Macmillan Journals Limited.

zeolite-catalysed reactions will have originated from within the interior of the crystallites in general. The geometrical selectivity is imposed then by the necessity for reactant and product molecules to pass through the pore apertures. In the case of ZSM-5, the largest dimension offered by the pore apertures is 0.56 nm. Taking into account the ability of molecules to 'wriggle' through the aperture to some extent, 0.6–0.7 nm seems likely to be a critical range of molecular kinetic diameters. Then towards the upper end of this range, a gas phase molecule would be expected to encounter severe resistance to its movement through the channel systems. The ease of this movement will be expressed by values of the internal diffusion coefficients, several illustrative values of which are indicated for aromatic molecules in ZSM-5 in Fig. 8.12. It is clear that resistance to movement

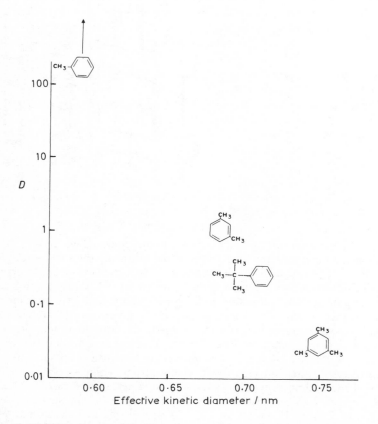

Figure 8.12 Diagram representing the variation of relative values of internal diffusion coefficients (D) of aromatic hydrocarbons within the pores of the zeolite ZSM-5 against the effective kinetic diameters.

through the zeolite structure increases sharply with the extent of methyl substitution of the benzene ring. This has implications for the products of reactions taking place within the zeolite; only molecules with the ability to move through the channel systems can emerge as gas phase products. Thus it is not surprising that the tetramethylbenzene represented in Fig. 8.10 is the largest aromatic molecule produced in significant amounts in the reactions catalysed by ZSM-5.

The basis of the M-gasoline process is that when methanol is contacted with the acidic zeolite HZSM-5 at temperatures of the order of 650 K, catalysed conversion occurs to produce a range of hydrocarbons and water. The general action is thus the separation of carbon from oxygen, the former being polymerized to a limited extent into hydrocarbon chains. In fact methanol can be converted to liquid hydrocarbons over many acidic catalysts; coking however accompanies the action usually and the catalytic activity is lost quickly as a consequence. ZSM-5, reflecting its geometrical selectivity, does not allow the formation of linked aromatic rings, which are the precursors of coke, within its structure and thus preserves its catalytic activity. This is the key factor for the usefulness of this most spectacular catalytic material.

The course of the conversion of methanol on HZSM-5 is indicated by the order of appearance of different products with increasing space time, as shown in Fig. 8.13. Space time in this connection is defined as the reciprocal of the liquid hourly space velocity (LHSV) and it can be regarded as a measure of the contact time with the catalyst. Dimethylether (CH_3OCH_3) appears only at short space times and is indicated to be a primary intermediate species. This appearance is unsurprising since many acidic solids, including silica–alumina and acidic forms of alumina, have the ability to catalyse the conversion represented as

$$2CH_3OH \rightarrow CH_3OCH_3 + H_2O$$

The next products with increasing space time are small alkenes (olefins). Dimethylether does not undergo a corresponding dehydration reaction in the presence of silica–alumina or acidic alumina. The generation of these alkenes in conjunction with further evolution of water, evident in Fig. 8.13, must then result from the influence of the highly catalytically-active microenvironment within the channel system of the zeolite. The actual mechanisms of elementary reactions involved at this stage have not been defined clearly as yet; at the level of this book it is not appropriate to review the several conflicting postulates which have been advanced. What is certain however is that the simplest dehydration process expressed by the equation

$$CH_3OCH_3 \rightarrow C_2H_4 + H_2O$$

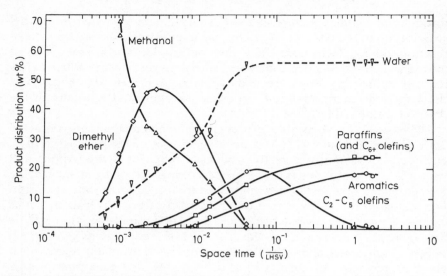

Figure 8.13 Profiles of detected product amounts (weight %) as a function of space time when methanol vapour is converted over HZSM-5 at a temperature of 644 K. Reproduced from *The conversion of methanol and other O-compounds to hydrocarbons over zeolite catalysts*, C. D. Chang and A. J. Silvestri (1977) *Journal of Catalysis*, **47**, 254 with permission of Academic Press Inc.

does not represent a correct description of the conversion mechanism. Beyond this stage, polymerization through the agencies of surface carbenium ions (Section 6.3) would appear to be the logical route towards larger hydrocarbon molecules, particularly as the temperatures concerned are only moderately high. The reaction-inducing microenvironment within the zeolite pore system appears to allow the exploration of alkane (paraffin), alkene and aromatic structures for the most stable range of products on a thermodynamic basis, with retention of hydrogen other than that emerging in the form of water. On a purely stoichiometric basis, what goes into these final stages of the conversion may be regarded as having the empirical formula CH_2, since two molecules of water are eliminated between each pair of methanol molecules consumed.

On a purely thermodynamic basis and without direct implications with regard to the detailed mechanism, values of standard Gibbs (free energy) function changes for various processes shown in Table 8.3 suggest the distribution of products to be expected from the full conversion of methanol on HZSM-5. The growing hydrocarbon chain within the zeolite might be expected to correspond to $(CH_2)_n$, which is isomeric with an alkene. But as illustrated in the Table by the large negative values of $\Delta G^{\ominus}$

Table 8.3 Standard Gibbs (free energy) function changes ($\Delta G^{\ominus}$) for processes at a temperature of 700 K

Process	$\Delta G^{\ominus}/\text{kJ mol}^{-1}$
1-nonene + 1-nonene → *m*-xylene + *n*-butane + 2 propane	-247
1-octene + 1-octene → toluene + *n*-butane + propane + ethane	-237
1-heptene + 1-heptene → benzene + *n*-butane + 2 ethane	-217
1-octene → 1-butene + 1-butene	-20
n-octane → *n*-butane + 1-butene	-21

Data derived from tabulated data in *The Chemical Thermodynamics of Organic Compounds*, D. R. Stull, E. F. Westrum and G. C. Sinke (1969) John Wiley & Sons Inc, New York.

for the first three processes, alkenes with more than six carbon atoms are unstable with respect to mixtures of aromatics and small alkanes. Also as indicated by the last two entries in the Table, longer linear chains are slightly unstable compared to shorter chains. Although limited, this selection of thermodynamic data suggests that the major products to be expected from the full conversion of methanol on HZSM-5 are smaller alkanes and aromatic hydrocarbons up to the geometrical selectivity limit (C_{10}) imposed by the pore aperture.

Table 8.4 lists typical distributions of the major hydrocarbon products resulting from the full conversions of methanol, ethanol and *n*-hexane over HZSM-5. Although the sets of yields differ in detail, they have a broad

Table 8.4 Representative distributions of major organic products from conversions of reactant vapours over HZSM-5 zeolite at temperatures close to 700 K

Products	Reactant		
	Methanol	Ethanol	*n*-Hexane
Propane	16	22	25
Butanes	24	30	17
Pentanes	9	10	5
C_{6+} aliphatics	4	4	1
Toluene	11	11	7
C_8 aromatics	17	15	29
C_9 aromatics	8	4	13

Yields expressed as weight percentages of the organic products.

degree of similarity. The data for *n*-hexane are included to make the point that the general distribution of the products does not appear to be influenced greatly by the processes of polymerization up to C_6 chains which are involved in the conversions of the alcohols. In concert these data justify in general terms the postulate that there is a strong measure of governance of the product distribution by thermodynamic considerations. The zeolite catalyst provides a microenvironment of high activity which induces rapid rates of the many reaction steps through which the conversions must proceed to yield the observed products. At the same time, the need for products to diffuse through the pore apertures of HZSM-5 ensures that species with more than 10 carbon atoms are insignificant.

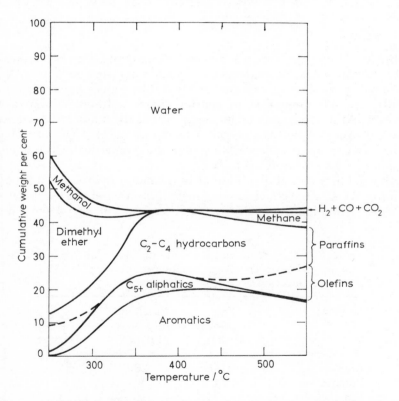

Fig. 8.14 Profiles of yields of categories of products from the conversion of methanol on HZSM-5 zeolite catalyst as a function of temperature at atmospheric pressure with liquid hourly space velocity of $0.6–0.7\,h^{-1}$. $T\,°C = (T + 273)\,K$. Reproduced from *The conversion of methanol and other O-compounds to hydrocarbons over zeolite catalysts*, C. D. Chang and A. J. Silvestri (1977) *Journal of Catalysis*, **47**, 255 with permission of Academic Press Inc.

The distribution of products obtained from the full conversion of methanol in contact with HZSM-5 varies with the temperature of the system, as shown in Fig. 8.14. At lower temperatures (below 350°C (623 K)) the conversion is incomplete, leaving dimethylether as a prominent product. At high temperatures (above 500°C (773 K)), methane and alkenes (olefins) become increasingly abundant at the expense of alkanes (paraffins, aliphatics). This diagram makes it clear that control of temperature to the vicinity of 370°C (644 K) is needed to give best yields of M-gasoline, when complete conversion of methanol is achieved within practicable space times.

On an overall basis the M-gasoline process is exothermic, releasing heat of around 45 kJ mol^{-1} of methanol converted. At first sight it might seem that this exothermicity could only be helpful in a reaction system which has to be maintained at elevated temperature. On the adverse side however, intensive release of heat within a catalytic system which is sensitive to temperature demands that preventative measures must be taken against temperature rise above the optimum range. In fact at the typical operating temperature, this total heat release could produce a temperature rise of some 900 K under adiabatic conditions (i.e. when heat losses to the surroundings are insignificant). In order to facilitate temperature control in large scale M-gasoline plants, two separate reactors have been used. The upstream reactor is packed with alumina typically, which catalyses only the initial dehydration step, resulting in the production of dimethylether in association with the release of about 10 kJ mol^{-1} with respect to the methanol consumed. In practice this means that just over 75% of the overall heat release of the M-gasoline process then takes place in the subsequent reactor containing HZSM-5, greatly easing the operations for temperature control therein.

8.10 Some processes using zeolite catalysts

Around half of the non-communist world's *para*-xylene is produced now by catalytic action on HZSM-5 catalyst. Toluene is the most abundant and cheapest aromatic hydrocarbon, which commends its use as an initial feedstock. There are two basic reaction strategies for the conversion of toluene to xylenes, represented overleaf.

It would be expected the *p*-xylene, with kinetic diameter tending towards that of benzene (0.57 nm), would be able to diffuse more easily through the ZSM-5 pore system than would *o*- and *m*-xylene (see Fig. 8.12). But when the processes represented overleaf are conducted with HZSM-5 itself, the mixture of xylenes which emerges from the internal structure of the zeolite has proportions of the xylene isomers which are not far removed from

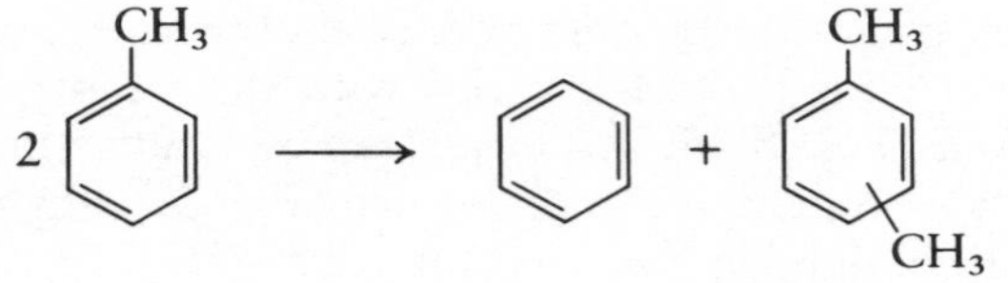

(Disproportionation)

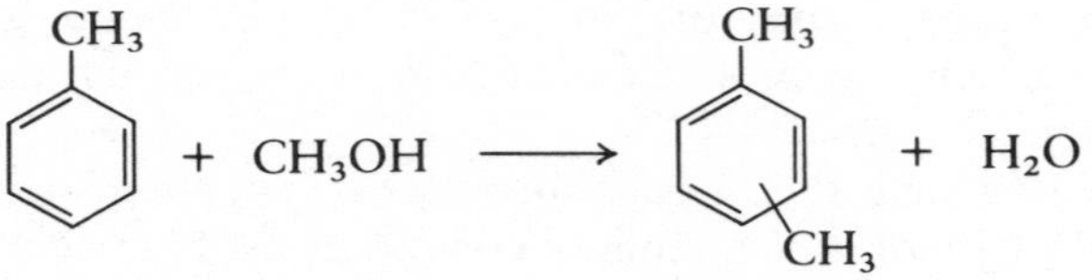

(Alkylation)

those expected in an equilibrated mixture at the typical reaction temperatures of 750–900 K. This suggests that the differences of kinetic diameters of the isomers are insufficient for the pore apertures of ZSM-5 to impose real selectivity. But much more selective action in this respect results when HZSM-5 has been impregnated with aqueous solutions of phosphoric acid or magnesium acetate and then calcined in air to leave the corresponding oxides deposited within the structure. Typically useful forms contain 8.5% of phosphorus or 11% of magnesium (by weight) respectively. These modified HZSM-5 catalysts show remarkably increased selectivities for producing *p*-xylene at the expense of the other two isomers. This is illustrated by the xylene isomer yields represented in Fig. 8.15. The spectacular selectivities for *p*-xylene formation in the lower half of this diagram are considered to originate in the occupation by the modifying species (phosphorus or magnesium oxides) of sites in the vicinity of the pore apertures. This restricts the dimension of the pores slightly in comparison with HZSM-5 itself. The attenuated pore aperture can still be penetrated with relative ease by benzene, toluene and *p*-xylene, but is almost impenetrable to *m*- and *o*-xylenes. The resultant situation is represented by a simple model in Fig. 8.16. It may be envisaged that thermodynamic equilibria between the xylene isomers is established with the zeolite supercages, but that only the *p*-isomer can 'leak' out to emerge into the gas phase. Continuous adjustment of the equilibria within the supercages to respond to the selective loss of *p*-xylene results, for example, in 97% production of this isomer into the vapour phase when the alkylation reaction is catalysed by the phosphorus-modified zeolite (PZSM-5).

Similar advantage can be taken of the enhanced selectivity of these modified ZSM-5 catalysts for the production of other *para*-substituted

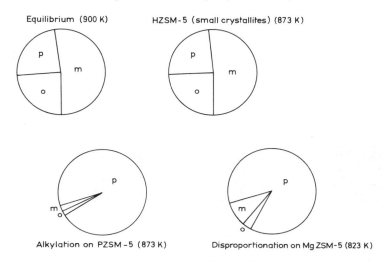

Fig. 8.15 Areas of sectors of circles corresponding to the proportions of xylene isomers (*ortho* (*o*), *meta* (*m*) and *para* (*p*)) achieved under the specified conditions. PZSM-5 is phosphorus-modified ZSM-5 and MgZSM-5 is magnesium-modified ZSM-5 (see text). Based upon data given by N. Y. Chen, W. W. Kaeding and F. G. Dwyer (1979) *Journal of the American Chemical Society*, **101**, 6783–6784 and the reference cited in the caption for Fig. 8.16.

products. For instance, alkylation of toluene using ethylene over ZSM-5 modified with silicon (SiZSM-5) has yielded a selectivity of over 90% for the generation of *p*-ethyltoluene, relative to the combined production of *o*-, *m*- and *p*-ethyltoluenes. SiZSM-5 has been produced by impregnation of ZSM-5 with a silicone oil followed by heating and then calcination to leave SiO_2 as the actual modifying agent. Dehydrogenation of *p*-ethyltoluene over a nickel catalyst (Section 6.1.2.1.) yields *p*-methylstyrene (CH_3—C_6H_4—CH=CH_2), the monomer for the production of the important polymer polymethylstyrene. An economically viable route to this material did not exist prior to the development of the modified ZSM-5 catalysts.

Small alkenes are vital feedstocks for many processes in the chemical industry. A route for the generation of these from methanol is likely to become of importance in the future when supplies of crude oil are less available. As indicated in Fig. 8.13, high-silica zeolites have the ability to catalyse the conversion of methanol to small alkenes (olefins); however with HZSM-5 these alkenes are intermediates on the pathway to other products. But a high-silica (or dealuminated (see Fig. 5.12)) zeolite with a smaller pore aperture than ZSM-5 might be expected to inhibit the conversion of methanol beyond the synthesis of short linear chains of

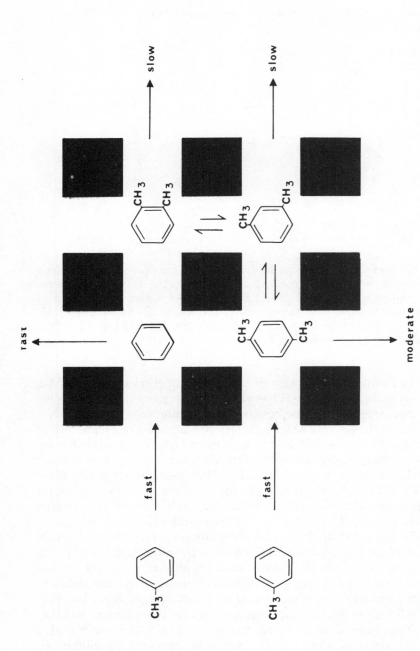

Fig. 8.16 Representation of the situation arising following the disproportionation of toluene within forms of ZSM-5 zeolite when the pore apertures have been attenuated by 'modifying' elements (see text). Black squares are used to represent the solid phase. Reproduced from *Shape-selective reactions with zeolite catalysts. III. Selectivity in xylene isomerization, toluene–methanol alkylation and toluene disproportionation over ZSM-5 zeolite catalysts*, L. B. Young, S. A. Butter and W. W. Kaeding (1982) *Journal of Catalysis*, 76, 430 with permission of Academic Press Inc.

Table 8.5 Representative yields from methanol conversion over small-pore, high-silica zeolite catalysts

Catalyst	T/K	Methane	Ethylene	Ethane	Propylene	Propane	Butenes	Butanes
Clinoptilolite	623	11	3	0	47	3	17	0
Zeolite T	633	4	46	0	30	0	10	7
Erionite*	643	6	36	0	39	2	9	6
ZSM-34†	673	14	43	0	33	5	3	1

* Dealuminated to Si/Al = 8 : 1. † Thorium-modified.
Yields expressed as weight percentage of the hydrocarbon fraction when the reactor temperature is T.

carbon. An A-type zeolite has this structural characteristic, but the low silicon-to-aluminium ratio in this (Table 3.7) does not induce the catalytic activity required. Fortunately there exist other zeolites with similar pore aperture dimensions to A-type zeolite but with higher silicon-to-aluminium ratios. Natural examples are the minerals erionite and clinoptilolite which have silicon-to-aluminium ratios of 3 : 1 (and can be further dealuminated) and 6 : 1 respectively. Synthetic materials designated as Zeolite T and ZSM-34 have corresponding ratios of 3.5 : 1 and 4–10 : 1 respectively. The pore aperture dimensions of these various zeolites lie in the range 0.36–0.52 nm, small enough to preclude the emergence of aromatic hydrocarbon molecules from within crystallites. Table 8.5 collects together some representative achievements of these catalysts in the conversion of methanol. These data indicate that catalysts are available to induce selectivities of over 70% for small alkenes in the organic products. The action is governed substantially by the strongly acidic centres within high-silica zeolites (Fig. 5.12 and discussion thereof) and the geometrical restrictions imposed by the pore apertures.

8.11 Concluding remarks

This chapter has been used to exemplify many of the basic principles of catalytic action on solid surfaces through discussion of processes of major importance for the chemical industry. It is evident that our present lifestyle is thoroughly dependent upon copious and comparatively inexpensive supplies of substances which serve as high quality fuels, plastics, fertilizers, solvents and edible fats. It should be abundantly clear that the comfort of people and satisfaction of their desires would be rather inhibited if efficient catalysts for the various production processes had not been discovered. We may all look forward in confident expectation of further good news and reports of exciting discoveries from the many scientists engaged in the search for new catalytic processes.

Further reading

This appendix presents a list of books and articles of potential interest in association with this book. These are ordered roughly in line with the progression of chapters, but in many cases there is spread beyond these confines, when the chapter heading will only indicate principal relevance. Particular attention has been given to items from the recent research literature which are of a review nature or are considered to offer appropriate development of basic principles.

General subjects and Chapters 1 and 2. Introduction and general aspects of catalysis at surfaces

Kirk-Othmer Encyclopaedia of Chemical Technology (3rd edn) (1978–1984) Volumes 1–26 (ed. M. Grayson), John Wiley & Sons Inc., New York.

Experimental Methods in Catalytic Research Volume 1 (1968) (ed. R. B. Anderson) Volume 2 (1976) (eds R. B. Anderson and P. T. Dawson) Academic Press Inc., New York.

Comprehensive Chemical Kinetics Volume 19 (1984) (eds C. H. Bamford, C. F. H. Tipper and R. G. Compton) Volume 20 (1978) (eds C. H. Bamford and C. F. H. Tipper), Elsevier Science Publishers B.V., Amsterdam.

The Chemical Physics of Solid Surfaces and Heterogeneous Catalysis Volumes 1–4 (1981 onwards) (eds D. A. King and D. P. Woodruff), Elsevier Science Publishers B. V., Amsterdam.

B. C. Gates, J. R. Katzer and G. C. A. Schuit (1979) *Chemistry of Catalytic Processes,* McGraw-Hill Inc., New York.

M. Boudart and G. Djéga-Mariadassou (1984) *Kinetics of Heterogeneous Catalytic Reactions*, Princeton University Press, Princeton, New Jersey.

Applied Industrial Catalysis, Volumes 1–3 (1983–1984) (ed. B. E. Leach), Academic Press Inc., Orlando, Florida.

W. M. H. Sachtler (1983) What makes a catalyst selective?, *Chemtech*, July, 434–447.

J. T. Kummer (1986) Use of noble metals in automobile exhaust catalysts, *Journal of Physical Chemistry*, **90**, 4747–4752.

K. J. Laidler and P. S. Bunting (1973) *The Chemical Kinetics of Enzyme Action*, (2nd edn), Oxford University Press, Oxford.

K. Hiromi (1979) *Kinetics of Fast Enzyme Reactions*, Halstead Press, New York.

Chapter 3. The constitution of catalytic surfaces

S. J. Gregg and K. S. W. Sing (1982) *Adsorption, Surface Area and Porosity*, (2nd edn), Academic Press, London.

J. W. Fulton (1986), Making the catalyst, *Chemical Engineering*, **July 7**, 59–63.

M. J. Yacaman (1984) Characterization of supported catalysts by transmission electron microscopy (review), *Applied Catalysis*, **13**, 1–25.

R. L. Burwell, Jr. (1986) Supported platinum, palladium and rhodium catalysts, *Langmuir*, **2**, 2–11.

P. Fouilloux (1983) The nature of Raney nickel, its adsorbed hydrogen and its catalytic activity for hydrogenation reactions, *Applied Catalysis*, **8**, 1–42.

B. H. Davis (1984) A comparison of surface areas derived from mercury penetration and nitrogen adsorption, *Applied Catalysis*, **10**, 185–198.

R. Datta *et al.* (1985) Supported liquid phase catalysts, Parts I, II and III, *Journal of Catalysis*, **95**, 181–208.

C. P. Tsonis (1984) Catalysis on polymeric matrices, *Journal of Chemical Education*, **61**, 479–483.

F. J. Waller (1986) Catalysis with metal cation-exchanged resins, *Catalysis Reviews–Science and Engineering*, **28**, 1–12.

A. M. Klibanov (1983) Immobilized enzymes and cells as practical catalysts, *Science*, **219**, 722–727.

T. Yoshioka and M. Shimamura (1986) Studies of polystyrene-based ion exchange fiber. V. Immobilization of microorganism cells by adsorption on a novel fiber-form anion exchanger, *Bulletin of the Chemical Society of Japan*, **59**, 399–403. (Parts I–IV cited).

K. Tanabe (1970) *Solid Acids and Bases*, Academic Press Inc., New York.

E. M. Flanigan (1980) Molecular sieve technology–the first twenty-five years, *Pure and Applied Chemistry*, **52**, 2191–2211.

J. M. Newsam (1986) The zeolite cage structure, *Science*, **231**, 1093–1099.

Chapter 4. The detection of adsorbates on solid surfaces

Characterization of Catalysts (1980) (eds J. M. Thomas and R. M. Lambert), John Wiley and Sons, Chichester, Sussex.

D. P. Woodruff and T. A. Delchar (1986) *Modern Techniques of Surface Science*, Cambridge University Press, Cambridge.

R. P. H. Gasser (1985) *An Introduction to Chemisorption and Catalysis by Metals*, Oxford University Press, Oxford.

S. Y. Tong (1984) Exploring surface structure, *Physics Today,* **August,** 2–11.

J. J. Weimer and F. A. Putnam (1984) Reactor for combined surface spectroscopic analysis and atmospheric pressure kinetic studies of catalysts, *Review of Scientific Instruments*, **55**, 238–243.

C. J. Powell (1985) Energy and material dependence of the inelastic mean free path of low energy electrons in solids, *Journal of Vacuum Science and Technology*, **A3**, 1338–1342.

J. E. Demuth and P. Avouris (1983) Surface spectroscopy, *Physics Today*, **November**, 62–68.

B.. J. Garrison and N. Winograd (1982) Ion-beam spectroscopy of solids and surfaces, *Science*, **216**, 805–812.

A. Brown and J. C. Vickerman (1984) Static SIMS for applied surface analysis, *Surface and Interface Analysis*, **6**, 1–14.

F. Jona, J. A. Strozier Jr. and W. S. Yang (1982) Low energy electron diffraction for surface structure analysis, *Reports on Progress in Physics*, **45**, 527–585.

G. T. Haller (1981) Vibrational spectroscopies applied to chemisorption and catalysis, *Catalysis Reviews–Science and Engineering*, **23**, 477–504.

P. Lagarde and H. Dexpert (1984) EXAFS in catalysis, *Advances in Physics*, **33**, 567–594.

Chapters 5 and 6. Chemisorption processes and catalytic actions on solid surfaces

G. A. Somorjai (1981) *Chemistry in Two Dimensions*, Cornell University Press, Ithaca, New York.

T. N. Rhodin and G. Ertl (eds) (1979) *The Nature of the Surface Chemical Bond*, North-Holland Publishing Co., Amsterdam.

R. A. van Santen (1982) Chemical-bonding aspects of heterogeneous catalysis. I. Chemisorption by metals and alloys, *Recueil–Journal of the Royal Netherlands Chemical Society*, 101/4, 121–136.

E. Shustorovich and R. C. Baetzold (1985) Towards a coherent theory of chemisorption, *Science*, 227, 876–881.

J. J. F. Scholten (1985) Some important aspects of chemisorption. Parts I and II, *Annales de Quimica*, 81, 475–494.

D. B. Dadyburjor, S. S. Jewur and E. Ruckenstein (1979) Selective oxidation of hydrocarbons on composite oxides, *Catalysis Reviews–Science and Engineering*, 19, 293–350.

K. Tanabe, T. Sumiyoshi, K. Shibata, T. Kiyoura and J. Kitagawa (1974) A new hypothesis regarding the surface acidity of binary metal oxides, *Bulletin of the Chemical Society of Japan*, 47, 1064–1066.

C. T. O'Connor, M. Kojima and W. K. Schumann (1985) The oligomerization of C_4 alkenes over cationic exchange resins, *Applied Catalysis*, 16, 193–207.

K. Hashimoto, T. Masuda, H. Ueda and N. Kitano (1986) Relationship between acid strength distributions of silica–alumina catalysts and their activities, *Applied Catalysis*, 22, 147–156.

J. A. Lercher and G. Rumplmayr (1985) Strength, type and catalytic activity of acid sites in ZSM-5 zeolites, *Zeitschrift für Physikalische Chemie Neue Folge*, 146, 113–128.

J. M. White and C. T. Campbell (1980) Surface chemistry in heterogeneous catalysis, *Journal of Chemical Education*, 57, 471–474.

G. A. Olah, G. K. Surya Prakash and J. Sommer (1985) *Superacids*, John Wiley and Sons Inc., New York.

H. Hattori, O. Takahashi, M. Takagi and K. Tanabe (1981) Solid superacids: preparation and their catalytic activities for reactions of alkanes, *Journal of Catalysis*, 68, 132–143.

Chapter 7. Catalytic action by enzymes

C. D. Garner and J. R. Helliwell (1986) Uses of synchrotron radiation in biochemical research, *Chemistry in Britain*, 22, 835–840.

Bioinorganic chemistry–state of the art (1985). A series of articles in the *Journal of Chemical Education*, 62, 916–1012.

M. Perutz (1985) The birth of protein engineering, *New Scientist*, 13 June, 12–15.

F. M. Menger (1985) On the source of intramolecular and enzymatic reactivity, *Accounts of Chemical Research*, 18, 128–134.

O. R. Zaborsky (1973) *Immobilized Enzymes,* CRC Press, Cleveland, Ohio.

R. A. Messing (ed.) (1975) *Immobilized Enzymes for Industrial Reactors,* Academic Press Inc., New York.

I. Chibata, T. Tosa and T. Sato (1986) Biocatalysis: immobilized cells and enzymes, *Journal of Molecular Catalysis,* 37, 1–24.

K. Yokozeki, S. Yamanaka, K. Takinami, Y. Hirose, A. Tanaka, K. Sonomoto and S. Fukui (1982) Application of immobilized lipase to regio-specific interesterification of triglyceride in organic solvent, *European Journal of applied Microbiology and Biotechnology,* 14, 1–5.

P. Linko (1983) Fuels and industrial chemicals (through biotechnology), *Biotechnology Advances,* 1, 47–58; (1985) 3, 39–61.

Chapter 8. Industrial processes based on solid catalysts

G. T. Austin (1984) *Shreve's Chemical Process Industries* (5th edn), McGraw-Hill Inc., New York.

M. Bowker, I. B. Parker and K. C. Waugh (1985) Extrapolation of the kinetics of model ammonia synthesis catalysts to industrially relevant temperatures and pressures, *Applied Catalysis,* 14, 101–118.

D. W. Goodman (1984) Model catalytic studies over metal single crystals, *Accounts of Chemical Research,* 17, 194–200.

R. J. Madix (1984) Reaction kinetics and mechanism: model studies on metal single crystals, *Catalysis Reviews–Science and Engineering,* 26, 281–297.

H. Praliaud, J. A. Dalmon, C. Miradatos and G. A. Martin (1986) Influence of potassium-salt addition on the catalytic properties of silica-supported nickel, *Journal of Catalysis,* 97, 344–356.

G. C. Chinchen, M. S. Spencer, K. C. Waugh and D. A. Whan (1987) Promotion of methanol synthesis and the water-gas shift reactions by adsorbed oxygen on supported copper catalysts, *Journal of the Chemical Society, Faraday Transactions I,* 83, 2193–2212.

R. B. Grant, C. A. J. Harbach, R. M. Lambert and S. A. Tan (1987) Alkali, chlorine and other promoters in the silver-catalyzed selective oxidation of ethylene, *Journal of the Chemical Society, Farday Transaction I,* 83, 2035–2046.

H. L. Hsieh (1984) Olefin polymerization catalysis technology, *Catalysis Reviews–Science and Engineering,* 26, 631–651.

D. L. Myers and J. H. Lunsford (1985) Silica-supported chromium catalysts for ethylene polymerization, *Journal of Catalysis,* 92, 260–271.

J. A. Maselli and A. W. Peters (1984) Preparation and properties of fluid cracking catalysts for residual oil conversion, *Catalysis Reviews– Science and Engineering,* 26, 525–554.

C. D. Chang (1983) *Hydrocarbons from Methanol,* Marcel Dekker Inc., New York, 1983.

I. E. Maxwell (1986) Shape-selective catalysis and process technology via molecular inclusion in zeolites, *Journal of Inclusion Phenomena,* 4, 1–29.

N. Y. Chen and W. E. Garwood (1986) Industrial application of shape-selective catalysis, *Catalysis Reviews–Science and Engineering,* 28, 185–264.

Index

Acetaldehyde 4, 60, 78, 190–1
Acetylene 92, 211
Acidic surfaces
    chemisorption on 27–31, 127–30,
        145–59, 161, 175–8, 180
    H_0 values 152, 157, 158, 177
    mechanisms on 174–8, 224–38
    titration of 151–2
Active sites of enzymes
    alcohol dehydrogenase 190–1
    chymotrypsin 185–6
    elastase 15–16
    general action 16, 186
    lysozyme 184–5, 189
    nitrogenase 191–2
Adsorption
    definitions 6
    energetics 28–36, 148–50, 174
    -immobilization of enzymes 79–80
    isotherms 17–24, 32, 33, 120
    -limited kinetics 43–4
    rate 20, 43
    thermodynamics 25–36
Alcohol dehydrogenase 190–1
Alkanes
    chemisorption 157–9, 164
    cracking 176–8, 223–4
    dehydrogenation 164, 179
    isomerization (skeletal) 164, 165,
        179
    reforming 178–82
Alkenes see Butenes, Ethylene,
        Propylene
Alkylation 234–5
Allyl radicals 144–5, 160, 173

Alumina
    acidic 152–3, 181–2
    desorption from 31, 33, 34
    M-gasoline process, use in 233
Aluminosilicates see Zeolites
Ammonia
    chemisorption on acidic surfaces 27,
        28, 30–1, 146, 148–50, 158–9
    oxidation 204
    synthesis
        industrial process 5, 203–4
        iron-catalysed 88–9, 114, 140,
            192–3, 203–4
        nitrogenase-catalysed 191–3
Anchored catalysts 59, 61–4
Aromatization of alkanes 164, 165
Aspartic acid (L-) 197
Auger electron spectroscopy (AES)
        110–14, 211

Back-donation 138, 140, 141, 145, 214
Band theory of metals 133–5
Benzene
    chemisorption on metals 141–2
    oxidation (selective) 170–1, 195–6
BET isotherm 23–4, 73
Bond energy trends 137
Brønsted acid sites 127, 146–50, 157,
        177–8
Butenes
    isomerization 38, 40, 63, 175–6
    oligomerization 176–7
    oxidation (selective) 42, 43, 79,
        173, 174
    synthesis from methanol 237

Calcination, definition 68
Calcium
    -exchanged zeolites 154–6
    phosphate catalyst 44
Calvet-type (micro)calorimeter 28–30
Carbenium ions 150, 157, 160, 175–7, 230
Carbon
    carbidic 112, 210–15
    graphitic 100, 165
    steam gasification of 9
Carbon dioxide 6, 94, 104, 145, 156, 167–8, 208
Carbon monoxide
    chemisorption
        dissociative 138–40, 211–13
        molecular 96–7, 125, 126, 128–9, 131, 138–41, 145, 208
        on
            iron 115–17
            nickel 95–6, 108
            platinum 128–9, 131
            transition metals 138–41
            transition metal oxides 145
        surface defects, role of 90, 140–1
    heats of chemisorption 139–40
    hydrogenation processes
        Fischer–Tropsch synthesis 111–13, 209–15
        methanation 98–100, 165–6
        thermodynamic parameters 209
    molecular orbitals 139
    oxidation 117–18, 167–8
Carbonium ions 177–8
CH_x species 99–100, 112–13, 210–12, 214
Chemical immobilization 81–3
Chemisorption
    bond parameters 103, 136, 137
    definition of types 25–6
    general features, on
        redox oxides 142–5
        solid acids 145–59
        transition metals 26–7, 132–42
Chromia catalysts 5, 12, 220–3
Chymotrypsin 14, 185–6, 189
Classification of catalysts
    enzymes 18
    solids 12–13
Clay minerals 53, 78
Cleaved faces 87–8, 90, 95–6, 127, 131, 142

Clinoptilolite 22, 237–8
Cocoa butter process 194–5
Coking 181, 229
Combustion 7–9
Copper, as catalyst for
    formic acid decomposition 93–4
    hydrogenation 201, 208–9
    methanol oxidation 109–10
    methanol synthesis 206–9
Coprecipitation 68, 75, 206
Corn syrup process 19, 193–4
Cracking 13, 176, 223–4
Cyclization of alkanes 164–5, 179, 181

Dealumination of zeolites 159, 238
Dehydration 13, 44–5, 229
Dehydrogenation 12, 93–4, 109–10, 164–5, 178–81
Desorption
    definition 6
    energetics 31–6, 44–5, 110, 159
    temperature-programmed (TDS) 31, 33–6, 95–7, 133, 149–50, 151–3, 158–9
Dispersion
    definition 55
    measurement 54–5, 120–1
    techniques for metals 64–5, 75–7
Dual function catalyst 179

Elastase 15–16
Electron
    Auger 110–11, 121
    energy loss spectroscopy (EELS) 94, 105–10
    escape depths 100–1
    wavelength 101, 124
Electronic promotion *see* Promotion
Enzymes
    active site 15–16, 183–6, 189, 190–2
    classification 18
    immobilization 16, 48, 49–51, 79–83, 193–4, 197
    kinetics 45–51, 186–90
    metallic centres 17, 190–3
    nature 14–17
    optimum pH 186–90
    turnover numbers 48–9, 186
    usages 17, 19, 193–9

Ethanol
 catalytic conversions, 4, 44–5, 231
 synthesis 213–14
Ethylene (ethene)
 chemisorption 25–6, 133, 150, 165,
  216, 221
 dehydrogenation 164–5
 desorption 31, 33–4
 hydrogenation 60, 61, 65, 162–3
 oxidation 60, 215–17
 polymerization 220–3
 synthesis 213, 235, 237
Ethylene oxide 5, 215–17
p-Ethyltoluene 235
Explosion hazards 9–10
Exposure 119
Extended X-ray absorption fine
  structure (EXAFS) 121–6, 191

Fermi level 134, 135, 136
Fischer–Tropsch synthesis 63, 166,
  212–15, 225
Formaldehyde
 desorption 110
 synthesis 5, 109–10, 171, 173, 174
Formate (HCOO) 94, 208–9
Formic acid 93–4
Functionality, definition 11
Functionalized supports 61, 81–3, 197

Gasoline, synthetic (M-) 224–33
Gel immobilization 80–1, 197
Glucose isomerases 14, 17, 80, 190,
  193–4
Glucose oxidase 80
Grafted catalysts 64–5, 223

Hammett acidity function (H_0) 150–3,
  157–8, 177
n-Hexane conversion, on
 platinum 165
 reforming catalyst 181
 ZSM-5 zeolite 231
High-silica zeolites 70–1, 73, 159, 226,
  235, 237, 238
Homogeneous catalysts
 general characteristics 4, 7
 heterogenized 59–64
Horiuti–Polanyi mechanism 163, 164,
  200

HREELS *see* Electron energy loss
  spectroscopy
Hydrodesulphurization 162–3
Hydrogen, chemisorption
 bond parameters 27, 103, 137
 dispersion measurement 54–5
Hydrogen peroxide 3, 10
Hydrogenation, on
 anchored catalysts 61–3
 grafted catalysts 65
 supported liquid catalysts 60
 transition metals 12, 42, 162–4,
  200–3
Hydrogenolysis 12, 90, 162–3, 166–7,
  209
Hydrolysis, enzymatic 184–6

Immobilization 16, 59, 61–4, 193–4
Impregnation 74–5, 77, 122, 212
Indicators 151–2
Infrared spectroscopy
 absorption 126–31, 145, 148,
  169–71, 219
 reflectance-absorption (IRAS) 94,
  127–9 131, 211
Inhibition 38
Iron
 as catalyst for
  ammonia synthesis 88–9, 114, 140,
   141, 203–4
  carbon monoxide hydrogenation
   111–13, 210, 212–13, 225
 crystal faces 86, 88–9
Isomerization 13, 38, 40, 63, 164, 165,
  175–6, 178–82, 193–4, 217
Isotopic labelling 144, 171, 208, 211

Kinetic behaviour
 enzyme catalysis 45–51, 186–90
 surface catalysis 36–45

Langmuir adsorption isotherm 19–23,
  31, 47, 120
Langmuir–Hinshelwood mechanism
  37–43, 117–18
Lattic entrapment 80–1, 197
Lewis acid sites 127, 146, 147, 157, 191
Lineweaver–Burk plot 47, 49, 189
Low energy electron diffraction (LEED)
  100–5
Lysozyme 14, 183–5, 187–90

M-gasoline 224–33
Maleic anhydride 5, 12, 171
Mars–van Krevelen mechanism 44, 169,
  171, 219
Mechanism
  definition 14
  of
    catalytic reforming 178–82
    Fischer–Tropsch synthesis 212–15
    hydrogenation (unsaturates) 163–6,
      201
    methanation 210, 212
    methanol synthesis 208
    oligomerization (alkenes) 176–7
    oxidation
      Mars–van Krevelen 44, 169,
        171, 219
      of methanol (selective) 172
      of propylene (selective) 173
      of sulphur dioxide 219
    polymerization (ethylene) 221
Methanation 98–100, 165–6, 210–15
Methanol
  conversion on zeolites 229–33, 235,
    237–8
  oxidation
    deep 42
    selective 143, 171–4
  synthesis 5, 42, 205–9, 214
Methoxy (CH_3O) 107–10, 208
Michaelis–Menten mechanism 45–51,
  187, 188–90
Microporous solids 56–9, 75–8,
  153–9, 175, 177–8, 224–38
Miller indices 86–7
Mixed-oxides, general features 65, 67–9
Molecular sieve action 58–9, 156
Molybdena catalysts 64–6, 172, 173,
  174
Molybdenum-containing enzymes
  191–2
Monolayer, definition 19
Mordenite 158–9

Nickel
  as catalyst for
    hydrogenation of
      carbon monoxide 98–100,
        211–12
      vegetable oils 201
    hydrogenolysis 90, 166

methanation 98–100, 166, 210–12
methanol oxidation 108–10
steam reforming 166
chemisorption on, of
  carbon monoxide 95–6, 138, 141,
    211–12
  hydrogen 26–7, 201
  vegetable oils 201
Nitric acid 5, 204–5
Nitric oxide 7–9, 113–4, 118–20, 204
Nitrogen chemisorption 140–1
Nitrogenase 191–2

Octane numbers 178–9
Oligomerization 13, 78, 176–7
Optimum pH, of enzymes 186–90
Oxidation
  deep 12, 42, 169, 215, 217
  selective 12, 42–3, 60, 64–6, 78, 79,
    80, 109–10, 143, 168–74,
    215–17
Oxygen, chemisorption 117–18, 143–4,
  169, 171–3, 204, 216, 219

Phillips process 220–3
Photoelectron spectroscopy,
  ultraviolet (UPS) 115–17
  X-ray (XPS) 115–21, 214
Photosynthesis 6, 7
Physisorption 6, 23, 27, 127, 130
Platinum
  as catalyst for
    alkane isomerization 164, 165
    ammonia oxidation 204
    carbon monoxide oxidation 8, 168
    hydrogenolysis 166, 167
    pollution control 8
    reforming 178–82
  chemisorption on 96–7, 128–9, 131,
    164–5
  model surfaces 87
  supported forms 73–7, 178–9
Polyethylene 5, 220–3
Polymerization 63, 176, 220–3
Polyphenylene 195–6
Poisoning 181
Pores, terminology 56
Potassium, promotion by 96–7, 114,
  140–1, 171, 211–13
Pressure-bridging systems 91, 98

Promotion 96–7, 114, 140–1, 171,
    211–13, 216–18
Propylene (propene)
    chemisorption 159–60, 173, 175
    oligomerization 178
    oxidation (selective) 44, 65, 144–5,
        173
    synthesis 237, 238

Raney metals 53, 54
Redox action 168–9, 171, 172, 219
Redox surfaces
    chemisorption on 142–5
    oxidation on 5, 12, 42–4, 64–6, 78–9,
        168–74, 217–20
Reforming of alkanes 178–82
REHY-zeolite 157, 223–4
Rhodium
    carbon monoxide chemisorption on
        103–4, 125, 126, 214
    grafted catalysts 65
    in ammonia oxidation catalyst 204
    in catalytic converters 8
    LEED patterns 103–4
    supported forms 60, 63, 65, 164
    synthesis gas conversion on 213–14

Sasol 215
Secondary ion mass spectrometry (SIMS)
    98–100
Selectivity, definition 3
SEXAFS 125–6
Silica–alumina
    acidity
        H_0 range 152–3
        nature 127–9, 146–7
        superacid forms 147–50
    chemisorption on, of
        alkenes 150, 176, 180
        ammonia 27, 28, 30, 146, 148–50
        pyridine 127–30, 148–50
    reforming catalysts 178–82
    spectra
        infrared absorption 128, 129, 130,
            148
        thermal desorption 30, 149
Silver 74, 94, 215–17
Sodalite cage 57
Space velocity 203
Steam
    -gasification 9

    -oxidation 12, 173
    -reforming 166, 203
Stereographic triangle 88
Structure sensitivity 90
Sulphides, transition metal 162–3
Sulphur dioxide, oxidation 60, 217–20
Sulphur poisoning 181
Sulphuric acid 5, 146, 147, 152, 217–20
Superacidity 147–50, 152, 157–9,
    177–8
Supercages, in zeolites 56, 57, 77, 226,
    234
Supported catalysts
    liquid phase 59, 60, 217–20
    metals 54–6, 65, 73–7, 118–21,
        122–4, 125, 127, 164, 167,
        181–2, 200–3, 206–9, 212–14,
        215–17
    oxides 52, 78–9, 123
Surface area, specific 23–4, 53, 73, 215
Synthesis gas, conversion on
    copper 42, 205–9
    iron 111–13, 209, 212–13, 215
    nickel 98–100, 165–6, 204–12
    rhodium 213–14

Temperature-programmed
    desorption spectroscopy (TDS) 31,
        33, 34, 36, 95, 151–2, 158–9
    reaction spectroscopy (TPRS) 92–8,
        164–5, 216
Template ions 70–1
TLK notation 87–8
Turnover frequency, definition 6
Turnover number 48, 186

Ultraviolet photoelectron spectroscopy
    (UPS) 115–17
UHV conditions, definition 90

Vanadia catalysts 5, 12, 13, 52, 60, 68,
    78, 169–72, 218–20
Vegetable oils, hydrogenation 5, 200–3
Volcano plot 162, 182

Water–gas shift reaction 9, 12, 63, 145
Wilkinson catalyst 61
Work function of metals 135, 136

X-ray photoelectron spectroscopy (XPS)
    115–21, 214

XANES 125
p-xylene synthesis 233–6

Yeast cells, immobilization 80–1

Zeolites
  A-type
    molecular sieve action 58–9, 156
    structure 56–7
    synthesis 69–70
  acidic forms 30–1, 70, 72, 156–9,
      177–8, 223–38
  erionite 237, 238
  high-silica forms 70–1, 73, 159, 226,
      235, 237, 238
  ion exchange 70, 78, 156–7
  surface areas, specific 53, 73
  T-type 237, 238
  X-type
    electrostatic fields (internal) 154–5
    rare-earth exchanged 156–7
    structure 56, 57, 154
    supported metals 75–6
    synthesis 69–70

Y-type
  rare-earth exchanged 156–7, 223
  structure 56–7
  supported metals 75–7
  synthesis 69–70
ZSM-5
  carbenium ion stability on 175
  crystalline form 72
  diffusion (internal) 228
  M-gasoline process 224–33
  modified forms 234–5
  p-ethyltoluene process 235
  p-xylene process 233–6
  products, from conversion of
      ethanol 4, 231
      n-hexane 231
      methanol 229–33
      toluene 233–4, 236
  size selectivity 226, 228–9, 233–5
  structure 226–7
  synthesis 71–2
ZSM-34 237, 238
Ziegler–Natta catalysts 63, 223
Zinc-containing enzymes 190–1
Zinc oxide 12, 145, 205–8, 209, 214